ADVANCED
TYPOGRAPHY

ADVANCED TYPOGRAPHY

FROM KNOWLEDGE TO MASTERY

RICHARD HUNT

BLOOMSBURY VISUAL ARTS
LONDON • NEW YORK • OXFORD • NEW DELHI • SYDNEY

BLOOMSBURY VISUAL ARTS

Bloomsbury Publishing Plc
50 Bedford Square, London, WC1B 3DP, UK
1385 Broadway, New York, NY 10018, USA

First published in Great Britain 2020

Cover and interior design: Richard Hunt

ISBN   PB: 978-1-3500-5591-9
        ePDF: 978-1-3500-5592-6
        eBook: 978-1-3500-5593-3

Printed and bound in China

To find out more about our authors and books visit
www.bloomsbury.com and sign up for our newsletters.

CONTENTS

Introduction

Typography, which began as the central technology of printing, remains the central technology of all graphic design. Typography is not just design with letters. It is communication of language. Typography classes are often taught as graphic design classes, with visual composition and the formal properties of letters as the main foci. Typographic conventions and subtlety often lack attention in both education and practice. Experimental type and compositions are technically easier to achieve than in the past, while deciding what direction to take has become more difficult, as the possible options have increased greatly. This also tends to focus attention on the visual possibilities, and take attention away from the communication of language.

Current media have changed the way that typography as a visual representation of language is produced, as well as changing the relationship of the designer and the viewer (and, we hope, reader), with that representation.

The most significant force in visual communication has been economic. Money has driven the development of communication technologies: the ratio of supply to demand for communication 'products' (and everything else) has moved toward the supply side ever since the Industrial Revolution. Beginning with the development of writing, visual communication technology has become

This book has several types of material in addition to the main text. They include:

- material related to the main text that appears in grey boxes set into the text.
- image pages, usually set with a grey background.
- information of general interest related to typography, which appears under a red dotted rule.
- practical tips, which appear in bold type with rules above and below.
- quotations about typography, set in condensed red type.
- marginal images with captions.

Protowriting

Protowriting, which emerged in many cultures on every continent, appears to have developed into complete language writing only in large agricultural and hierarchically-organized societies.

Complete language writing

Although protowriting systems arose in many cultures, scripts able to represent complete language are rare. The only entirely independent complete language writing systems that we are aware of are Egyptian hieroglyphics (which led to the first known alphabet in the Middle East that later developed into the Roman and other alphabets), Chinese logographic script (which evolved into modern Chinese and Japanese), and Central American logographic scripts (which were destroyed in the course of European colonization). Other complete language writing systems may have existed, but there is no evidence of them today. Damper climates and writing on perishable materials may have led to their disappearance.

ever more important, with only a few exceptions, such as the loss of literacy in the Homeric Age in Greece, or the Middle Ages in Europe. Computers and online communication are only the most recent examples of this trend. Competition for readers and viewers has become increasingly fierce.

This evolution in visual communication since literacy first arose has been punctuated with technological milestones. The first of the two most significant is the printing press, which increased the availability of visual representation of language and resulting literacy by orders of magnitude. The second is the development of the personal computer and its associated technologies, which have done the same thing. Both of these changed the relationship of readers to the written word.

HOW IS THIS TYPE BOOK DIFFERENT FROM OTHERS?

This book is not intended for beginning students. There are no extensive recapitulations of the history of writing and typography, no diagrams explaining the anatomy of letters. Neither are there explanations of the basics of page layout software. It is presumed that the reader of this book either already knows these things or is able and willing to find them out.

What this book does do is focus on the culture and systems of typography as they apply to modern design practice using the Roman alphabet. It refers to what is common knowledge to the senior design student and practitioner, but those references are intended to be a baseline from which the discussion is carried further, encouraging readers to consider their own relationships with the practice of typography.

The relatively recent technology of the internet has changed how typography is practiced and presented, but the essential typographic principles have not changed. Although the control of type on the Web is still not as sophisticated as it is in print, and although some of the principles are difficult or impractical to fully address on screen, the ability to control typography on screen is constantly improving.

This book also pays more attention to those aspects of design practice that have changed radically since the Bauhaus and Basel schools which still influence much contemporary graphic design education. While typographic conventions change slowly, how typography is practiced has changed a lot. An entire craft trade has been eliminated and replaced by computers and software developers. This is not new: the history of typography and printing is largely a history of labour being replaced with technology. But now, creators of typographic works have ceased to need expertise to produce it. Whether it is produced well is another matter.

Some of the information about aspects of design or software included in this book may seem elementary. My rule of thumb in deciding whether I should include something is, 'Am I answering a question that, by action or word, design practitioners have shown needs answering?'

WHAT IS TYPOGRAPHY?

Today, much of what we call typography appears on screen. Other typography exists in explicitly physical form, most often in architectural practice. But for physical or print work, the *design* of typography is today practiced almost exclusively on screen using computer software (although handset letterpress printing still exists, done mostly by aficionados and artists).

However, the evolution of today's typography, whether on screen or in physical form, has evolved from the use of various kinds of inks printed mostly with metal type, on various kinds of surfaces, mostly paper.

Typography is a practice that combines art, skill and craft. Good typography needs art in the aesthetic aspect, skill in creating effective and appropriate communication, and craft in execution. Today the art and skill are as important as they ever were, but now, the craft also falls to the designer, and attention to it is something that current design education doesn't always successfully address. The current typographer needs knowledge of history, technology, human vision, culture and psychology.

Technology and workers

Replacing human labour with technology long predates the current fears that Artificial Intelligence (AI) will take over from humans. Typography and printing have shown this trend since the 15th century. The effect of this on employment was the opposite of what might be expected, as an ever-growing demand for printed materials led to employment in printing and related industries increasing until the 21st century.

- Printing and moveable type replaced writing and scribes.
- Mechanical type casters replaced hand production of type sorts by type casters.
- Rotary presses, increasingly large, greatly reduced hand printing by press workers.
- Typesetting machines replaced typesetting by human typesetters.
- Pantographic machines replaced human punchcutters.
- Photographic typositors reduced the work of lettering artists.
- Phototype and computer-driven typesetting systems reduced work for typesetting machine operators.
- Desktop computer replaced the work done in type shops.

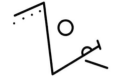

Example of Nsibidi, an Eastern Nigerian protowriting system, dating from as early as 1500 BCE.

On the left is the Phoenician ancestor of the capital A we use, originating around 1200 BCE, derived from Egyptian hieroglyphics. On the right is the Egyptian symbol for water, for which the Phoenician word was 'mem', a direct ancestor of our 'M'.

Saki Mafundikwa's book surveys twenty systems of visual communication that arose in Africa before colonialism.

TYPOGRAPHY IS A TECHNOLOGY

Like most technologies, typography is based on other, preceding technologies. When Bi Sheng invented moveable type, about 400 years before Gutenberg, typography united the already ancient technology of writing with then new technology of carving relief images into wood and then inking and pressing them onto a paper surface for multiple copies. Bi Sheng's moveable and reusable type was made of fired clay and consisted of durable, separated models of characters that could be rearranged, inked and used to print multiple copies as needed.

Since that time, there have been many technological advances in communication technology, and many other script traditions have adapted those technologies. The visual representation of language itself changes little, hiding the technological changes from the observer. Scripts evolve slowly, much more slowly than the languages they represent or the technologies used to reproduce them. The principles and conventions of typography have also changed little over the past few hundred years. The practitioner must observe those basic principles and at the same time adapt to technological, societal and economic changes.

CULTURAL CONTINUITY

Typography both embodies and transmits culture over time and across space. Many of the letter forms we use can be traced back five thousand years to the alphabet that arose in present day Syria, which itself was an adaptation of characters from Egyptian hieroglyphics. Phoenician traders and colonists spread the alphabet around the Mediterranean, and descendants of that alphabet eventually spread throughout the world. The current form of our capital letters has endured, mostly unchanged, for two thousand years. The forms of the lower-case roman letters we use are essentially and visibly those of the Carolingian Renaissance of over 1200 years ago, and have remained more or less unchanged through the evolution of the Latin language that they were originally used to express, and the adoption by, and imposition of the alphabet on, other languages.

We see the same thing in another widely used major writing system: Chinese script. Many contemporary Chinese characters are clearly based on the earliest Chinese writing.

REFLECTION OF CULTURE

Visual typographic styles change much more quickly than typography basics. Although essential typographic forms are constant, their appearance and how they are used are strongly influenced by contemporary culture. Typography also reflects culture back to itself. In textual communication, it is an almost unnoticed medium that carries the thoughts and beliefs of culture. In display type and layout, it reflects and influences contemporary cultures, and can enrich (or impoverish) the private and public visual environments.

The contemporary communication environment means that cultures are less local than they were in the past. So typographic culture becomes somewhat flattened as trends and fashions are not constrained by geography. Instead, because of different communities on the internet, typographic fashion becomes, to some extent, part of societal, rather than geographic, communities.

CONCLUSION

The technologies of producing type, and of setting and communicating type, change suddenly, as do typographic fashions. The forms of the alphabet and typographic conventions in text change very slowly, if at all. Craft, in the sense of doing things properly, doesn't change much either, though the skills of craft change with every change in technology.

Whether you are setting radical display type, or setting text for reading, the intention of this book is one, not of art or typographic direction, but in advising designers how to make good typographic decisions and how to achieve a high quality of execution.

IMP. CAESAR
NEPOTI DIVI

The majuscules of the Roman alphabet are based on Roman square capitals, particularly those found on inscriptions.

A B C D E
F G H I J
K L M N O
P Q R S
T U V W
X Y Z

The Roman alphabet gained a few letters during the Republic (to better write Greek words), and more since the time of Trajan's column (to better write languages of the Roman Empire).

We do not have to learn the techniques of the past, but we do have to learn how to manage and carry out aspects of typography that used to be delivered by professional typographic service providers. At the same time, there are freedoms and possibilities attached to type that were never possible before. Designers must be prepared to explore new and changing technological possibilities.

Changing technologies and practice

There is no question that the way people read now is different than it was in the past. People's attention spans are shorter, and there is far more to read, across a wider choice of media. Although this trend has been connected to the advent of the internet, it can be traced to the Industrial Revolution, when increased production efficiencies, marketing and the increase in wage-earners with some disposable income meant that more and more reading material became available to an increasingly literate public. Newspapers and illustrated magazines gave citizens more to read, leading to more competition for their attention. The amount of typographic material has exploded again with the internet, while the volume of printed type has diminished surprisingly little.

In a typical printed book, the reader's experience is largely controlled. The text is linear and is unfolded page by page, and books are largely self-contained. Some books may refer to other books, sometimes in text, often in footnotes or endnotes, but in most cases, a book is still expected to be something that can be used without reference to other works. The reader's expectation is for a book to be a complete experience. A table of contents and an index may give readers options in how they engage with parts of a book, but the basic reading structure is influenced and formed

The invention of typography confirmed and extended the new visual stress of applied knowledge, providing the first uniformly repeatable "commodity," the first assembly-line, and the first mass-production.

Marshall McLuhan, *The Gutenberg Galaxy*

Roman cursive handwriting was a quickly written version of the Roman capital form. The quick nature of the process led to strokes overshooting the capital height, which eventually resulted in the ascenders and descenders of minuscule script.

by the book's structure. Books can be skimmed and the reader can choose to read some parts and not others, but all the content is available to the reader on the same level.

Newspapers and magazines are less linear, but they are also self-contained, though unlike many books, it isn't expected that people will read all the content of such publications.

The structure of an internet reading experience is much different: the experience is not linear but divergent. Someone looking at an internet page is usually offered a number of choices within the site, may encounter links to other sites, and may easily choose to go to another site.

Whatever the technology, one thing has not changed: in most cases, information is still communicated by typographic form.

. . . .

Economies of scale

The unit cost of a book is reduced as more copies are produced – a powerful incentive to get more people to order a copy – making market appeal more important than the quality of a manuscript – unlike the case with expensive, hand-copied manuscripts. This is an unchanging characteristic of industrial production, of which printing is a foundational example: printing 1000 books today will result in a cheaper cost per book than printing 500.

Print and Web

Typographic principles and practice develop over time. The enormous change from handwriting to the printing press caused remarkably little immediate difference to the appearance of visual language. The advent of typesetting machines similarly made little change, and actually led to a revival of historical typographic forms. The internet is an even more radical change, but the biology and psychology of the reader remains the same, and typography continues to evolve from the cultural foundation of handwriting and printing. As a result, typographic principles are largely the same in print and on the Web. The biggest difference is that the reader is now an actor in shaping typography, whether by choice of device, by user controls or how they engage with interactive features on a site, or by the interactive nature of the internet itself.

TYPOGRAPHY ENTAILS TECHNOLOGICAL CHANGE

Typography, in both print and on screen, as opposed to writing by hand, has always been technically sophisticated, making use of developments in industrial technologies. While the forms of typography usually evolve slowly and incrementally (though an explosion in how basic forms were treated began with Victorian advertising in the Industrial Revolution), the methods of producing and reproducing typography have had both disruptive radical changes and ongoing technical development. The essential physical processes of most printing remained unchanged from the mid-1400s to the mid 20th century, as the process was continually refined and increasingly automated. New methods of creating and reproducing type changed the methods of producing type, increased the amount of typographic production, and, more recently, made it possible for designers to create their own typefaces.

Radical technologies, conservative aesthetics

The introduction of the printing process itself is an example of a new function following an established visual form. Gutenberg was trying to closely duplicate the slowly evolved written form as closely as possible while using a radically innovative process.

Typographic practice changes slowly and is highly resistant to innovation. While visual aspects can be innovative, the art of making things readable can't be blithely innovated. Like efforts to regularize spelling, efforts to reform alphabets have been failures, except in gradual increments. Many of the typefaces we use for text today aren't much different from those of the early 16th century. Sans serif typefaces, while relatively recent innovations, can work well for text, but again, they must be fairly conservative in form, that is, of similar proportion and weight to serif typefaces commonly used for text.

Before the development of typesetting machines, the setting of text by hand was the most time-consuming part of producing a printed document, and was therefore the economic driver of technologies such as typesetting machines and the typewriter.

Typography and alphabets

One of the reasons that typography took off in Europe, rather than in China where it was first invented, is that four thousand characters are needed for normal communication in Chinese writing: essential forms communicate words through visual association with meaning, though include categorical and phonetic information. The need for so many characters meant that type was impractical

The Roman alphabet on the other hand, needs only twenty-six essential characters to represent the sound of words, so even with capitals and punctuation, fewer than 100 characters are needed, making moveable type a more practical system.

Logograms in phonetic scripts

Alphabetic systems do use logographic elements; examples are symbols, punctuation and numbers, and today, emoticons and emojis. Few people would understand all of the following:

hai mươi sáu nhân với hai bằng năm mươi hai

sechsundzwanzig mal zwei ist gleich zweiundfünfzig

twenty-six multiplied by two equals fifty-two

двадцать шесть, умноженное на два равно пятьдесят два

However, people from most cultures would understand the logographic expression:

$$26 \times 2 = 52$$

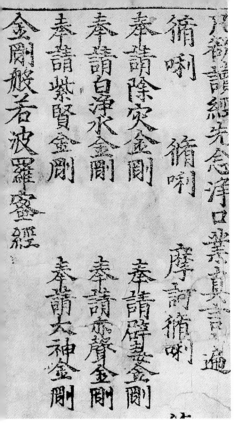

A detail from the earliest preserved printed book: the Diamond Sutra, *inked and printed using carved woodblocks in China, 868 CE, 300 years before the first known moveable type, and 800 years before Gutenberg.*

graphus

Example of the humanist manuscript style of the 1400s that was the basis of Roman type.

BIRTH OF THE PRINTING PRESS IN EUROPE

Carved and inked wooden printing blocks were used to reproduce multiple copies of pages a long time before the printing press. Woodblock printing arose first in China, and had spread to Europe by the early 1400s.

In Europe, typographic form began with a faithful imitation of the Gothic script that was the dominant formal writing style in Northern Europe. It was soon supplanted by type based on the humanist writing style, using Roman capital forms and humanist minuscule, modified to have Roman inscriptional style serifs. The basic technology of printing remained largely the same from the 1400s to the late 1800s. The method of producing type depended on the use of hand-carved metal punches used to produce copper moulds of each character, which in turn were used to produce multiple reverse images of the characters in a mixture of lead, tin and antimony. These were set into position by hand to form a raised reverse image of a page, then inked and pressed onto paper, enabling the production of multiple copies. When a print run was finished, the typeset page could be dismantled, and the type then reused to produce other documents.

In the earliest days of printing, decorated caps and other graphic elements were added to the page by hand. Soon, wooden, and later copper, engravings were introduced (which could be printed in other colours of ink), so that before long all graphic elements could be printed instead of being added by hand. These new technologies were eagerly adopted by printers all over Europe faster than new technologies had been in the past, because examples of them were, for the first time, mass produced.

PRINTING LEADS TO THE MODERN WORLD

Moveable type, once created, could not only reproduce manuscripts more quickly, but could produce multiple copies thousands of times faster than the scribe, with the amount of time needed for each copy being reduced as the number of copies increased. Previously, copying two identical manuscripts had taken more or less twice as long as producing one. Using a printing press, the more copies produced, the cheaper the unit cost, at least in terms

& molte genti
& molte genti

The difference between the original printed Jenson type from around 1475 and a PostScript version of 1996 is one of technology; the forms are essentially the same.

of labour. The first printing presses were an early iteration of the assembly line that became the basis of efficient manufacture of automobiles and other mass-produced products.

In a sense, the printing press was the industrial robot of its day, replacing human labour with technology.

The development of the printing press in Europe anticipated production processes in other fields. The production of printed matter with a press became a model for the division of labour of mass production in the Industrial Revolution, something that has culminated in today's industrial methods.

While the work of the scribe became unnecessary, more and more printers and other craftspeople associated with printing were needed. By 1500, less than fifty years after Gutenberg's Bible, there were printing presses in over 250 cities across Europe, with more than 20 million books estimated as having been printed. The increased availability of reading material encouraged more people to learn to read, which in turn led to an even greater demand for print. Some of the information contained in these books led to developments in science and technology. Previously, most learning had to be started from scratch by each person in each field, because previous knowledge developed by others elsewhere was inaccessible.

Printing also led to the communication and development of new political and religious thought, which led in turn to the Protestant church, which was, at least to some degree, predicated on the ability of individuals to read the Bible (and other religious

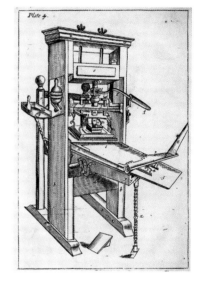

This press shown in Joseph Moxon's Mechanick Exercises, Or the Doctrine of Handy-Works Applied to the Art of Printing, published in 1683, though showing developments in the details of function, is essentially the same as the presses of 200 years earlier, and remained the model for most hand presses until the 20th century.

opine
opine

The Jenson face, shown top, based on Nicolas Jenson's 1475 typeface is strongly influenced by the model of a flat-nib pen held at a more or less constant angle. The Garamond, shown below, has more variation in angles between the letters, as their being carved from steel begins to influence the forms.

abcdefg
abcdefg
abcdefg

These typefaces from different centuries are different in style, but their essential form is the same.

Top: Garamond's basic form is from the flat-nib pen held at an angle of about 30° from the horizontal.

Centre: Bodoni is influenced by engraving methods and the split nib pen, for which the stroke weight varies according to the pressure of the pen on paper.

Bottom: Clarendon has similar features to the Bodoni, such as round terminals on the a, c, f, and g, but exaggerates them, and reverses the trend towards higher contrast between thick and thin strokes.

documents) for themselves, resulting in a breaking away from the Catholic church, which relied on the model of literate priests interpreting religious material for an illiterate populace.

INDUSTRIAL PRODUCTION METHODS

As printing became more mechanized and systematized, the tasks associated with it also became increasingly specialized. Even in the early years, the person who designed typefaces, the person who cast type, the press operators and inkers who set and printed type, and those who proofread type, were often different people with separate skills and tasks. All of them were needed to run a printing press. This specialization increased in typography and printing until close to the end of the 20th century. There were ongoing incremental technological improvements, such as iron presses, moving from hand-cast letters to machines that did the casting, and taking impressions of flat 'formes' of type, so more than one press could print the same page. Later, techniques were developed for forming the impression of a handset page on cylinders for rotary presses. Most advances focused on making the production of printing faster. However, the basic processes of making multiple copies of letters, setting them by hand, and then inking them went unchanged until the typesetting machines of the late 1800s. By the end of the 1800s, colour lithography had also become a common typographic medium, especially for packaging.

This was followed by the developments of the 20th century: the offset press, phototype, computer-driven typesetting systems, the typositor, and finally, the desktop computer.

TECHNOLOGY AFFECTS TYPOGRAPHIC FORM

The appearance of type itself also evolved, though slowly, with the introduction of new technologies. The first type was strongly influenced by the technology of the flat-nibbed pen that had been used to that point. However, because the metal punches were carved, serif forms like Roman inscriptional capitals soon replaced the curved endings and diamond-shaped serifs that were the result of the scribe's pen: the consistently angled lettering soon became more varied. The advent of the split nib pen and engraved type led to new developments of type form in the 1700s. Still, the essential forms changed little.

Production of the display type needed for public advertising during the Industrial Revolution also led to inventions for the creation and reproduction of type, such as the pantographic wood type cutter, which enabled the copying of letters in a range of sizes from a single pattern, as well as the large type sizes for advertising that would have been impractical in metal. Increased ease of type production helped create the unprecedented explosion in styles and variations of typefaces in advertising.

Linn Boyd Benton's punchcutting machine, arriving at about the same time as the Linotype and Monotype machines, and his matrix cutting machine of the early 1900s, enabled the precision cutting of type matrices of varying sizes that could be produced on an industrial scale. They were based on copying from a pattern, using a technically refined and engineered version of the cruder pantograph that was already being used to produce wood type.

Graphic designers, since the introduction of the term in the early 20th century by William Addison Dwiggins, normally worked with typesetters (who produced type for printing in graphic design), and occasionally with type foundries (in those rare cases when the designer designed a typeface). The graphic designer would also often direct or collaborate with illustrators or photographic technicians of various kinds. Beginning with print, this division of labour continued with type on screen (in television and cinema), when again, typography and image experts would contribute to the production of typographic design. This division of design and production ended with the desktop computer and design software, giving designers the tools do it all.

THE DESIGNER REGAINS CONTROL OF TYPE

When the personal computer, page layout and other graphic software were introduced, the designer suddenly gained control of most of the process of execution.

This has had both advantages and disadvantages.

. . . .

Skills typographers need to have that they didn't need in the past

- An ability to think systematically in the process of typographic production. (Style sheets, master pages, CSS, the effective use of search and replace, tagged text, etc.)

- A command of the conventions and aesthetics of typography in terms of execution rather than simply critical judgement.

- A willingness to engage with, benefit from, and if necessary, learn complex technical systems.

WHAT TOOLS ARE AVAILABLE? HOW DO YOU USE THEM?

The larger and more complex the project (or series of projects), the more it is worth investing the time to learn any techniques or systems that will help you do the job. It is always worth investigating possible methods and techniques you may not be aware of. The Internet has all the information needed, and the best and clearest explanations are often not on the sites of the software manufacturer.

PHOTOVISION

AT LAST... HERE IS SOME GOOD NEWS

Good news about no longer having to spend thousands of dollars on rub-down type sheets and type bills...with nothing to show for it at the end of the year. Now you can automate your layout dept., and save. **Good news** about a headline setter designed just for creative people. The **Spectra Setter 1200** is the designer's answer to the sky-rocketing cost of rub-down letter sheets and headline type bills. Now you can design and set your headlines right in your own studio...in less time than it would take you to rough out a comp or 'rub down' a headline layout. You have probably already paid for a **Spectra Setter 1200** in just the rub-down sheets you have...unusable with missing letters. We don't know how much **good news** you can stand in one day...but the **Spectra Setter 1200** is the most versatile setter made in the U.S.—yet is priced far below less comparable units. You can set any size headline you need, on paper or film, from 1/8" to 7" high letters—plus you can condense, extend, italicize, backslant, etc.—all from one inexpensive film font. You have over 2500 designer type styles to choose from. You can stack line over line and you see each letter as you set it for creative, visual spacing—and you never run out of letters! Automated, easy push-button operation. No hand cranks to turn. You change letter sizes easily in seconds so you can mix sizes as you set. Put

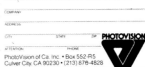

frequently used logos on film and make your own stats, at any size, in seconds—even step and repeat patterns on a large 9" x 20" table area. If you're spending $15 a week on type or rub-down sheets you are paying for a **Spectra Setter** without having any of the benefits of ownership, convenience, and being able to design your headlines—*How* you want them, *When* you want them. And the very **best news** is that it's so super easy to use! After only a few minutes' practice you could set our 'good news' headline in 5 to 10 minutes, save a $12. to $30. bill, and have the headline now, when you need it.

Return this coupon now and we'll send you more **good news**—a free $200. font offer, a fully detailed brochure, a sampler and a listing of over 2500 type styles that are available to fill your every creative need.

YES, SEND ME SOME MORE GOOD NEWS!

COMPANY

ADDRESS

CITY   STATE   ZIP

ATTENTION   PHONE

PHOTOVISION

PhotoVision of Ca. Inc. • Box 552-R5
Culver City, CA 90230 • (213) 876-4828

PHOTOVISION

We license and supply all ITC faces with many extra exclusive swash & biform characters designed in our studio.

Top left: Rubdown letters were used for design mock-ups, and sometimes for final display type.

Top right: The typositor was revolutionary: it allowed small companies to make display typefaces relatively easily, and made it possible to set type very tightly both horizontally and vertically. It was not suitable for text setting.

Bottom: The typositor gave more typographic options to designers: more typefaces, more weights, more effects. VGC specimen book.

It sometimes appears as if technology has simply made graphic design and typography easier. In many ways this is true, but on the other hand, every increase in technology increases the choices available to designers (and choosing takes time and thought), and the responsibility for the craft of those choices (which takes time and skill).

The computer also changed the typographic workflow. Until the personal computer, the graphic design process was largely linear. The designer analysed the communication intention of a project, conceived the aesthetics, and then supervised its production. Every job went through orderly stages of approval, as it passed through the phases of a project, each carried out by different experts such as editors, proofreaders, typesetters, photography technicians, film strippers, and so on.

Through most of the previous century of graphic design, the designer had a supervisory rather than functional role in production. While a designer would conceive of and specify type and image treatment, much of the actual execution would be done by type shops, photographic services, illustrators, photographers and others. Although the designer would have a more or less clear vision of what the final outcome would be, the end result would be strongly affected by the service providers. The tools of the designer were the pencil and visual judgement. Now the designer also needs the expertise that was previously held by those specialists, and typography is the most significant of those basic and essential skills.

On screens, typographic control moves toward the user

The choice of different-sized screens and the ability for users to resize type also means that the reader has some control over typography, both in the choice of devices to read it on and the appearance of the type on those devices, especially with responsive design, which is now the expected standard.

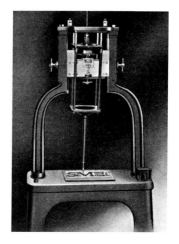

The Benton Pantograph of Linn Boyd Benton marked the end of the human punchcutter and the beginning of scalable typefaces.

Advertisement from 1992 for a type shop trying to hold onto the business that the desktop computer was soon to take away.

A CHANGED GRAPHIC DESIGN PARADIGM

Before the desktop computer, the designer's function was supervisory and intermediary as much as it was conceptual and aesthetic, and was part of a sequential process of development. The computer blurred the lines between tasks, and made the designer responsible for executing the tasks that were previously done by specialists in different technologies and areas of design.

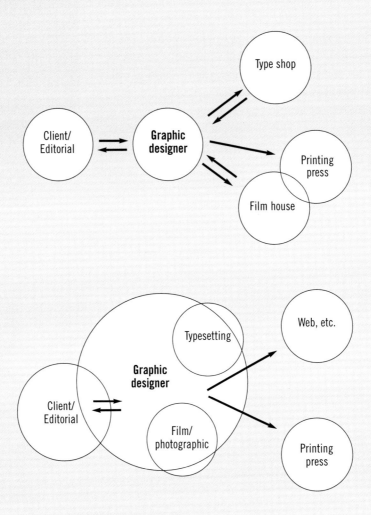

Top: The pre-desktop-computer graphic designer as central figure in a discrete system, where most tasks were done, in order, by different people.

Bottom: The post-desktop-computer graphic designer, with more technology available, and more tasks to accomplish, with tasks less linear and clearly defined.

DESIGNERS LOSE (SOME) CONTROL OF TYPE

There are three different factors that take the control of typography away from the designer. The first is that anyone with access to a page layout application or web creation software will be able to produce work without really understanding the programs, and they may even look 'professional' to those with little understanding or knowledge of typography. So work that would have once fallen to typographic designers is now sometimes done by individuals with little or no design training. Also, clients have been known to use their own software to make typographic or other changes to a designer's work without consulting the designer.

The second is the nature of current screen technology, which allows users to see typography in different forms depending on how they view it.

The third is that the networked and linked aspect of the internet mean that the organization and sequence of typographic communication is often less than it would be in traditional media, so design becomes to some degree a matter of anticipation rather than control.

DESIGNERS NEED TYPOGRAPHIC KNOWLEDGE MORE THAN EVER

This need for increased technical typographic knowledge and skill applies to designers in all media. In the past, a book designer, for example, although choosing the typeface, sizes, leading and layout, would rely on the type house or printer to produce the type. At this stage, attention would be given to things like the rag or justification, the finessing of the typographic details, and the printer or type house might make suggestions to the designer on how to improve the typography. For another example, the director of a television advertisement would rely on outside typographical expertise to produce any type for the screen, and this typography would also incorporate the typographic knowledge of the supplier.

Now that the designer is often expected to execute as well as design a project's typography, there is often no second set of expert eyes to refine or correct the type.

Current work process

Today, designers are often expected to complete many of the following tasks:

- Evaluate the content (includes reading the content, breaking it down, and creating different text treatments for the various features and voices).
- Develop the design / develop the typographic system.
- Develop the design file.
- Prepare the text (in the early stages of a large job, it may make sense to have a type work file separate from the design file, in which all type is contained in single text thread).
- Develop / adjust / execute the display type.
- Develop / execute the text type.

Text coding in page layout programs

A tagged text file such as those that can be generated from InDesign allows for changes and global alterations that would not be possible in the file. The file below shows the beginning of this chapter exported to tags. Many designers never use this feature, but it can be useful to solve problems that would be hard to manage with menu items.

```
<ASCII-MAC>

<vsn:13.1> <fset:InDesign-Roman> <ctable:=<PANTONE
P 48-8 U:COLOR:CMYK:Spot:0,0.99,0.91,0> <UK Text
Black:COLOR:CMYK:Spot:0,0,0,1>>

<dcs:Th lig removal=<Nextstyle:Th lig removal> <clig:0>
<cotfdl:0> <cotfcalt:0>>

<dps:Text=<Nextstyle:Text> <cc:UK Text Black>
<cs:11.000000> <ctk:4> <ptc:HL Composer> <phll:2>
<pli:2.000000> <palp:2.000000> <cl:14.000000>
<clang:English\: UK> <pmcbh:3> <pmcah:3> <pswh:7> <pt
r:16\,Left\..\,0\,\;40\,Left\..\,0\,\;102.85000000000
001\,Left\..\,0\,\;109\,Left\..\,0\,\;233.9\,Left\..\
,0\,\;474.90000000000003\,Left\..\,0\,\;> <cf:Garamond
Premier Pro> <cfs:Proportional Oldstyle> <pdws:1.040000>
<pmaws:1.250000> <pmaxl:0.030000> <pminl:-0.010000>
<pmaxgs:1.010000> <pmings:0.990000> <pkfnl:4> <pknl:3>
<pkl:1> <pta:JustifyLeft> <phwt:8> <pshadc:Black>
<pga:BaseLine> <pbmcb:0>>

<dps:Chapter number=<BasedOn:Text> <Nextstyle:Chapter
number> <cc:Pantone P 48-8U> <ct:Extra Condensed>
<cs:90.000000> <ctk:80> <ccase:Small Caps>
<pli:0.000000> <cf:Franklin Gothic Std>>

<dps:Large chapter head=<BasedOn:A subhead sidebar>
<Nextstyle:Large chapter head> <ct:Bold> <cs:22.000000>
<capk:Optical> <cvs:1.030000> <cl:26.000000> <ph:0>
<psb:14.000000> <pdws:0.800000> <pga:None>>

<cc:PANTONE P 48-8 U>1<cc:> <cc:UK Text Black>
<ct:Regular> <cs:11.000000> <ctk:0> <ccase:Normal>
<cf:Garamond Premier Pro>>

<cc:> <ct:> <cs:> <ctk:> <ccase:> <cf:> <pstyle:Large
chapter head>Changing technologies <0x000A>and practice

<pstyle:Text>

<pstyle:Text> <cstyle:Th lig removal>Th<cstyle:>ere
is no question that the way people read is different
than it has been in the past. Peoples<0x2019> attention
spans are shorter, and there is far more to read, on
more media. Although this change been connected to the
advent of the internet, this trend can be traced to
the Industrial Revolution, when increased production
efficiencies, marketing, and new technologies meant
that more and more reading material became available
to the public. Newspapers, and illustrated magazines
gave citizens more and more to read, leading to more
and competition for their attention. <cstyle:Th lig
removal>The<cstyle:> amount of typographic material has
exploded again with the internet.
```

NEW TYPOGRAPHIC MEDIA

To make all this more complicated, typography appears on the Web, where type is not only read but is also part of interactive experiences. It can also be animated on screen. Software such as Adobe AfterEffects and Maxon's Cinema 4D lets designers do not only basic animations, but also apply many visual and animation effects. These may or may not contribute to the aesthetic or communicative success of a project, but are a great temptation to use nonetheless.

Producing and editing video for the Web or other screen environments usually requires at least some typographic elements, even if just for the title and credits—things that can make a big difference to a project. The films *Seven* and *Catch Me If You Can* are early examples of how software can apply to title and credit typography, contributing to a project's success.

Continual skill acquisition

Before the desktop computer, the technical skills designers learned at school and early in their working lives would serve them for the rest of their careers. This has changed. The complex and developing abilities and wide variety of software packages mean that knowledge and expertise must be acquired on an as-needed basis.

An early initialism on the internet was the advice 'RTFM', standing for 'Read The F***** Manual' as an answer to questions asked by users of software on forums. Fortunately, the greatly increased technical possibilities and attendant difficulties of learning software and using it to its best advantage are accompanied by the greatly increased resources on the internet.

Knowing what can be done is more important than knowing how to do something, because you can look anything up once you know it exists.

MORE KNOWLEDGE NEEDED, MORE KNOWLEDGE AVAILABLE

A search of the internet is often the equivalent of the manual. The internet is also quite possibly where you can find a PDF of the traditional manual itself. It is (usually) easy to find information you need, and what you find may well be better or clearer than the software manufacturer's official explanation. This is not to say that it is necessarily easy to become competent with an unfamiliar software tool, but given time (admittedly often in short supply), what you need to know to develop competence is at least available.

The increasing possibilities of different kinds of practice also means that after the initial trend to generalism that resulted from the personal computer, there has been a new tendency towards specialization. Some designers are developing more focused practices in motion graphics, web, print, or wayfinding, etc. Whatever their area, all graphic designers need to have a good general knowledge of the different design tools, and an ability to supervise or collaborate on, if not actually execute themselves, typography in different media.

FROM APPRENTICESHIP TO SELF-EDUCATION

Historically, typographers and designers were taught, or at least exposed to, the technical skills needed to practice design. As well as learning concept development, aesthetics and layout, the designer would receive some training in typesetting, illustration, photography and printing, but might not expect to do these professionally, as these tasks would be performed by outside services. As in most trades, they would then move on to an apprenticeship, in which they would learn how to work as their mentor did.

Currently, designers must learn many of the necessary skills themselves, which also change and develop very quickly.

Motion graphics designers will need to be able to design and produce good typography in two- and three-dimensional animation software.

A designer working on complex books will have to be competent with page layout software features for controlling and styling text and pages if he or she hopes to develop and execute typographic design efficiently and accurately.

USE THE RIGHT TOOL FOR THE JOB

When working on long documents, usually supplied in MS Word or other word processing software, doing some initial work in that program before bringing it into your design software can be helpful, as style sheets can be applied and imported into the major page layout programs. By working in a word processing program, the designer is less likely to be distracted too early by matters of typographic design. Word processing software also has better spelling and grammar tools than design software.

DON'T WORK ON DESIGN AND THE EXECUTION OF TYPOGRAPHY AT THE SAME TIME

Typographic design takes creativity, trying different things, and visually evaluating the result. Working on typographic execution takes attention to detail, systematic thinking and attention to the reader's experience.

Fontographer, first released in 1985, was the first affordable commercially available font editor. It put type design into the hands of the individual.

A designer working with architectural or other applications that include three-dimensional lettering will have to understand drafting and rendering software.

Someone designing typefaces will need an understanding of the technical aspects of Bezier curves, different font formats and how type renders on screen, and will benefit from an understanding of OpenType tables, and other parts of font structures. Python programming scripts and tools such as TTX, which can convert OpenType and True Type fonts to and from XML (a human- and machine-readable data format, something like HTML), can save time, improve the quality of the typeface and reduce the chance of missing something. Some Python scripts for type editing programs are available, and you can edit existing scripts, or write your own, if you have interest and ability in programming.

All these things are not usually taught thoroughly, if at all, because of time constraints and the fact that instructors don't have technical knowledge in all areas. The best design students are often well ahead of their instructors in their ability to both learn and use software when necessary.

Working designers must adapt to using new tech, and like their instructors, supervisors are quite likely to be unable to teach them. Supervising designers or 'art directors' have to be able to understand the capabilities of technology and keep track of changes and innovations, but are in the position of directing rather than executing. They are likely to fall behind and be less capable than their juniors in terms of execution, and have less understanding of current tools.

ECONOMIC FORCES CHANGE

Traditionally, the high cost of buying typography from a supplier had the effect of making designers more cautious and more reliant on techniques and decisions that had worked well for them in the past. The fact that typographic and most other production was farmed out also allowed designers to focus on design rather than spending a lot of time on production. There were a few production jobs in graphic design studios. Pasting-up waxed galleys of type onto boards was a common entry-level job, as was operating the camera apparatus that many studios had which was used for resizing or otherwise preparing images for print.

These production jobs could be done with a limited amount of skill and training. The closest graphic design occupation to this today is that of the much more highly skilled back-end coder.

Designers now rely little on outside suppliers, so can take more exploration to a 'final' stage. This means that costs of typographic experimentation have moved away (from the point of view of the designer) from money and toward cost in time. Production, too, is time consuming. It can take much more time than necessary, unless the designer develops an organized work process that uses available software and other systems to their best advantage.

NEW ECONOMIC MODELS FOR TYPEFACES

The economic landscape of typography has changed in other ways, and the way that typefaces have become part of on-screen design work is an example of that. In the days of letterpress printing, in the most common model, type was either sold to printing companies in the form of the metal type itself (known as 'foundry type'), for hand setting, or as matrices for mechanical typesetting machines, so that printers with the right equipment could cast their own metal type automatically, using a keyboard. As new technologies arose, the model remained of suppliers selling type to designers as a service, with only larger design and publishing companies paying foundries for the equipment and right to use fonts supplied by those foundries.

Leasing the right to use typefaces has become the common model. Although people talk about 'buying' fonts, they are actually buying a license to use the font software. In some cases, the right to use the typeface software is assigned at no cost, as part of computer operating software or a software application package, or simply as a free font. In other cases, the right is assigned to the user for a one-time fee, paid when a designer decides they want to 'buy' a particular typeface. With web fonts, the licence may allow a certain number of page views. This is the most common model today, though Google fonts and other free typefaces are increasingly popular, as 'free' things tend to be.

. . . .

End User License Agreements

Fonts almost invariably have EULAs, license agreements that specify how you may use them. Some are quite open, others very restrictive. Using an unlicensed font could result in the user being sued by the foundry.

The birth of font piracy

The development of electrotyping in the 1800s allowed for the beginning of typeface piracy: metal type could be copied almost exactly and then be sold by the copier to the ever-growing number of printers.

PRINT MEDIA

The colour, weight, smoothness and stiffness of the medium on which type is printed all affect the appearance of typography. For type on screen, the size and colour of both the type and background are the variables. When using CMYK printers, the absorbency, colour, and smoothness of the paper all affect how the type appears.

Intellectual property laws protect font software, rather than the forms themselves. However, since the forms are created from software, commercial typeface designs are practically, if not literally, protected.

In the past, there was a capital barrier to the creation of typefaces: fonts were expensive to make and had to be manufactured on a large scale to be profitable. This barrier diminished with the introduction of filmstrip photo typositors in the 1960s, which allowed for the possibility of individual production of display typefaces. In the 1980s, relatively inexpensive type editing software made it possible for individuals to independently produce and distribute display and text faces as computer files. This has made type design accessible to anyone.

There are many digital type foundries that create typefaces that are both aesthetically and technically excellent. There are even more typefaces of lower quality, many of which are made by designers with more enthusiasm than expertise. The number of fonts available has increased a thousandfold since the mid 1980s, and more become available every day.

A factor that made for high typeface quality in the past was that the direct market for type foundries was composed of type shops and printers, who had an interest in and knowledge of good typefaces, which they in turn would promote to publishers and designers. Now typeface licenses are usually sold directly to designers, who, while somewhat expert, are less attuned to the details of good typeface design than the typography specialists of the type shop.

The growing number of free typefaces is also a factor that has led to a decrease in technical typeface quality. This lack of quality, beside problems of form, spacing and kerning, may affect a font's behaviour on screen, which can cause unexpected problems at different size use and in different browsers (though high-resolution screens make this increasingly a smaller risk). The fact that typefaces are often obtained through informal and unpaid channels is a pressure against the production of new and high-quality typefaces. Since creating and distributing a font is much easier than it was before the desktop computer, there as been an overall trend toward quantity over quality.

Free fonts from sources such as Google, though not all of great quality and design, do include some good options, which means that a non-existent font budget allows a range of typeface choices. On the down side, this is yet another pressure on type designers and foundries who inevitably lose market share, and possibly, their financial viability.

DIFFERENT MEDIA, DIFFERENT KNOWLEDGE

The Web is now the principal professional field for most graphic designers. A designer working with typography on the Web or another interactive medium will need to understand css, Java-Script and HTML capabilities as they apply to typographic design, whether or not he or she is actually the person doing the coding. Like a building contractor, designers must have an understanding of the technical aspects, even if they are not responsible for them.

The larger and more complex the project (or series of projects), the more it is worth the time to learn any techniques or systems that will help you do the job, unless experts in those technologies are available to do the project. A problem that design school projects often have is that they do not demand mastery of the tools.

Gantt chart for a typographic design project

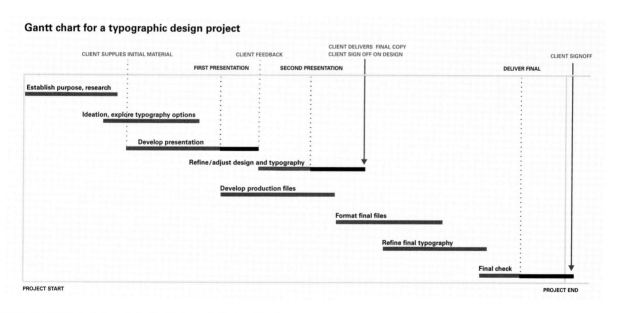

The red bars indicate design activity, the black bars indicate waiting for a client response. A project doesn't work quite as neatly as this indicates, and a Gantt chart is usually revised and updated as the project progresses.

For example, they might ask the student to design a book title page and sample spread, or magazine cover and spread, or an index page and site map for a website, but largely ignore the typographic requirements of actually building the complete project.

This seems a dated, almost archaic, model, at least for those schools that imply that their graduated students will be qualified to find employment in graphic design. In the past, a designer's time would be spent conceptualizing, sketching and mocking-up a design, with type shops producing the typography that would be pasted down to create 'camera-ready art'. A designer today is likely to be spending more of their time executing their design (or someone else's design) than in the design phase.

Designing a system for execution might not be worth the time for a typical course assignment, but it is absolutely invaluable if one actually has to produce an entire publication or website. Design instructors might reasonably argue that they are teaching design, not systems. However, students still need to learn how to deal with and use various systems to successfully work in the design world. Typography classes seem the appropriate place to learn this, though many skills will inevitably be self-taught, due to the fast-evolving changes in technology.

This kind of systematic thinking is part of training for web designers or coders, and coding for the Web is closely related to the proper use of software for projects in other media. Some training in web coding is helpful for print practice as well as web design. Conversely, of course, the coder who ends up working in design is likely to benefit from more education about typography and design, something that is often largely neglected in more technically-focused courses.

USE OF AVAILABLE TIME

Just as design schools have to weigh up the benefits of teaching a particular skill given the limited amount of time in the curriculum, the designer must weigh up the benefits of learning a particular piece, or feature of, software with the time required to learn it. The typography for a simple single-page project can be done visually, with little benefit from using many of the systems available in

AVOIDING LAST-MINUTE CLIENT CHANGES

In the past, the rigidity and linear aspect of production meant that text was finalized early in the process. Now clients know that they can change or add text at any time in process. Establishing an agreed-upon workflow early in the project can at least discourage this kind of thing, if not eliminate it.

software. (In fact, some excellent contemporary typographic works are designed without using any software at all.) Still, even for a simple project, knowing when (and how!) to adjust kerning and leading, and depending on the design, other abilities of the applications being used, is indispensable. Just as web coders do not code each element as they come to them, instead relying on Cascading Style Sheets, so professional designers need to make use of the same systems, or same kinds of systems, that are available in page layout or other software they might be using.

The same need for understanding available systems applies to font design. The designer can use auxiliary software tools to speed up and improve the technical quality of a typeface development project. As with the other examples, it is not necessary to know these things to execute a project, because, as with design software, the typeface editing software is sufficiently accessible that a non-expert can still get results, but the execution is likely to be faster and have better results when the designer understands and uses the tools and methods available.

In the case of an art director or other kind of supervisor of design, a strong ability to use current software is not necessary. However, few people become supervisors without proving themselves in the design trenches. While web designers often work with coders from the beginning of their careers, print designers are almost always expected to execute designs. And even supervisors have to stay abreast of developments in technology. Knowledge of new developments and techniques will make for a more effective (and respected) supervisor in any field.

COLLABORATION WITH SOFTWARE INSTEAD OF PEOPLE

Most of the time, the closest modern equivalent to a type shop is the software that we use, so in a sense, we are collaborating with the designers of that software.

Photography and other visual assets often come from an online stock agency rather than collaboration with a photographer.

Relationships that haven't changed much are those between the designer and the client, and that of the designer with the printer and illustrator, or other technician or artist.

WORKING WITH TECHNICAL EXPERTS

A designer may not be executing the technical aspects of design, but will still have to communicate with the specialists who do. Just as graphic design students used to get training in typesetting in order to understand the systems being used to execute their design, current designers need a broad understanding of technologies to communicate effectively with the coders, programmers, fabricators or other technicians they might collaborate with.

Because increasing capabilities and complexity of software make it harder for an individual to master the necessary skills for all kinds of work, the division-of-labour model that was common before the personal computer has returned, at least in web design, with designers designing the 'front end' of the function, appearance and user interface, and coders programming the 'back end'. The coders working on the back end are usually not trained or responsible for, and quite possibly not particularly interested in, the typographic aspects of the job. Those responsibilities rest with the designer.

....

New work flow, new problem

Today's clients know that they can add copy at the last minute, when in the past, once the type was set, any changes would be very expensive. This kind of request can mean that design decisions have to be remade late in the process and carefully crafted earlier work can be rendered useless.

....

New typographic characters

Icons, emojis and widely understood abbreviations have become part of visual communication conventions. You can probably read these as well as as you could their equivalents in English.

LOL   YOLO   WTF   IDK

The end of the type shop

Before the desktop computer, designers got type from a type shop. After specifying the typefaces and size, and other typographic details, the designer would send the typewritten copy to the type shop, from a few words for an advertisement, to an author's typed manuscript for a book.

Type shops had the expensive equipment to use the typefaces, usually licensed by the same company that made the equipment, and the skilled operators needed to produce good type from it. Type shops also had the supporting technologies, such as resizing cameras and film developers, that were needed for the phototype that began to dominate in the second half of the 20th century. Some shops also had hand lettering artists on staff.

All work would be reviewed by typographic proofreaders, who made sure that all the type was set without typographical errors, and check and correct kerning, justification, rag shapes and other visual aspects of the type. These proofreaders would also correct grammar, if necessary, and make suggestions for improvement to the designer's type specifications.

Many, if not all, of the tasks of the type shop now fall to graphic designers.

CHANGING PROCESS / WORK FLOWS

Every design job is a process with a beginning and end (we hope!), and different projects will have different workflows. Some will be quite simple, others, especially if you are dealing with many other individuals or organizations, will be more complex. It is important that parts of the workflow be communicated between all parties. Not only is it necessary to meet the deadlines established with collaborators, clients or others, but approaching a project in an organized and linear way will let you properly focus on typographic aesthetics and details. When suppliers were involved, this happened naturally, but when one person (the designer) is able to do everything without suppliers, misunderstandings about schedules and deadlines can lead to trouble. Establishing and agreeing on a schedule, such as a Gantt chart or workback schedule, will help keep a complex job on track.

Also, a clearly communicated workflow will save reduplication of work. For example, a final pass of adjusting the setting of text should be done only when the copy is final, to avoid wasting time. This kind of reduplication can't be completely avoided, but a well-organized project will help minimize it.

DESIGN WORKFLOW BOUNDARIES WEAKEN...

If in the past, the designer's workflow was dictated by requirements of production (ideation, sketching, selection of images, if needed, choosing and specifying type for display and text type, getting images resized, and specifying colour treatment, etc., if necessary, with frequent client approval stages and collaboration with suppliers), that procedural structure has disappeared.

Designers may have excellent conceptual and aesthetic skills as well as typographic skills, but will have great trouble employing them simultaneously. You may consider yourself a good multitasker, but multitasking doesn't really exist: even for computers themselves, multitasking is basically just rapid task switching, and people aren't as good at that as computers are.

The text of this 1970s ad was aimed at advertisers and gives an idea of what place type shops played in design typography.

Being able to change typographical decisions at any time can lead to disaster. If you decide late in the process to change a typeface or other typographical parameter, errors such as overset text or bad line breaks could arise. These outweigh any advantages that might come from a slight improvement in a design, that after all, you had considered good before changing your mind. Having a 'no design change' deadline for yourself can save you some grief.

Quality control

Graphic designers used to be able to rely on the process of design, which included stages of approval, proofreading, and higher costs bringing more attention to design, all of which led to many people checking the type. Attention to typographic detail now falls to the designer.

TYPE TAKES ATTENTION

A place to work without interruptions is the best place to focus on all parts of the design process, but especially the design and execution of complex or text typography. Turning off the internet doesn't hurt either.

In a graphic design project of significant complexity, there will be many tasks which you may feel tempted to work on more or less simultaneously, because for one thing, you are likely to be responsible for executing all the aspects of the design, and for another, the computer makes it possible to work on anything at any time. While this ability is sometimes useful, it also encourages a kind of artificial attention deficit disorder. Lack of focus is particularly a problem when dealing with the execution of typography, where losing or reduplicating a line or a paragraph can lead to memorable instances of typographic error, which people will unfortunately often remember for longer than your otherwise good typographic design, especially with printed work.

The fact that a website can be easily changed after publication takes off some of the pressure to do a 'perfect' job, but it is still better to deliver a project without errors and avoid the embarrassment of making changes after the project has been delivered.

A large print job with designer-caused errors is a disaster that can be a fireable offense.

...SO WE HAVE TO DESIGN THE WORKFLOW

Designing typography and other graphic elements is something we all expect to do, and something that is a basic element of design education. Designing a *system* for implementing a design is something that doesn't happen enough in design schools. Planning the stages of a project and using the affordances of the software as much as possible is indispensable to effective use of time, helps maintain consistent quality, and helps avoid missed deadlines.

For a book or other long publication, or a complex website, a typical effective workflow is to develop the design, then design the job flow. Some thinking ahead about how a project will be executed should be a part of the design process. Implementing a system that is difficult or impossible to execute efficiently will take away from time spent on design, and less efficiency usually means more errors. This doesn't mean that we should seek the easy path: most conceivable designs can be systematized one way or another. But it is also possible to work unsystematically. It will just take longer and tend to be of lower quality.

TRADITIONAL AND 'OBSOLETE' PRACTICES

These days, there is a tendency for designers' entire practice to take place on the computer. Their inspirations themselves often come from the internet, and designers' ideation, tools, and execution take place on their computers. As a result, design often refers very strongly to current visual culture fashions. Experimental work is similarly often influenced and driven by the tools that exist within software. This is not a bad thing in itself, but there are things that the designer will discover, and ideas and aesthetic effects that are unlikely or impossible to come up with on the computer. Experimenting with wood or foundry letterpress, silk-screening, paste-up, transfer lettering, hand lettering, etc., will enlarge your practice. These methods are not 'efficient', but their inclusion can create, or at least play a part in, striking and effective typographic design.

CONCLUSION

Typographic technology has changed several times since printing was invented, with the internet being the most recent example of this. Designers have taken on the control of, and responsibility for, typography, and this takes new ways of working. Media have changed, but typographic principles remain essentially the same. Type continues to be the main means of communication on the Web and in print. Excellent typography is now possible in all the media we work in, but it doesn't happen by itself. Software gives the tools but doesn't make good typographical decisions or autonomously execute good typography. Typography education often lags behind the discipline in terms of new technologies and at the same time has forgotten much of the knowledge that was held by the typographic specialists of the past. There is a tendency for people to teach as and what they were taught, rather than on the basis of their current practice. Adding to this is the fact that people teaching typography are often generalist graphic designers who didn't have access to a type-focused education. This is not to say that these typography courses aren't valuable, but they are not in themselves enough to give you typographic expertise.

Typography provides the most characteristic picture of a period.

Peter Behrens

Well-executed typography that has no particularly creative concept or originality may (or may not!) serve the transmission of language. Typography that is not well executed will at best be unprofessional, and at worst drive readers away. The designer must first think about the purpose of the work; second, explore the possibilities; third, conceive a coherent vision; fourth, execute the project well. It is difficult, if not impossible, to work on all these approaches at the same time. Designers, who may begin with intuition, should finish with the systematic approach of the typographer-technician.

Typography: art and craft

For the title of this chapter to be useful, we must define art and craft. There will be, inevitably, a lot of overlap between the two.

The creative potential of typography has expanded enormously with the advent of computer software and new communication technologies. The student of typography should be prepared to employ the software and other technologies when it makes sense, while retaining the attention to detail and understanding of the reading experience, which is formed by long-standing cultural and craft traditions. Good typographic design can attract readers. Bad typographic craft may drive them away.

ART...

By art, we mean the visual and creative aspect of typography. There is no strict right or wrong about composition or visual typographical decisions. These decisions are subjective and dependent on the designer's individual vision of how to communicate given content. Any but the simplest and most straightforward composition will be laid out in very different ways by different designers (see page 46) even if they are using the same typefaces. And two designers are unlikely to choose the same typefaces for any given purpose, yet both may be making excellent choices.

Aesthetic and function

In the same way that a designer's relationship with a typographic design changes as the design develops, the reader's relationship changes from an initial visual and aesthetic experience, that depends on the designer's creativity and aesthetic judgement to a communicative experience that depends on the designer's craft knowledge and execution.

**Design is often intuitive.
Production should be systematic.**

Using design tools in an intuitive way
is fine for the initial design phase, but
software systems allow a high level of
systematization and organization. This
should be taken advantage of for complex
projects. Designing the structure is part
of design.

THE FUNCTION OF TYPE
CAN BE COMPROMISED
FOR REASONS OF
AESTHETICS.

CRAFT...

Craft, on the other hand, is the right and wrong, the quality of
adjustments, the knowledge and application of typographic conventions, and the attention to typographic detail in both display
and body type. Good typographic craft, too, will vary with each
designer but more subtly than the larger aesthetic decisions.

Much of typographic craft is something that most designers
will agree on. These include basic typographic decisions as choosing the parameters of a block of type, good visual alignments, the
quality of justification or rag (though there might be disagreement
on how tight or loose a rag should be), and other aspects of execution. A lot of it has to do with attention to detail. Part of most
successful typography, no matter how effortless it might look, is in
careful refinement.

There is also an aspect of typographic craft that has returned
with the computer, and that is the craft of production, which today
usually is mostly to do with the use and management of computer
software. In most computer applications, there are many ways that
we can produce a page that looks a certain way, but using the tools
in an organized and effective way directly affects the efficiency and
adaptability of our work.

... OR BOTH

Aspects such as hierarchical and other relationships, page structures, etc.—in other words, the construction of the elements of
typographic communication—lie somewhere in between art and
craft. For a simple example, the colour of a piece of type can't
really be incorrect, but choosing a colour that doesn't contrast well
with the background will cause problems with legibility and visual
balance. If the text is being used visually, though, and either doesn't
need to be read, or is repeated elsewhere, this may be a reasonable
design decision.

So, typography is sometimes mainly an art and sometimes a
mainly a craft but is almost always, to some extent, both.

In the past, a professional designer needed the ability to critically judge typography without necessarily having the ability to produce it, as the relationship between graphic designers and those who executed typography was a collaborative one: the designer had to be able to tell good typography from bad, without needing to know the decisions that went into that production. An important part of being a good designer was in the recognition and choice of a good type shop.

Generally, display type and layout, and the relationships of typographic elements with each other and with other elements of the page, are on the art end of a continuum that has art on one end and craft on the other. At the same time, display typography has craft elements such as kerning and other space relationships.

Text typography tends toward the craft end of that continuum, though the larger decisions about typefaces, spacing and location of typographic elements on the page are aesthetic and compositional choices that are more art than craft.

Designing page size and layout, the treatment of chapter heads, running feet and folios is typographic design. The setting and adjustment of them is typographic craft. In the setting of page 188 of a novel, for example, there is probably very little artistry. After the initial design decisions, setting type is a matter of craft and attention to detail. There may not be many opportunities to do something brilliant, but you can help keep the reader enjoying reading, and avoid weakening the visual communication interface between author and reader.

There is a skewing towards the art aspect in the kind of typographic design that wins awards, but in most practice, typography's purpose of communicating information has to be the priority. If winning awards is what you are trying to do, that's fine. But most of the time the main purpose of typography is communication served by art. It is the success of the communication of the author or designer's intent that is the measure of typography's success.

To over-simplify, the difference is between inarticulate practice with the materials of production ('printing'), and conscious shaping of the product, by instruction ('typography')

Robin Kinross, *Modern Typography*

DIVIDE TASKS

Designing and crafting type take different mindsets. It is best to wear the designer 'art' hat when designing type, and wear the typographer 'craft' hat when setting type.

We do not read everything that appears in print, but do read that which appears interesting.

Edmund G. Gress, *Fashions in American Typography 1780–1930*

The purpose of typography

The first purpose of typography, some suggest, is to clearly convey language. This presumes that the main intention is to communicate language, which is what the vast majority of typographic practice is, and continues to be about.

Emil Ruder, a founder of the Schule für Gestaltung Basel (Basel Design School), wrote, 'Typography has one plain duty before it and that is to convey information in writing.' But is this true? The *most important* purpose may be to clearly convey information, but in most cases (the exceptions being when the reader has already decided to read the content), the *first* purpose is to get the reader to engage with it. Part of typography's usual purpose is to signal to the reader that there is content worth further reading.

Casting against type

It is worth considering the idea of casting against type for display type, that is, using an unexpected type face for the subject, (as long as it makes sense), as a visual version of the rhetorical device antiphrasis (see page 49).

What's the use of being legible, when nothing inspires you to take notice of it?

Wolfgang Weingart

Beware of bathos

Bathos is a negative term that comes from overdoing pathos, which can result in the opposite of the intended effect: instead of evoking empathy, for example, it evokes laughter.

TYPE AS ART OR HYBRID PRACTICE

Most professional typographic practice is intended to communicate and contexualize language.

However, there are other equally valid practices of typography. These include the purely expressive, the experimental and the self-indulgent, all of which can stand on their own, as well as informing more traditional communication practice, and these practices are often what get the most attention from other designers and design critics.

Often, design school gives many opportunities for this, while the professional dimension of typography gets little attention in comparison. Graduates of design programs often find the opposite when in employment: they spend their days and evenings setting type, but have little opportunity for wide exploration or typographic play. The pressure of time discourages many designers from immersing themselves in pure exploration on their own time, but we should all try to find time to work on projects that have nothing to do with our professional obligations.

The art of persuasive rhetoric was part of higher education in the Western tradition until the 20th century. It was considered an important part of the education of a citizen, as it concerned the craft of argument and debate, leading to finding the best way forward through the decisions of a democracy. As type is a visual representation of language, the principles of rhetoric often apply well to it.

Rhetoric is today sometimes thought of as being 'empty', but it really means putting forward an argument as well as possible, appealing variously to logic (logos), to emotion (pathos), and to ethics (ethos). This clearly applies to typography, not only in the content of the words that are chosen, but also to how that content is presented, especially on the macro-typographic elements of display typography and layout. Rhetoric in typography is always *related* to the content of the text, and *applies* principally to display text and page layout.

Purely visual creativity is not linguistic, though imagery itself may have rhetorical qualities. Typography in particular has rhetorical dimensions both visual (in how it looks) and linguistic (in what it says), and ideally, these should work together, and certainly, they should not work against each other.

Elocution, one of rhetoric's most obviously relevant skills, deals with volume, pitch and pacing. Size or weight of type is analogous to volume, typeface and some punctuation is analogous to pitch (a question mark suggesting a rising voice), while commas and periods (or full stops) suggest pauses. Typeface choice contributes to tone. Placement of letters, words and lines are analogous to pacing. These apply very much to display type, but also to text type, where the type choice and setting may have some rhetorical qualities such as suggestions of importance, seriousness or frivolity.

However, most rhetoric is found in the words of the text rather than in its visual quality. When a reader begins to read text, visual rhetoric falls away, as the reader moves from the visual experience of looking at the page, to the semantic experience of reading the content and experiencing the text's rhetorical qualities. Both are important; the visual perception of the type provides the context

What?

What?

The word in both these images is identical, but they communicate different messages. This is an obvious example, but this kind of effect is always present, though usually more subtle.

within which the reader engages with the content. Even more crucial, it can also determine whether the potential reader reads the type at all.

This is not to say that the rhetorical aspect is always the most important aspect of typography. Sometimes, the visual qualities may supersede, override or simply ignore rhetorical considerations.

TYPE HAS DIFFERENT FUNCTIONS IN DIFFERENT CONTEXTS

Designers understand that while typography works more or less the same way in most applications, it has different purposes in different kinds of work. In each case, the designer has to balance the art and craft, the aesthetic and semantic aspect, and consider the context of the typographic design. There is obviously a difference between work that is intended to have some kind of permanence (most books, architectural typography, institutional websites, logos and so on) and that which is by nature ephemeral (package labels, periodicals, brochures, advertisements, web banners, event flyers, etc.). It is still worth taking time to analyze the purpose of typography in an application rather than simply relying on instinct.

More permanent work functions over a longer time, so it is best to avoid too much focus on fashion, and pay more attention to functional communication of content, though the design will still likely reflect the time and place of its creation. Ephemeral work usually provides more typographic freedom, as it is expected to communicate for a short time in a certain context. Conversely, because it has a particular purpose, it is also expected to be particularly appropriate for that purpose, which suggests that there is more of a 'right' kind of typographic approach. Ephemeral works can be a good focus for personal projects or exercises.

THERE IS A PLACE FOR IMPROVISATION

Like the grid, a systematic approach is a useful tool you have at your disposal; it is not a requirement for every project. Approaching type as visual or conceptual art is usually less systematic than the approach to type as communication of content. Creative design takes intuition and improvisation that is by nature *not* systematic. Part of design practice is approaching the project intuitively and

Emil Ruder's 1967 book takes a modernist approach to integrating function with aesthetics.

experimentally (though informed by research), and then moving toward a more rational, systematic approach in developing and executing those experimental iterations.

The need to communicate effectively can sometimes seem a hindrance to creativity, but in the context of typographic design, it is a framework that gives direction and purpose to the designer.

There is an infinite number of ways that typography can be approached and refined. The designer must not only *choose* an approach that works but also be able to *support* why the chosen direction and final piece is particularly suited to the project. The designer doesn't necessarily begin with a logical concept. However, being able to argue how intuitive decisions achieve a rational purpose is often necessary to get approval to actually use them.

Research

Research into typography is something that we all do unconsciously to varying degrees. Even if, in the interests of developing unique and original approaches, a designer avoids the millions of examples on the Web, just by living in a culture, seeing current graphic design is unavoidable and will have an influence on the designer's work.

And since we are developing communication, which depends on the creator and audience having a common language, then research is necessary when we are designing for a demographic or culture other than our own.

Research for typography balances primary research (experimentation and evaluation of your own work), and secondary visual and other research (research about the subject, visual and technical research, scoping and competitor research).

Some research is project specific, but ongoing study of on technique and cultural changes is an important part of maintaining typographic currency and expertise.

. . . .

Three audiences

The client / instructor These may be more focused on one or the other of the two categories. Graphic design instructors are interested in creativity and exploration, and thus often pay relatively little attention to details in typography. The typical client is more interested in the function of design, and may need to be 'sold' on typographic decisions that do not resemble similar work.

The end user / reader These may be people looking for entertainment or information, people conducting research, people interested in buying a product or service, etc. They may be expected to have different levels of education and interest. User-focused design implies prioritizing navigation and functional typography over visual creativity, though such creativity is important to engage the reader on the visual and cultural levels.

Other designers Your professional reputation depends on them (and they may be in a position to hire you, recommend you to others, or give you an award). Designers, like clients and instructors, tend to focus on innovation and aesthetics, but they will also appreciate your well-crafted typographic systems.

CRAFT IN TYPOGRAPHY

These two recto pages of the same basic design show the importance of typographic craft. The page on the left has errors in attention to typographic detail. The page on the right shows much better craft.

Chapter number is set in reduced caps rather than true small caps.

Chapter head is set at text weight. (This is not bad, but using the available display cut is an option to consider.)

Drop cap is too close to following text, also set in reduced caps rather than true small caps.

Bad hyphenation parameters ('essential-ly').

Widow is made worse by the large paragraph indent.

Lining figures and all cap settings are distracting.

Ligatures not used (ff, fi, fl).

Double hyphens not changed to emdashes.

Some double word spaces, the worst being in the middle of sentences.

Whole paragraph has been negatively tracked to bring up a line, which changes the typographic colour of the paragraph.

Marginal text is too small and narrow to lock to baseline grid. Having things line up is nice, but this is a case of 'lesser of evils'.

Running foot is too tight and weak, using capitals rather than small capitals.

CHAPTER ONE

Technology

THE TECHNOLOGY OF TYPE has affected its appearance since its introduction, even though the makers of type have generally tried to minimize this as little as possible over most of its history. Although the method of printing from inked metal (or wood) letterforms was essentially unchanged, evolution of form was slow and incremental until the Industrial Revolution, and although new and original forms were created, it was rare for typefaces to reflect the medium in which they were made until the late twentieth century. (With a very few exceptions: Rudolf Koch's Neuland typeface of 1923 was carved onto the type punches without drawings.) Only in the late twentieth century did the medium of typographic technology begin to inform its appearance.

Typeface editing and creation software led to the most notable instances of this. The work of Zuzana Licko of the Emigre type foundry is a good example of this. She used the bitmap form in which fonts were rendered on screen as inspiration for PostScript type designs created in the 1980s and 90s. Conversely, the versatility of the vector format made it possible to imitate other technologies, leading to faces more or less unclassifiable under the VOX-ATYPI system: the imperfections of old wood type, handlettering, graffiti and other visual sources became popular sources of inspiration for the independent type designers, who previously--for better or worse--had to choose from typefaces produced by commercial type foundries.

As a result there are many, many more typefaces available today than there were before the accessibility to type design software, and it has meant that designers must develop a good critical sense. There are no typographic gatekeepers now.

Typefaces did reflect the medium in which they were made, but not deliberately: improved type metal, the use of etching tools and development of the pantograph did change the appearance of typefaces since the 15th century.

TYPOGRAPHY 13

Technology

THE TECHNOLOGY OF TYPE has affected its appearance since its introduction, even though the makers of type have generally tried to minimize this as little as possible over most of its history. Although the method of printing from inked metal (or wood) letterforms was essentially unchanged, evolution of form was slow and incremental until the Industrial Revolution, and then, although new and original forms were created, they did not deliberately reflect the medium in which they were made until the late twentieth century. (With a few exceptions: Rudolf Koch's Neuland typeface of 1923 was carved onto the type punches without his first making design drawings.) Only in the late twentieth century did the medium of typographic technology begin to inform its appearance.

Typeface editing and creation software led to the most notable examples of this. The work of Zuzana Licko of the Emigre type foundry is a good example of this. She used the bitmap form in which fonts were rendered on screen as inspiration for PostScript type designs created in the 1980s and 90s. Conversely, the versatility of the vector format made it possible to imitate other technologies, leading to faces more or less unclassifiable under the Vox-ATypI system: the imperfections of old wood type, handlettering, graffiti and other visual sources became popular sources of inspiration for the independent type designers, who previously—for better or worse—had to choose from typefaces produced by commercial type foundries.

As a result there are many, many more typefaces available today than there were before the accessibility to type design software, and it has meant that designers must develop a good critical sense. There are no typographic gatekeepers now.

Typefaces did reflect the medium in which they were made, but not deliberately: improved type metal, the use of etching tools and development of the pantograph did change the appearance of typefaces since the 15th century.

TYPOGRAPHY 13

True small caps are used, and given extra tracking.

Display cut of Garamond used. Caps in text have been made small caps.

The left margin has been adjusted to create a stronger visual line.

Space has been added after the drop cap.

Like the design shown on the facing page, tabs have been used for paragraph indents but adjusted in the style sheets to an appropriate width.

Leading for short line length reduced.

Ligatures applied throughout.

Emdashes have been used to replace the double hyphens. On a narrow measure, a space-endash-space would probably work better.

Adjustment of typography using true small caps for acronyms and old-style numbers.

Text hyphenation and justification parameters have been adjusted, and some lines have forced breaks to avoid widows.

PAGE DESIGN VARIATIONS

Using only two weights from the Univers family shows that typeface choice is not the most important thing in having typographic control and creativity. Even with the same typefaces, the page format, use of white space, visual balance, hierarchy and typographic contrast all present the same information in a different way.

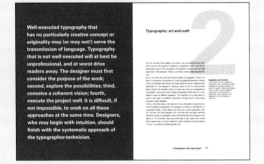

DEGREES OF FREEDOM

In typographic practice, the amount of freedom we have varies. Working on a project for a client may come with a typeface and compositional style that has already been established. In cases like this, although we may some have agency in creating a layout, the main task may be mainly in setting the type as well as possible in terms of justification and rag, and adjusting and finessing other typographical details.

In other cases, we may have carte blanche and be able to make all typographic decisions. In cases like this, we will inevitably bring more of our own perceptions and preferences—what we might call our style—to produce creative solutions for the communication of content.

Avoiding the mediocre middle

Typographic design should avoid the mediocre. Excellence in display type and layout is largely a matter of art: typographic choice, treatment and placement. It is often a case of taking risks and discovery of the unexpected.

Excellence in text type is largely a matter of execution and craft, though the typographic design choices of placement, use of space and typographical parameters is, at its best, an art.

Very good execution of typography is relatively rare now, as the days of professionals completely focused on its execution are a distant memory. Even teachers of typography are usually generalist graphic designers who are interested in typography, and who focus on typographic design, but who probably didn't have much training in the tradition of typographic craft.

As a result, almost every designer who has a deep understanding of the practice of type is more or less self-taught. Because of this, it is common to find text set acceptably, but quite uncommon to find text type set really well.

Many designers make the relationship of visual elements (syntax) their primary concern. In practice, their stress on visual syntax often detracts from meaning (semantics) and each element's effect and affect on the reader (pragmatics). In the initial stages of a design, visual syntax should not be the main concern, because a message is never communicated on a purely syntactical level.

Willi Kunz, *Micro and Macro-typography*

___

QUESTION SOFTWARE'S AUTHORITY

Accepting the choices and structures suggested by the software is unlikely to produce the best possible work. The most basic aspects of software have their own aesthetic (even rhetorical) qualities that may or may not work well in a given project.

___

CONCLUSION

Display type and layout are where you can make the big typographic decisions. This is where originality and creativity come in. That isn't to say that craft is absent here. Kerning, leading and other visual relationships in display type require attention and craft, and there is an artistry in the larger decisions about text type, such as page format and page composition. Display type can be evaluated by its appearance and meaning. Text type on the functional scale can only be tested by reading it, something that is often neglected in design education. Allowing students to set type in 'lorem ipsum' text is a tacit acknowledgement of this neglect. The tasks facing the designer when dealing with typography include both the art practice of typographic design and the craft practice of setting both display and text typography.

In spite of — in fact because of — the unevenly inked type, rough edges, the odd gouge and absence of kerning, this poster evokes the event better than clean computer type does.

Common rhetorical devices that can apply to typography

Alliteration The repetition of an initial consonant sound. Example: Repeating a letter form or other graphic treatment to initial letters. Repeated drop caps are a form of visual alliteration.

Antiphrasis A figure of speech in which a phrase or word is employed in a way that is opposite to its literal meaning, in order to create an ironic or comic effect. Example: see margin, page 72.

Antithesis The juxtaposition of contrasting ideas in balanced phrases. Example: Contrasting conceptually or aesthetically typographic treatments in close proximity.

Ellipsis Leaving out part of a phrase without changing the meaning. Example: Leaving out a letter or part of a letter (but leaving the space) without losing meaning.

Hyperbole Extravagant statement; the use of exaggerated terms for the purpose of emphasis or heightened effect. Example: Making a word or phrase more visually significant than warranted.

Understatement (or litotes)
The opposite of hyperbole. Example: Setting display type you would expect to be large at a small size.

Metaphor A reference to something by comparison to a different thing with which it has something in common. Example: Setting type in a way that visually (but not pictorially!) represents what it means.

Personification A figure of speech in which an inanimate object or abstraction is endowed with human qualities or abilities. Example: Making a word resemble the thing it represents.

Pun A play on words, sometimes on different senses of the same word and sometimes on the similar sense or sound of different words. Example: Using a typeface whose name means something relevant to the text.

A pun/in-joke: the cover of this book on David Rockwell is set in the Rockwell Extra Bold typeface.

Having an understanding and command of the tools you use is necessary for success in any kind of work, including typography.
In the past, graphic designers were expected to have skill in concept development and illustration, as well as an understanding of the printing process. They understood type from a critical and creative point of view, particularly display type, but often had little knowledge of the craft of actually setting it. Typesetters understood the craft of type, but their creativity was generally focused on solving technical problems, or the adjustment of difficult settings or letter relationships. The graphic designer now has both the tools and the responsibility for doing that work.

Type is technology

Typography is, and always has been, a technology. Writing systems themselves are also technologies. Writing was produced by the technology of the writing implement and the surface. The writing itself was accomplished through the technical skills and knowledge of the scribe. The development of parchment made of animal skins, and paper to write and print on were also innovations in technology, as are the screens we work and read on. As a more complex technology than handwriting, typography requires more knowledge and expertise to manage and use to its full potential.

New technologies both further enable the practice of typography and influence typographic form.

When the printing press was developed, the efficiency and quality of printing depended on the quality of the tools (the design and manufacture of the press and the typefaces used), as well as the technical collaboration of the inker, press operator and proofreader. This model of collaboration between designer and craft experts continued for 500 years. The present era has brought the technology of typographic production into the computer and software programs, which the designer now uses to produce the typography that is the essence of most visual communication. The collaboration has become mainly one with the anonymous designers of the technologies that we use.

The mechanization
of the scribal art
was probably the
first reduction
of any handicraft to
mechanical terms.

Marshall McLuhan, *The Gutenberg Galaxy*

The graphic designer in the past was analogous to a film director. The designer would deal with the client, sketch possible approaches, present a visual and visual mock-up, then collaborate with and manage the production of suppliers who were experts in their fields. This would include typography and its technologies, as well as illustration, photography, film preparation and printing.

On the positive side, a designer could expect high-quality work from these collaborators.

On the negative side, these services were expensive. Any changes made to typography and other services cost money. The designer is now free of that particular economic pressure, giving more freedom to experiment and refine.

TIME

QUALITY   RESOURCES

The production triangle

A design project is usually firmly within the production triangle restrictions of time, cost and quality. Effective understanding and a degree of mastery of available technologies can help the designer with both time and quality, both of which are directly related to cost. Time, because making efficient use of the abilities of type software makes the job faster. Quality, because making full use of style sheets and master pages, and using search and replace functions, can make it practical and easy to automate processes and change design parameters if necessary, thus reducing the number of mistakes. Resources are your ability to design and the abilities of the software used. The more resources we can use effectively, the more we can do in a given amount of time.

TECHNOLOGY ENABLES EXPERIMENTATION

In the past, when typographic possibilities were limited by the constraints of the workflow, the technologies of the time and the cost of typography, innovative typographical approaches were more difficult. Camera effects or physical innovation were the only way to work with typographic form, and camera work on typography needed expertise and expensive equipment that were

Keyboard from the dedicated Alphatype typesetting system of the 1980s.

not available to the designer. Even trying different measures and typefaces or sizes would mean a new charge from a type supplier. So experimentation was expensive in terms of time and money, because type shops took time to deliver a new setting and would charge more if you wanted it in a hurry. Working on the computer, experimentation is easier, and there are many, many more possibilities. On the other hand, physical experimentation is not much easier now than it has been in the past (though the computer can make the materials for experimentation more easily available, as when laser-printed type is a basis for pasted-up compositions). Experimentation on the computer still takes time, though. The temptation is to do all experimentation on the computer, but working with pencil, pasting-up type or using another medium will lead to work that would not come from the computer itself, even if the computer is later used to execute ideas that come from these physical experiments.

ZONE

Distorting type (in this case, Times Roman) had a period of popularity in the 1980s after it became a commonly available modification on computer typesetting system.

CURRENT TECHNOLOGIES

Today, most typography is executed using software applications. Depending on the project, a page layout program is normally used for creating complex print documents, a vector program is used for manipulating type forms themselves, an image program might be used for creating some typographical effects, a motion program for animated typography, a code editor for web design or a font editor to create fonts.

There is disagreement about the various ways to define the following words, but this is the way they are used in this book.

Font The computer file that is the source of the forms of a typeface shown on screen and printed.

Typeface A particular set of characters, such as Times Roman.

Type style A particular style of a type family, such as Times Roman Italic.

Type family The collection of all styles of a typeface. This can be as few as two to over fifty.

Glyph Any character in a font that has a separate place in the font. So the 'fi' ligature is a glyph made up of the 'f' and 'i' glyphs.

After a period during which a single person could hope to have sufficient expertise in all areas of typography, we are returning to a point where we are starting to collaborate with others, because few can maintain a high level of expertise with all the increasing capabilities and complexities of programs that work with typography. But, as in the past, when we do work with collaborators, we have to be able to both communicate and critically evaluate the typographic execution of others.

THE RIGHT TOOL FOR THE JOB

Using the right tool for a job is worth doing. Although many of the software programs are able to do tasks better suited to another program, it is usually inefficient and frustrating. We might be tempted to use a program we know better rather than the program best suited to the task, and if it is a small and simple task, it might be easier than learning how to do it in the most appropriate program. Usually, though, learning how to do something the right way will pay off, as you are likely to run into it again, and even if you don't remember the details, you'll know where to start.

If it is complex and a one-off task, hiring or bartering services with an expert for a project may be worthwhile.

Typography's function is to c sage quickly and easily. The should be to aid easy legibilit y choosing the most readable

Typography's function is to sage quickly and easily. The should be to aid easy legibility y choosing the most readable

Typography's function is to
Typography's function is to convey
TYPOGRAPHY'S FUN

Typography's function is to c
Typography's function is to co
TYPOGRAPHY'S FUNCT

The 1960s Alphatype digital system maintained the historical practice of having different drawings for different sizes. The lighter weight, narrower forms, and more complex details of the display cut are typical of the tradition of the hand-cut punches used to produce the moulds for the final pieces of type. Shown here are 12 point and 72 point Alphatype Caslon, resized for comparison. This attention to scale almost completely disappeared with the advent of scalable computer fonts.

Variable fonts offer the potential for this kind of typographic subtlety to be restored in a single font file. The image above shows the same text set in Adobe's Minion Concept variable font. The font has two variable axes, weight and optical size. In the example above, the weight setting is 400 for both, with the optical size setting at 12 for the top and 36 for the bottom. The differences are not as dramatic as they are in the Alphatype example at left, but the general effect is similar.

In coding for typography, as in all coding, the code should be well commented, not just so others can work on your files but so that you can navigate your own code, and remember how and what you were thinking when you first wrote it. Commenting is a basic part of good web-coding practice. The closest equivalent in page layout programs is giving useful titles to master pages and style sheets. Good organization and systematic use of both is indispensable, to you or anyone else working on your files.

And sometimes, still, the right tools for a job might be a pen and a sheet of paper.

FONTS

The change in font technology from physical to photographic to digital didn't take long. Newspapers were still using hot-metal Linotype machines until the 1970s. Now a font is a piece of software that describes the vectors that shape the letterforms and other glyphs, the widths of each form, and kerning table, as well as other information, such as how the font will be rasterized at low resolutions, and what font will be used when software is used to italicize or bold the typeface.

SCALABLE FONTS

One of the biggest changes from traditional type is the advent of the scalable font.

Until the 1800s, every size of every typeface was cut at actual size by hand. Except in the case of large woodcut fonts, the initial type forms had to be cut in steel, using small metalworking and etching tools.

Smaller sizes were simpler and bolder, at least partly because the punchcutter's fingers and eyes were not scalable. So the smaller letterforms were necessarily simpler, and larger sizes would be narrower in form, set closer together, and have more complex curves and finer serifs. These characteristics worked well for the reader, because the form suited the size from a visual point of view. This also made for good visual balance between different sizes, as the visual weight and level of complexity of the 'same' typeface were harmonious at different scales.

KEEP TYPE AS TYPE

Type forms should remain type if possible. Outlining type not only makes it uneditable but also loses the 'hinting', something that can be important when printed at small sizes or in some screen applications. Failing that, type forms should remain in vector format unless there is a good reason to rasterize them, and even then, only rasterize the type that needs it (usually for some visual effect). The rasterized type should be imported into a vector or page layout program. Otherwise it will appear visibly bitmapped in final display form at any size larger than intended. Even if the font is not available, creating vector forms will at least keep them scalable until they are finally rasterized at output or on screen.

The Linotype machine replaced hand type-setters in the late 1800s, and its speed enabled the modern newspaper with many sections and more pages.

The mechanical pantographic punchcutting machine (see page 18) designed by Linn Boyd Benton in the late 1800s let typefaces of different sizes be cut from a single pattern without the hand work in miniature that had previously been required to cut text sizes. However, the typeface manufacturers recognized the significance of different treatments of type at different sizes, and often continued to adjust the forms of the characters for the range of sizes produced. This was not just a whim of the type foundries; the presses who used type would demand this kind of subtlety for the type that they were paying for. And since type was expensive, many of those who bought type (small printers and publishers, and to a lesser but growing extent, suppliers of type to designers and advertising agencies) would be only able to afford a limited range of fonts (as the set of characters of one size of typeface was called in the days of metal type) for a few typefaces, and would thus be very aware of the visual quality of those types.

The character of typefaces themselves changed when they were produced for the typositor (shown in the advertisement on page 20), as the final typeface forms were drawn instead of being cut out of steel. As they were only used for display, the fact that they were scalable wasn't a problem.

When digital type systems were introduced, the problem of the same typeface for all sizes began, because these systems were scalable, and different cuts for different weights became rare in most fonts. Font editing software gave those who were interested the tools to create vector fonts that were both easy to produce and completely scalable. Few type designers (even at the major foundries), designed more than one version of a set of characters, so one font would be used for all sizes, for text and display.

Type forms changed again with the computer, as even typeface designers who began their work on drawing boards eventually had to transform their work into the geometric curves that describe typefaces. Not only does the medium, by its nature, affect the letterforms but also makes it easy to clean up and rationalize them. In the case of designs that start on the computer with Bezier curves, as many are, the process of creation itself makes it easy to fall into a mechanical sterility.

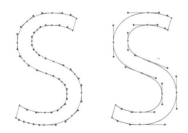

On the left is a character from a TrueType version of a font, on the right, one from a PostScript OTF font. PostScript is capable of drawing more complex curves, as are vector programs such as Adobe Illustrator. So if you are modifying or customizing type outlines, using PostScript fonts is the better choice. For other uses, there isn't much difference, though TrueType faces may appear better on lower-resolution screens on Windows machines, as TrueType has more developed hinting parameters.

Scalable faces have become the norm, with a still small number of exceptions which have different cuts intended for different sizes (see page 162), often given names such as 'display', 'text', 'caption', 'web' etc. Typefaces with a single version are often designed to work well in a display showing, because that is how they are often chosen, even when they are intended for text cuts. A frequent result is faces that work as display type but are somewhat weak and dazzling at small sizes or (more rarely) faces that function well at text sizes but are heavy and badly spaced for large sizes, or, most commonly, faces that function adequately, though not excellently, for either purpose.

The development of variable fonts, which have a range of versions within a single font file, promises to improve this.

Working with type on computer screens

One factor leading to the acceptance of single-cut scalable fonts is the ease of scalability, and the fact that working on screen often tends to cause the designer to be unaware of the subtleties of scale. On a computer screen, a print designer will zoom in to look at the type at a virtual size of up to several hundred points, and therefore be perceiving it in a way that has little to do with how it will be seen on the page.

s, or (more rarel

badly spaced a

:tion adequately

One factor leadir

the ease of scala

ls to cause the d

This is a screen capture from a page layout program. Most designers who want to look at type closely on screen look at it at this kind of size. It gives little information on how it will look and work in final text.

Although the subtler dimensions of typography may get overlooked as a result of technological innovation, the technology that causes the problem also provides the tools to solve them: page layout programs and, increasingly, css, are able to deal with the subtleties of type relationships.

Vector based programs such as Adobe Illustrator let you adjust the forms of characters for a small amount of display type. If you are ambitious and have the skills and interest, font editing and creation programs, such as FontForge, FontLab or Glyphs, give you the tools to create fonts for print or screen.

For the even more ambitious, such programs make the creation of variable fonts a possibility.

Neither the full page view nor a view suitable for reading gives the designer a real understanding of the reader's experience of the final printed work.

Typography
Typography

Top: 12 point type as it appears rasterized in a 300 dpi laser proof on bond paper.

Bottom: type as it is rasterized in high-resolution printing. It appears lighter.

Another advantage of traditional design was that the job usually existed at the same scale from beginning to end, with the type, after the sketching stage, being seen in something close to its final form early in the process. Working entirely on the computer, where visual scale is almost infinitely variable, means that we may not really understand how the typography works until we see it in its final form, a significant problem for print designers. Almost every graphic design student has had the experience of printing a final copy for submission, and being horrified at the size of the type, because that is the first time it has been seen in its final form. Most often, the type is bigger than expected.

Design for screens doesn't have this problem, because the medium of display of design is essentially the same as the display of the final. However, every design for screen has, in effect, to be designed several times for the different devices on which it may be accessed.

PROOFING FOR PRINT

Proofing systems can mask the problems with scalable fonts in the print environment, though this factor will no doubt decrease as technology provides better proofing devices. Ironically, laser prints provide a result that misleadingly compensates for the faults of scalable type. Because of its low resolution and the characteristics of powdered toner and rough paper, the laser printer tends to make body size type bolder and less detailed, more the way that smaller cuts of type necessarily were before the 20th century. Laser proofs are adequate for layout and display type but are not a reliable representation of what the final text will be if the project is to be printed on a good-quality press.

It is not uncommon for even experienced designers to be disappointed in the appearance of body type when a printed piece is seen for the first time. It is often lighter than they expect, because they have been looking at laser proofs printed on bond paper, which usually gives type a darker look than it will be in its final printed form. If a book is entirely typographical, this can be to some extent corrected on press, but if there are images, any darkening of type will also darken the visuals, causing a different problem.

Proofing websites needs a different approach. While a final form of the design is immediately apparent to the designer, what works perfectly on a designer's computer and phone will not necessarily work when it is seen by viewers with different operating systems, browsers and screen sizes.

Designers have to test their work to know how it will appear to final users with different systems and devices. Experienced web designers know this, but they still can get caught out with typographic elements that don't display or function as expected on a particular combination of screen and operating system.

User testing

Testing a design with users is helpful for any project to understand how an audience will perceive and interact with it. It becomes even more necessary for complex websites, as the user experience of typographic navigation is accordingly more complex. Designers are so close to the project that they are likely to be unable to put themselves in the place of a user who is encountering the site for the first time. This kind of testing can be formal or informal, depending on the available resources.

Technology provides many more typographic options

For most of the history of typography, print was almost the only medium; and most involved the inking of physical forms of the letters and pressing them on paper. Although the technology for designing typefaces and printing them made advances, the essential technology stayed the same until the development of lithographic printing in the late 19th century. Lithography was adapted for typography in the 20th century, though much of the original type was still produced by letterpress before being printed lithographically.

Now there are no limitations or divisions between type and image. In the computer environment, everything, including type, is described by bitmaps or by mathematical descriptions of curves, which can be manipulated an infinite number of ways.

While the World Wide Web consortium is continually upgrading web standards, different browsers still often interpret the same type differently, which means that typography needs testing on the likely platforms that the site will be encountered on. There are websites that will allow you to test prototypes on different devices and screens.

Adoption of new CSS standards also are adopted at different times by different browsers, so features may work on some but not on others. Many people don't frequently update their browsers, so it is normal practice to make sure that a typographic design works sufficiently well on older versions of the common browsers.

DEMOCRATIZATION OF TYPOGRAPHY

The personal computer has raised the typographic consciousness of everyone, not just designers. This is good, in that to some degree, it has raised many people's interest in, appreciation of, and respect for typography.

It can be bad, in that people are able to produce typography themselves, often poorly. This was not possible before the availability of design software. Clients may know just enough about typography to lead them to argue about typographic decisions on the basis of what are often subjective and uneducated opinions. Much of design work has become collaborative, instead of the model of the past, when the designer was usually the acknowledged master of arcane aesthetic and technical knowledge.

As a result, you must rationalize your typographic decisions, so you are ready with an answer when a client asks you to use Papyrus or some other typeface that has caught his or her attention, or has some other typographic preference that might undermine your design.

> **No longer the province of the lone practitioner, design has become a broad, collaborative process.**
>
> Tim Brown, CEO of IDEO

The importance of communicating about type

In the past, designers commanded knowledge of processes and production that were mysteries to most clients. Now that the technology to produce design and typography is widely available and easier to use, your knowledge of design, typography and typographic technology become more important in a decision to hire you or take your advice seriously. Typography, more than other aspects of design, is an area where you can demonstrate clear and concrete knowledge of type and how to use it, which can be hard to do with the more subjective aspects of design. Clients can easily get access to the same resources as you, so the difference between you and a client is not only creativity, knowledge and experience of graphic design, but also in your greater ability to use available tools to produce effective graphic design, and to make the typographic choices that are a central part of that design.

CONCLUSION

A mastery of typographic technology and a competent employment of the systems available will make a designer who is executing any but the simplest job more efficient. This efficiency will allow more time to actually design, and make it easier to make minor or even major changes to the design later in the process. Many projects given in design school would need a structured production system if they were fully executed, but setting up style sheets and master pages can seem like a pointless make-work assignment when you are only dealing with a couple of sample pages.

In practice, with a job of any size, effective use of the technology will allow faster execution, less chance of errors and more control of your project's typography and more ability to refine your design. These skills make you more valuable, which make you more employable and more profitable, whether you are working independently or for a studio. They also let you spend less time on production, and thus more of your time on design.

It is also necessary to understand the technologies of print and Web, whether or not you are the one actually doing the printing or coding. The same applies to motion typography, or any other typographic environment. A good sense of what can be done and how is necessary to design in any medium. Additionally, understanding the capabilities of design tools (even if you don't know how to use them well) is important if you are supervising others as part of the production of a design.

Finally, it has more important than ever to be able to explain and defend your typographic choices. The computer has made many people more aware and opinionated about type. Designers in the past were the gatekeepers of typography, as not everyone made typographic choices every day. Now that everyone does, designers have to prove their expertise, instead of having it automatically accepted.

MASTERING THE CREATIVE TOOLS

Understanding the capabilities of typographic technologies and systems doesn't only give designers more time and help them do a better job. It also gives a better understanding of what the possible and practical creative typographic choices are. Typographic design always uses and is influenced by available technologies. For example, the tight settings that were popular in the second part of the 20th century were largely a result of the new photographically based typesetting tools that made tight kerning and leading a possibility.

Mastery of type as visual and type as text are not the same thing, but they are both needed for effective typographic control of almost every project. Awareness of the differences, and making use of the visual and textual elements of typography, as well as recognizing their intrinsic duality, are important design skills. It is also necessary to recognize the different craft dimensions of the visual and textual functions and be able to execute them both well.

Type as visual / type as information

This chapter focuses on the typographical choices in communication design, and how type works both as a visual element of design and as a communicator of language.

Typography works visually first: it must draw attention to itself, or have attention drawn to it. It will work best if it is attractive, intriguing, or best of all, compelling. At almost the same time, except in unusual cases, it will communicate language content, as well as something about that content. Until you begin to read, type may communicate almost nothing beyond 'this is language'. This will also be the case if it is in a language you can't read. You might not be familiar with words from your own language that are used in a text. And you may not be able to read the type because of distance or some other limiting factor such as only being able to see a part of it. If, however, the text is in a language you understand, and you are able to make out the letters, you will transition from having only a visual impression to having an understanding of language. You will be reading.

Sometimes you might experience the visual effect and meaning almost instantly and simultaneously. This is the aim of most headlines or advertising typographic communication, at least at first, though there is often text that supports or expands the initial communication. Sometimes, though, it is just a simple message or

The way something is presented will define the way you react to it.

Neville Brody, typographic designer

the name of a product that is being communicated, often with an image to develop or reinforce your perception of that content.

In most cases, there is a mixture of the two. The reader starts with the initial visual experience and recognition of a few words. If it holds their attention (potential) readers will move on to a deeper engagement.

In print and large screen environments, we have space for typographic composition. On small screens, with little room for white space, the visual qualities of the typography itself become more important in the structuring and communication of content.

DIFFERENT KINDS OF READING EXPERIENCE

Some type must communicate quickly and efficiently. It may be for navigation, which can range from road signage to architectural wayfinding, to the navigation of a website or the index of a book. It may be to communicate a single message, as in some advertising or political messages.

Other kinds of typographic material have to be read completely and in sequence to be effective; still other kinds of material can be skimmed, with the reader entering and leaving engagement with the content. For example, a technical manual needs to be easy to navigate but once the appropriate section is found, the delivery of the material and presentation of any images must let the reader clearly understand sometimes complex material.

Putting yourself in the place of the reader

The typographic designer has an influence on and exerts some control over how a viewer engages with content. Although typographic design is rooted in intuition, experimentation and personal approaches, if it is to communicate effectively, you must consider how a potential reader will encounter and engage with what you have created. This will inevitably lead to refinement and adjustment, which will lead to more effective typographic design.

Even at the same typeface and size, typographic colour varies with tracking and leading, as shown here. This can be done in page layout software, and with the CSS controls 'line-height' and 'letter-spacing'.

Typographic colour applies mainly to text, though the visual darkness of display type can also be considered as colour. The term refers both to the overall darkness of an area of text, a result of the darkness or lightness of the typeface itself, size, leading and any adjustment of the overall letterspacing (or 'tracking').

Typographic colour applies mainly to text, though the visual darkness of display type can also be considered as colour. The term refers both to the overall darkness of an area of text, a result of the darkness or lightness of the typeface itself, size, leading and any adjustment of the overall letterspacing (or 'tracking').

FORM AND COMMUNICATION

Type that is successful in visually engaging the reader is not necessarily the same as type that communicates effectively. Type can be formally beautiful, interesting, provoking, or engaging, yet not communicate. This is not always a bad thing: effective communication is usually, but not always, the goal. And even the most utilitarian typography has visual form. On the whole, a need for effective communication means that there will almost always be a compromise between aesthetic and utility.

A typographic treatment that is visually attractive may be difficult to read, or communicate poorly or inappropriately. Conversely, type that would otherwise communicate well may not be read if it doesn't appear interesting or relevant. A successful initial impression will attract the eye and communicate relevance. Once the reader has chosen to engage with the work, communication should shift to be as seamless and clear as possible: the visual impression will fall away, and the reader will be engaged in the text.

TYPOGRAPHIC COLOUR

Typographic colour applies mainly to text, though the visual weight of display type can also be thought of as colour. The term refers both to the overall darkness of an area of text, a result of the visual darkness or lightness of the typeface itself, the size and leading, and any adjustment of the overall letterspacing (or 'tracking'). For screen design it is common to also adjust colour with lightening the actual colour of the type, for example, by changing the value of black from 100 per cent to 90 per cent. There is no 'right' typographic colour. It must work with the page and balance with any images or other graphic elements, so testing a setting in the planned design context is important. In the case of print, this should be done with samples that are as close as possible to the final printing. When proofing for offset printing on 600 dpi laser printers, printing the type and images at 200 per cent can give a better idea of how type and image will balance. Laser printing on coated paper is another way of getting a better idea of how type will appear when printed lithographically.

Look Before You Leap.

Look before you leap.

Title case or sentence case?

Title case balances well in short titles but looks old-fashioned, even a bit pompous, in longer titles. If your heading is a sentence, it makes sense to use sentence case.

Readers usually ignore the typographic interface, gliding comfortably along literacy's habitual groove. Sometimes, however, the interface should be allowed to fail. By making itself evident, typography can illuminate the construction and identity of a page, screen, place or product.

Ellen Lupton, *Thinking with Type*

TYPOGRAPHIC COLOUR

Typographic colour is a function of typeface choice, size, leading, tracking and quality of setting. Shown here are settings with significantly different typographic colour.

Rockwell Regular 8.5/11.5, track 10

Typographic colour also refers to the *evenness* of the colour of text, in terms of regular word spaces and overall spacing in justified setting. A loose or uneven ragged edge affects visual colour, which in turn affects both the appearance of the page, and the reading experience. Colour works both on the visual aspect of a page — as the reader's eye first registers it, as poor colour may persuade readers that their attention is better turned elsewhere — and in the experience of reading the content.

Univers Bold 8/14, track 5

Typographic colour also refers to the *evenness* of the colour of text, in terms of regular word spaces and overall spacing in justified setting. A loose or uneven ragged edge affects visual colour, which in turn affects both the appearance of the page, and the reading experience. Colour works both on the visual aspect of a page — as the reader's eye first registers it, as poor colour may persuade readers that their attention is better turned elsewhere — and in the experience of reading the content.

Janson Text 9.5/11, track 0

Typographic colour also refers to the *evenness* of the colour of text, in terms of regular word spaces and overall spacing in justified setting. A loose or uneven ragged edge affects visual colour, which in turn affects both the appearance of the page, and the reading experience. Colour works both on the visual aspect of a page — as the reader's eye first registers it, as poor colour may persuade readers that their attention is better turned elsewhere — and in the experience of reading the content.

Grotesque 8/11, track 0

Typographic colour also refers to the evenness of the colour of text, in terms of regular word spaces and overall spacing in justified setting. A loose or uneven ragged edge affects visual colour, which in turn affects both the appearance of the page, and the reading experience. Colour works both on the visual aspect of a page — as the reader's eye first registers it, as poor colour may persuade readers that their attention is better turned elsewhere — and in the experience of reading the content.

SYNCOPATION

SYNCOPATION

Colour also applies to single lines of type: the looser the type the lighter the colour.

Typographic colour also refers to the *evenness* of the colour of text, in terms of regular word spaces and overall spacing in justified setting. A loose or uneven ragged edge, especially on a narrow column, affects visual colour, which in turn affects both the appearance of the page, and the reading experience. Typographic colour works both on the visual aspect of a page — as the reader's eye first registers it, as poor colour may persuade readers that their attention is better turned elsewhere — and in the experience of reading the content, as bad spacing or variation between dark and light lines can interfere with the reading process.

Typographic colour in text is first a result of design decisions such as typeface choice, point size and leading; second, a result of typesetting parameters such as overall letterspacing and H&Js; and third, how the designer deals with exceptions that these parameters are not able to deal with successfully. In the case of print, the amount of ink on the press can affect typographic colour.

TYPOGRAPHIC RHYTHM

Typographic rhythm is a commonly used term that applies to different things. Vertical rhythm is related to the baseline grid and proportions between elements.

It applies to typeface weight and leading: heavier type makes stronger rhythmic lines, and more leading increases the rhythm of lines, as the difference between lines comes clearer. Even tightly leaded lines have some rhythm, as the space between the lines is formed by the distance between the x-height and baseline above.

Rhythm also applies to the horizontal distribution of spaces within and between letters and words in a line of text (which also affects typographic colour).

On the page level, an even, regular rag has rhythm while an uneven rag with odd shapes doesn't. Rivers or uneven letterspacing in justified text also destroy rhythm.

Letterspacing in heads or other graphic type element can add visual rhythm. Subheads, drop caps or other typographic elements such as rules can add rhythm to an otherwise monotone page. Rhythm also applies to the layout of text and images on the page.

Literal rhythm. The relationships on this page are roughly related to the ratio of 1 to 1.41 (the square root of 2). The relationship of leading and text size, the text area and the page size, the type size of the headline to the text, and the space between the capitals and the cap height are all 1 to 1.41.

The sizes of the large type are slightly different on this poster as a way of expressing restlessness.

A good typographer is always a good reader.

Stephen Coles, author of *The Anatomy of Type*

Rhythm in size differences is another aspect. The basic principle is that as type sizes increase, the difference in sizes should be proportionally greater. As with the grid, there are various theories about type size relationships, but in the end the designer's eye is the best judge. The traditional type size relationships shown on page 129 work well as a starting point.

Finally, rhythm applies to document pacing, most relevant to works that have visual variety between pages, such as magazines or other browsing material. This is often accomplished with images but can also be done with typographic visual elements.

ANALYSING TYPOGRAPHY

Typographic analysis has two main aims: one, to determine our approach to a given typographic challenge and two, to evaluate type that already exists, whether our own work or that of others.

We usually start our analysis from the point of view of our intention, that is, make some rough typographic choices about size, placement and typeface from the innumerable possibilities available, based on our intuitive analysis of the project. We then try those choices, then analyse the degree to which they are successful. This continues, iteratively, until we are satisfied, or all too often, until we hit the deadline. Good designers are seldom easily satisfied, often experimenting and refining until time runs out. This is dangerous, though, because it can lead to errors in the final work.

Designers' control over the many possibilities of typography, makes the experimental possibilities even greater. What we do not have control over is how others might perceive it, and thinking about that can help us focus our work.

Thinking about typographic design analytically and critically helps to understand what is good or not good about your own and others' work, and helps put you in the place of someone encountering your work for the first time.

No matter what your initial design process is, you must be able to critically evaluate what you have done. In much of graphic design, including typography, there is a subjective aspect. But with typography, more than other aspects of graphic design, there are some things that can be at least argued to be objective. Designers evaluate typography frequently, sometimes objectively, sometimes more subjectively, though we have a tendency to be better at (and more enthusiastic about!) critically evaluating others' typography than our own, especially once it has been finalized. Both objectively and subjectively based decisions can be defended, but the more objective argument is usually more convincing.

Sometimes something is missing, sometimes something is wrong, sometimes the typographic decisions are good but badly executed. Sometimes it is more subtle: for example, otherwise good typographic elements might not work well together or not have an effective relationship with each other.

There is no fixed method for typographic design, which is a good thing, because otherwise design would be formulaic and unoriginal. This can become a problem for design students who have early success and praise from their instructors: they may end up with a few reliable methods or variations on a single theme, and adapt a successful formula to different projects, rather than exploring and experimenting.

Relying heavily on what has worked well in the past may end up producing visually pleasing work, but it is unlikely to produce either innovative work or work that is ideally suited to its content. Not that we shouldn't learn from our own past successes, but too much dependence on a personal style can end up resulting in a routine design process and results.

Good designers continually evaluate and critique both their own and others' typographic decisions. There are frameworks and principles that are useful for helping the critique and analysis of type. These can help evaluate existing designs, be used to refine design in progress or lead to a complete rethink of the typographic decisions made. Analysis raises questions more than it supplies answers. The process of answering these questions is likely to lead to good typographic design.

Questions are the essence of the analysis of any kind of graphic design. Although display and text type have different requirements, within these requirements, the analytical frameworks in the following pages will apply to most typography.

The book designer strives for perfection; yet every perfect thing lives somewhere in the neighbourhood of dullness and is frequently mistaken for it by the insensitive.

Jan Tschichold, *The Form of the Book: Essays on the Morality of Good Design*

POINTS OF ENTRY

If we are dealing with design that is likely to include browsing, such as a magazine or large website, we should have many points of entry. Captions don't just refer to the image, they also relate to any other text content. A good pull quote brings the reader into the text by suggesting that more information can be found in the text. If we are dealing with something like a novel, the cover, inside flap and the appearance of pages are points of entry. Once engaged, the reader will (or won't) continue the engagement, at which point the job of the typography shifts to make the reading as pleasant as possible. If the reader disengages, they may re-engage through another point of entry.

These two versions of the same text taken from Wikipedia show the difference that typography can make to the way we interpret the content. The version on the left seems objective and factual. The version on the right conveys a more subjective stance towards the content. The text is the same in both, and the experience of reading it will be similar, but the way the reader comes at it has been framed by the appearance and visual emphasis.

Postmodernism

Postmodernism is a broad movement that developed in the mid- to late-20th century across philosophy, the arts, architecture, and criticism and that marked a departure from modernism. The term has also more generally been applied to the historical era following modernity and the tendencies of this era.

Definition

While encompassing a wide variety of approaches, postmodernism is generally defined by an attitude of skepticism, irony, or rejection toward the meta-narratives and ideologies of modernism, often calling into question various assumptions of Enlightenment rationality. Consequently, common targets of postmodern critique include universalist notions of objective reality, morality, truth, human nature, reason, language, and social progress. Postmodern thinkers frequently call attention to the contingent or socially-conditioned nature of knowledge claims and value systems, situating them as products of particular political, historical, or cultural discourses and hierarchies.

Accordingly, postmodern thought is broadly characterized by tendencies to self-referentiality, epistemological and moral relativism, pluralism, subjectivism, and irreverence.

Influence

Postmodern critical approaches gained purchase in the 1980s and 1990s, and have been adopted in a variety of academic and theoretical disciplines, including cultural studies, philosophy of science, economics, linguistics, architecture, feminist theory, and literary criticism, as well as art movements in fields such as literature and music. Postmodernism is often associated with schools of thought such as deconstruction and post-structuralism, as well as philosophers such as Jean-François Lyotard, Jacques Derrida, and Fredric Jameson. Some philosophers have criticized the term.

postmodernism

Postmodernism is a broad movement that developed in the mid- to late-20th century across philosophy, the arts, architecture, and criticism and that marked a departure from modernism. The term has also more generally been applied to the historical era following modernity and the tendencies of this era.

While encompassing a wide variety of approaches, postmodernism is generally defined by an attitude of **skepticism**, **irony**, or **rejection** toward the meta-narratives and ideologies of modernism, often **calling into question** various **assumptions** of Enlightenment rationality. Consequently, common targets of postmodern critique include universalist notions of objective reality, morality, truth, human nature, reason, language, and social progress. Postmodern thinkers frequently call **attention to the contingent or socially-conditioned** nature of knowledge claims and value systems, situating them as products of particular political, historical, or cultural discourses and hierarchies.

targets universalist notions of objective reality, morality, truth, human nature, reason, language, and social progress.

Accordingly, postmodern thought is broadly characterized by tendencies to **self-referentiality, epistemological and moral relativism, pluralism, subjectivism, and irreverence.**

Postmodern critical approaches gained purchase in the 1980s and 1990s, and have been adopted in a variety of academic and theoretical disciplines, including cultural studies, philosophy of science, economics, linguistics, architecture, feminist theory, and literary criticism, as well as art movements in fields such as literature and music. Postmodernism is often associated with schools of thought such as deconstruction and post-structuralism, as well as philosophers such as Jean-François Lyotard, Jacques Derrida, and Fredric Jameson. **Some philosophers have criticized the term.**

adopted in a variety of academic and theoretical disciplines

ANALYZE THE CONTENT

To effectively design visual communication we need an under-standing of the content that is to be communicated. So the first task of analysis should be of the content. Good typography for one text may not be good typography for another. On the other hand, we can't usually can't change the typography in a single project or series just because the content changes. So we may have to balance appropriateness to content with consistency. Periodicals, anthologies, book cover series, and websites that have many kinds of content are examples of this. In these cases we have to design a system that typographically interprets and represents the over-arching editorial voice of the anticipated content.

AIDA

An old (early 20th century) acronym from advertising applies to how a successful advertisement works. AIDA stands for Attention, Interest, Desire and Action, with Action referring to buying the advertised product. This acronym can also be usefully applied to the analysis of graphic design and typography.

Thinking through these steps helps put you in the place of someone encountering your work for the first time. What is the first impression? What makes the viewer want to engage with the content and become a reader? How does the reader perceive the content of what they are reading? And, finally, what information and perceptions does the reader take away?

Attention comes from the appearance of the layout and head-lines or images that the potential reader sees at first glance.

Interest depends on whether the potential reader perceives that the content is worthy of increased engagement, which leads to the *desire* to further engage with the typography, with the *action* being the reading of the content.

This sequence may be repeated several times when a viewer is interacting with a piece of communication design.

In successful typographic communication, all these steps must take place. How we experience these steps depends on the context: our engagement with an email in our inbox goes through these steps differently than it does with a website or a book.

The rhetoric of pull quotes and subheads

The text chosen as content for pull quotes influences the reader's perception of content, and communicates what the designer thinks is interesting.

COMPLEX HIERARCHIES

Hierarchy is not always as simple as order of importance. A cover for a book in a series is an example, as is some forms of product literature. A typographic symbol (or logo) can be recognized first and be what causes the potential reader to engage. So in some sense it is higher in the hierarchy than the principal subject or name of the work. Subheads and pull quotes are another example: the subheads in an article have a higher importance in the hierarchy of text, but the pull quotes have a higher place in the visual hierarchy.

SEMIOTICS

While semiotics is derived from linguistics, originating in the work of Ferdinand de Saussure and Charles Peirce, and developed by Charles W. Morris, it is frequently applied to the analysis of visual communication. A full discussion is outside both the scope of this book and its author's expertise. Essentially, it is the study of how people make meaning from what they see and experience. With typography, the relationship between the literal meaning of the words that are set (denotation) and how they are set in terms of what the visual experience and understanding of the viewer is (connotation) are the essential aspects of this. In a sense this is just a codification of what designers do naturally. (See page 146 for more on connotations.)

However, it is important to pay attention to how this works, because connotations intended by the designer may or may not be recognized in the culture of the reader, and with an international audience, we must recognize that typographic forms and their use may carry meaning that the designer can't easily anticipate.

An awareness of semiotic principles is useful in the analysis of typographic decisions: some of the decisions we make can affect the reader and express things we may not intend. This is often thought of as being more applicable to image choice and treatment, but also is relevant to typography, where the choices we make have meaning beyond the aesthetic and practical. The relationships and treatments of typography not only suggest something about the content but also about the designer's relationship to the content.

Semiotics is also relevant to the design of symbols and icons that are important in screen design and typography, as well as in wayfinding and industrial design.

Semiotic principles can also help us to understand why typographic decisions work or not, for ourselves or in communicating with others. Attention paid to the cultural and social meanings that are attached to typography can usefully influence design and help broaden concepts beyond the aesthetic. It can also help avoid unintended meanings that may sabotage communication.

Semantics, syntactics, pragmatics

These words used in semiotics have frequently been applied to graphic design, notably in Massimo Vignelli's 'Vignelli Canon'. Applied to typography in particular they can be described as follows.

Semantics relates to the content of typography, from the point of view of the establishing and communicating an intended meaning.

Syntactics has to do with the structure of the typographic content such as layout and hierarchy. Readers bring an understanding and experience of syntax to typographic works.

Pragmatics is concerned with how readers interpret the typographic form and content.

The typeface affects how we interpret this word. It doesn't evoke danger, at least in the conventional sense. It might imply danger that is disguised or attractive, or be ironic, depending on the context.

Visual semiotics applies mainly to layout and display type; text type has the function of communicating language, where more conventional linguistic semiotics come into play. However, the way the text is presented will affect the overall perception of the text that it is associated with, to the extent of being the difference between whether it is read or not.

HIERARCHY

Visual hierarchy is a basic part of typographic practice, and we all have a practical understanding of how it depends on contrast with other elements. But spending some time on analysis of what makes a hierarchy functionally successful is also useful. Relative sizes, positions, colour, white space and other visual elements don't only work as aesthetics, they also contribute to how readers perceive content.

Visual hierarchy also influences the order in which a reader engages with typographic elements, which influences perception of content. Elements that visually contrast with other elements are what attract the eye. Hierarchy both tells the reader what the designer considers important in the text, and is a tool for the reader's own navigation.

Working with typographic contrasts is part of early design education, but contrast is often approached more intuitively and compositionally rather than as a systematic way of analysing and developing the order and communication of content.

The basic rule of functional hierarchy is that it should be sufficient and not much more than that. This doesn't mean that it can't be exaggerated for aesthetic effect and visual interest, but doing this suggests that elements are doing something beside indicating hierarchy. The more levels of hierarchy that are needed, the less it makes sense to sacrifice hierarchy to aesthetics.

As always, trying to put yourself in the position of the reader will help your typography communicate more effectively.

In this advertising for an art and design school, not only is the joining of the H and U harmful to the typography, but it resembles the trap under a sink, perhaps inadvertently suggesting plumbing, rather than art, as a career.

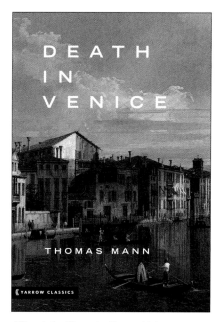

Although the title and author are higher in the visual hierarchy, the series title in the bottom left corner may be the most important typographical item for those who are not familiar with the work or its author.

This page prioritizes communication of language over visual appeal. The hierarchy is simple, clear, and everything is legible and easy to read. However, it is not particularly visually interesting.

This page takes a much more visual approach, with attention paid to composition and the visual properties of type. The text is dark and heavily leaded to create a horizontal bands. It is more apt to attract attention than the page above this one, but reading may be discouraged.

COHERENCE

Aesthetic coherence is necessary to any kind of typographic design. Having several good individual elements in design doesn't matter if they are incompatible with each other. Using very well done Victorian-advertising-inspired typography for part of a layout, and excellent Swiss design for another part is unlikely, as a whole, to work. (Though coherently integrating elements from both would be an interesting challenge.)

LESSER OF EVILS

Typography involves compromise. Not just with clients or instructors but with the material itself.

Sometimes a previously determined typeface must be used to signal an institution, even if it isn't appropriate for a particular piece of content. Setting such content in a different typeface may make for a better individual piece, but in the context of work for a client, the more important thing is that the individual piece function within the context of the overall communication approach. A piece of copy may have letter combinations or word lengths that cause problems, but addressing them is probably a lesser evil than insisting the writer to rewrite the copy. (Though in the type shop where I worked in the 1980s, we routinely added or removed paragraph breaks to make type work better visually. And you can always ask if you can make a change to text, if it makes a significant improvement.) A narrow justified column might be ideal in terms of page layout, but if it results in holes in the lines, and difficult-to-read content, then the lesser of evils might be to widen the column, or set the type flush left, even if the composition suffers a bit. Possibly a different (though less-preferred) typeface will be more effective in a particular situation.

In designs that have many different kinds of material in them, the design that suits one kind of content may not suit another, while a consistent appearance is likely to be needed. So what is a good typeface for one part may not be good for another. Again, a lesser-of-evils approach is often a useful one: it is better to take a neutral approach that will accommodate different kinds of content even if it does not suit any of the content perfectly.

NEWSPAPER SETTINGS

Newspapers usually use narrow justified settings. Part of this is tradition: it makes a newspaper look like a newspaper. The short measure also helps disguise the short sentences that are typically used in newspaper writing. Finally, short lines make tighter leading possible, so more articles can fit into the available space, which both gives the newspaper more perceived value, giving the paper a visual density that signals that a lot of information is being presented.

Typical newspaper setting

Typeface choices have become more important for websites and publications.

Before the desktop computer made its appearance in the 1980s, typefaces were expensive and the choice was limited.

Now thousands of new typefaces are available.

With the introduction of font creation software, even custom typefaces are within in reach of the smallest newspapers and the graphic designers who create the look of the publication and manage the reading experience.

This allows any publication to develop a distinct typographical look that helps set it apart from its competitors.

Some typeface designers have made careers of designing custom faces for media and other companies. General graphic designers sometimes use font creation software to make create custom icons or other graphic elements used in publications.

The general public is more aware of typefaces than they were before the computer. Although some continue to use the default typeface offered by software, many deliber- ately choose which typeface to use.

This also makes many people have a stronger opinion about the type- faces that they encounter and read every day, and to develop a critical appreciation of different typefaces.

Not every graphic designer approves of these typographic developments. Massimo Vignelli, the famous New York designer, wrote "the prolifera- tion of typefaces and type manipula- tions represents a new level of visual pollution threatening our culture."

One the other hand, many design- ers believe that the ever-increasing choice of typefaces make it easier to choose the 'perfect' type for each job, and will sometimes decide that no existing typeface is suitable for a given project, and will commission a new one.

This can be a selling point to cli- ents, particularly large corporations, who not only gain a unique brand identifier, but also avoid what may be high licensing costs to use an ex- isting typeface.

Two companies that rely on cus- tom typefaces for their visual iden- tity are the automobile manufactur- ers Mercedes and Volvo.

These narrow settings cause problems with loose lines and hyphenation, as can be seen above. The fact that newspapers tend to use shorter words makes excessive hyphenation less of a problem than it otherwise might be.

Same text across two columns

Typeface choices have become more important for websites and publications.

Before the desktop computer made its appearance in the 1980s, typefaces were expensive and the choice was limited.

Now thousands of new typefaces are available.

With the introduction of font creation software, even custom typefaces are within in reach of the smallest newspapers and the graphic designers who create the look of the publication and manage the reading experience.

This allows any publication to develop a distinct typographical look that helps set it apart from its competitors.

Some typeface designers have made careers of designing custom faces for media and other companies. General graphic designers sometimes use font creation software to make create custom icons or other graphic elements used in publications.

The general public is more aware of typefaces than they were before the computer. Although some continue to use the default typeface offered by software, many deliberately choose which typeface to use.

This also makes many people have a stronger opinion about the typefaces that they encounter and read every day, and to develop a critical appreciation of different typefaces.

Not every graphic designer approves of these typographic developments. Massimo Vignelli, the famous New York designer, wrote "the proliferation of typefaces and type manipulations represents a new level of visual pollution threatening our culture."

One the other hand, many designers believe that the ever-increasing choice of typefaces make it easier to choose the 'perfect' type for each job, and will sometimes decide that no existing typeface is suitable for a given project, and will commission a new one.

This can be a selling point to clients, particularly large corporations, who not only gain a unique brand identifier, but also avoid what may be high licensing costs to use an existing typeface.

Two companies that rely on custom typefaces for their visual identity are the automobile manufacturers Mercedes and Volvo.

This setting shows the same piece set in a more traditionally readable format on the same column grid. The short paragraphs become more obvious, and cause potentially insoluble widows as does the greater space necessary for this format, because of greater need for leading with this line length. Also note that the typographic colour on the right is significantly lighter due to the increased leading.

X-HEIGHT AND LEADING

After layout decisions and typeface choice, how type appears on a page, and the experience of reading it, is largely controlled by decisions about type size, leading and indents. In terms of perception, the x-height is more significant than type size, and needs consideration when establishing leading and indents.

Communication is the principal reason type appears on a piece of graphic design. Certainly type may be used almost purely as decoration, but in most cases, it is set in words that are intended to be read by the viewer, and often the information that has to be conveyed is to some degree at odds with the requirements of a design. Type, both literally and figuratively, is shaped by its content.

Communication is the principal reason type appears on a piece of graphic design. Certainly type may be used almost purely as decoration, but in most cases, it is set in words that are intended to be read by the viewer, and often the information that has to be conveyed is to some degree at odds with the requirements of a design. Type is shaped by its content.

This Perpetua is set solid, that is, 9-point type on 9 points leading; the ratio of x-height to distance between x-height and baseline is about 1:1.5.

This Trade Gothic is also 9/9, and the distance between x-height and baseline is less than the x-height. Much too tight for text.

Communication is the principal reason type appears on a piece of graphic design. Certainly type may be used almost purely as decoration, but in most cases, it is set in words that are intended to be read by the viewer, and often the information that has to be conveyed is to some degree at odds with the requirements of a design. Type, both literally and figuratively, is shaped by its content.

The Trade Gothic on the left is set 7/9. The space between the top of the x-height and the baseline above is about the same as the Perpetua setting. Note that the lines look slightly more open, because of the shorter ascenders and descenders. Also note that the sans serif text with the smaller point size now fills almost the same amount of space as the serif text.

LINE LENGTH, LEADING AND INDENTS

Because the line length and leading are related, it is best to avoid having the same size and leading of type in different measures, except on rare occasions, such as pull quotes or images that may occasionally make incursions into the text block. The type shown below on the left would be too loose if set on the measure on the right, while the type below on the right would look vertically fragmented set on the measure on the left. Longer lines also need longer indents.

The graphic design elements, such as decorated capitals and marginal decoration, even running heads, continued to be left to the handwork of craft-artists with pen and ink, who would be engaged after the printing of the book to decorate each copy individually. Gutenberg was not primarily an artist; he was rather the Henry Ford of the fifteenth century.

His aim was not to create something new, or find a new mode of visual expression. Instead, he was attempting to imitate on a mass scale, as closely as possible, the existing visual representation of language, the Gothic manuscript scribal hand.

The graphic design elements, such as decorated capitals and marginal decoration, even running heads, continued to be left to the handwork of craft-artists with pen and ink, who would be engaged after the printing of the book to decorate each copy individually. Gutenberg was not primarily an artist; he was rather the Henry Ford of the fifteenth century.

His aim was not to create something new, or find a new mode of visual expression. Instead, he was attempting to imitate on a mass scale, as closely as possible, the existing visual representation of language, the Gothic manuscript scribal hand.

The longer the line length, the more leading that is needed. The indents should also be greater. For this reason, using the leading amount as the indent is a good place to start; a line with 10-point leading would have an indent of 10 points, while a setting with a leading of 14 points would have an indent of the same size. This is not a hard rule: shorter line lengths can get away with slightly less, longer line lengths might work well with more.

PARAGRAPH BREAKS

The normal ways of indicating text paragraph breaks are the paragraph indent and the line space. Because they are what readers are used to, they are usually a good choice, because they do not distract from the reading. They separate paragraphs, but do not make the paragraph too important a division.

Indent

The graphic design elements, such as decorated capitals, marginal decoration and running heads, continued to be left to the handwork of craft-artists with pen and ink, who would decorate each copy individually after printing.

Gutenberg was not primarily an artist; he was the Henry Ford of the 15th century. His aim was not to create something new, nor to find a new mode of visual expression.

The indent is appropriate in terms of how important a paragraph division is; it is a pause for a slight change of thought. A major change of subject or theme can be indicated with a line break (with no indent).

Line space

The punchcutters who created the types were primarily craftsmen and mechanics, not artists, and their aesthetic skill was in the balance of letterforms, in the refinement and development of the characters that had come before and not in self-expression or radical innovation.

This tradition of craft production of type, with incremental advances made by skilled craftsmen who essentially built closely on what had come before, continued until the 19th century.

The line space is the current standard on the Web. On the whole, a half line space is better than a full space. This can lead to a minor problem when two columns are set beside each other, because sometimes the adjacent lines will align, sometimes they will be unaligned by half a line space. This is not too bad. However, slightly unaligned is distracting and should be avoided by using exactly a half line space. Line spaces can tend to break up a page, especially if there are many short paragraphs.

No indication

It was then that the demands of advertising provoked the development of more unusual faces in order to make advertisements stand out from their surroundings.
Predictably, many of these faces were culturally ephemeral. They were often not designed with an eye to aesthetics but merely to be loud and attract attention. As a result, on the whole, they were typographically unconsidered.

Quite popular with German and Dutch designers is having no paragraph indication at all. This works okay if the last line on a paragraph is not too long (as in the first paragraph here). If the last line is long, as in the paragraph ending with the word 'ephemeral', the paragraph division is weak. The result is that some paragraph breaks are stronger than others, which is a problem.

Graphic element

When a major typographic innovation (such as Egyptian or sans serif faces) is introduced, the typefaces gain a foothold as display type. It is still considered somewhat daring to set a novel, say, in a sans serif typeface. ¶ Even relatively minor innovations, such as ITC's body faces with their unusually large x-heights introduced in the 1970s, tend to fall quickly out of favour after initial popularity. ¶ If the designer proposed using a 16th century page layout and decorative conventions to advertise a highly technical new product, they would no doubt be criticized. ¶ On the other hand, a typeface closely based on 16th century type might be an excellent choice.

Line shift

When a major typographic innovation (such as Egyptian or sans serif faces) is introduced, the typefaces gain a foothold as display type. It is still considered somewhat daring to set a novel, say, in a sans serif typeface.
　　　　Even relatively minor innovations, such as ITC's body with their unusually large x-heights introduced in the 1970s, tend to fall quickly out of favour after initial popularity.
　　　　If the designer proposed using a 16th century page layout and decorative conventions to advertise a highly technical new product, they would no doubt be criticized.
　　　　On the other hand, a typeface closely based on 16th century type might be an excellent choice.

Hanging indents

When a major typographic innovation (such as Egyptian or sans serif faces) is introduced, the typefaces gain a foothold as display type. It is still considered somewhat daring to set a novel, say, in a sans serif typeface.
Even relatively minor innovations, such as ITC's body faces with their unusually large x-heights introduced in the 1970s, tend to fall quickly out of favour after initial popularity.
If the designer proposed using a 16th century page layout and decorative conventions to advertise a highly technical new product, they would no doubt be criticized.
On the other hand, a typeface closely based on 16th century type might be an excellent choice.

Type treatment

When a major typographic innovation (such as Egyptian or sans serif faces) is introduced, the typefaces gain a foothold as display type. It is still considered somewhat daring to set a novel, say, in a sans serif typeface. **EVEN** relatively minor innovations, such as ITC's body faces with their unusually large x-heights introduced in the 1970s, tend to fall quickly out of favour after initial popularity. **IF THE** designer proposed using a 16th century page layout and decorative conventions to advertise a highly technical new product, they would no doubt be criticized. **ON THE** other hand, a typeface closely based on 16th century type might be an excellent choice.

There are many possibilities for indicating paragraph breaks, all of which would take some getting used to, some with intrinsic problems.

*Using a **graphic element**, such as a pilcrow, was common in the early days of printing.*

*The **hanging indent** (or **outdent**) is distracting, bringing your eye to the new paragraph too soon.*

*The **line shift** is likely to lead to problems when a line doesn't end in a suitable place.*

*Using **type treatment** can give an odd emphasis to the treated words.*

DROP CAPITALS

Drop caps are useful as a typographic element that usually has no relationship to the meaning, so they can be used as visual punctuation. Normally they are understated, that is, set in the same typeface as the text. However, using stronger visual differences can also work to add more visual interest or to resonate with the design or the text. All the examples at the bottom of the page can be constructed as style sheets, so could be easily applied throughout a document.

Though we have the choice to decide what information we focus our attention on and use, that information is presented to us in a designed form, which affects both our initial decision to pay attention to that information, and our subsequent thought about and any analysis we may make of it. Graphic representations of information, and visual explanations and interpretations of that information are appealing because they offer the possibility of a simple and concise representation of relationships and trends and a means of presenting large amounts of information. As Jacques Bertin wrote in his comprehensive and authoritative *The Semiology of Graphics*, "It would take at least 10,000 successive instants of perception to compare two data tables of 100 rows by 100 columns. If the data are transcribed graphically, comparison becomes easy; it can even be instantaneous."

At the same time, visual representations unavoidably simplify the reality of almost any relationship. This is true of any form of communication, but it is at least possible to express uncertainty and ambiguity with semantic communication in a way that is more difficult with visual communi-

cation. Real world relationships are complex, and while visual representations of them are useful, their analysis and commentary generally require the use of language. Tools such as graphs, diagrams and maps are aids to and particularly suitable for understanding relationships, but are in a way incomplete, because it is difficult, if not, impossible for them to explain the reasons for relationships.

This tendency of visual communication to present unanalyzed conclusions is inevitable to some extent, but should not be simply accepted. There are many choices that are made when creating visual representations of "real world" relationships. There is the choice of what to portray, how to portray it, (i.e. scatter plot, graph, chart [and what kind of chart: bar, pie, or other], diagram, etc.). Elements such as composition, typography, organization and emphasis are design elements that shape the information, and consequently, its interpretation. But in most cases the intention of visual explanations is to clarify, often by means of simplifying, the information presented, (though Edward Tufte, a well-known contemporary writer on information

design, would disagree, claiming that "graphics can be more precise and revealing than conventional statistical computations"). Revealing, certainly, but almost never more precise. Graphical representation of statistics can show trends and comparisons, but precision must be left to the numbers themselves. Precision is not always necessary, or even desirable, as precision can distract from the more significant trends and relationships, but if quantitative precision is needed, visual representations on their own are seldom able to convey it. Consequently, when possible, the underlying data should also be made available to users, whether or not they choose to avail themselves of it. The world is complex, and the use of visual explanations may simultaneously enable a grasp of the significance of a complex set of information, and at the same time, give a misleading oversimplification of that information.

A page like this may be readable but lacks visual interest.

Though we have the choice to decide what information we focus our attention on and use, that information is presented to us in a designed form, which affects both our initial decision to pay attention to that information, and our subsequent thought about and any analysis we may make of it.

Graphic representations of information, and visual explanations and interpretations of that information are appealing because they offer the possibility of a simple and concise representation of relationships and trends and a means of presenting large amounts of information. As Jacques Bertin wrote in his comprehensive and authoritative *The Semiology of Graphics*, "It would take at least 10,000 successive instants of perception to compare two data tables of 100 rows by 100 columns. If the data are transcribed graphically, comparison becomes easy; it can even be instantaneous."

At the same time, visual representations unavoidably simplify the reality of almost any relationship. This is true of any form of communication, but it is at least possible to express uncertainty and ambigu-

ity with semantic communication in a way that is more difficult with visual communication. Real world relationships are complex, and while visual representations of them are useful, their analysis and commentary generally require the use of language. Tools such as graphs, diagrams and maps are aids to and particularly suitable for understanding relationships, but are in a way incomplete, because it is difficult, if not, impossible for them to explain the reasons for relationships.

This tendency of visual communication to present unanalyzed conclusions is inevitable to some extent, but should not be simply accepted. There are many choices that are made when creating visual representations of "real world" relationships. There is the choice of what to portray, how to portray it, (i.e. scatter plot, graph, chart [and what kind of chart: bar, pie, or other]). Elements such as composition, typography, organization and emphasis are design elements that shape the information, and consequently, its interpretation.

But in most cases the intention of visual explanations is to clarify, often by means of simplifying, the information presented, (though Edward Tufte, a well-known contemporary writer on information design, would disagree, claiming that "graphics can be more precise and revealing than conventional statistical computations").

Revealing, certainly, but almost never more precise. Graphical representation of statistics can show trends and comparisons, but precision must be left to the numbers themselves. Precision is not always necessary, or even desirable, as precision can distract from the more significant trends and relationships, but if quantitative precision is needed, visual representations on their own are seldom able to convey it. Consequently, when possible, the underlying data should also be made available to users, whether or not they choose to avail themselves of it. The world is complex, and the use of visual explanations may simultaneously enable a grasp of the significance of a complex set of information, and at the same time, give a misleading oversimplification of that information.

Drop caps don't interfere with long reading and can make a page more initially appealing, and give it a visual rhythm.

D rop caps work mainly as visual elements, most of the time to add visual interest to text-heavy pages. They normally don't have any meaning, unlike subheads, which cannot be placed just anywhere, because they relate to the text, and only make sense in the place they belong.

This kind of drop cap, of the same typeface as the text, can be used (sparingly) several times in a long text block. They often need a little space added to the left of the capital.

D rop caps work mainly as visual elements, most of the time to add visual interest to text-heavy pages. They normally don't have any meaning, unlike subheads, which cannot be placed just anywhere, because they relate to the text, and only make sense in the place they belong.

More decorative drop caps like this, as well as those below, are most suitable for beginning an essay or a chapter. They are too visually assertive to be used as frequently as the more conventional version above. Also, the fact that this drop cap rises above the paragraph would make it impractical in continuous text

D rop caps work mainly as visual elements, most of the time to add visual interest to text-heavy pages. They normally don't have any meaning, unlike subheads, which cannot be placed just anywhere, because they relate to the text, and only make sense in the place they belong.

Knocking the cap out of a coloured shape is another possible approach that should be used sparingly.

D rop caps work mainly as visual elements, most of the time to add visual interest to text-heavy pages. They normally don't have any meaning, unlike subheads, which cannot be placed just anywhere, because they relate to the text, and only make sense in the place they belong.

A drop cap can hang out of the measure. This would tend to bring the eye to the cap too soon if it were used frequently in text.

Choosing the lesser of evils is sometimes easy. It becomes more difficult when it is not clear what the lesser of evils is. There may be a question of whether the benefit of a choice outweighs any problem it may cause. Nevertheless, it does help with the analysis of typographic decisions.

A lesser-of-evils analysis is also often a good way to challenge typographic specifications or requirements that might be part of a design brief or to help articulate design decisions to an instructor or client.

STRUCTURE OF ELEMENTS

Analysis of structure focuses on how typographic elements relate to each other and to other design elements, conceptually, visually and logically. The analysis can be project wide (for example, how pages relate to each other) or on a page or spread (how the elements on the layout relate to each other). This analysis also includes less visual structures, such as that of the relationship of the typography to different kinds of content, to the relationships of the typographic elements of design to each other (in terms of logic relationships of elements of content, or visual relationships of similar items) and whether typographic hierarchies are clear and logical. Finally, structure also refers to how different parts of a project relate to each other.

Every visual arrangement has some kind of potential structure, even if that structure appears chaotic. The onlooker focused on a design will usually find or impose a perceived structure of some kind even if the composition essentially *is* chaotic. This is unlikely to lead to successful communication, because part of the mind of a person looking at it is likely to be occupied in mentally imposing a structure. However, it may make for a successful visual composition.

Control of typographic structure will help achieve a clear path through the design execution, create a strong first impression, and pave the way to engagement by the reader.

Lacking analytical, consensual terms, decisions become based on vague notions, 'gut' reactions and unproven authority, prejudicing discourse among designers and their clients.

Willi Kunz, *Micro- and Macro-aesthetics*

SOME STRUCTURE CONSIDERATIONS

- Document or site structure
- Different level of type styles, such as heads and a hierarchy of subheads, if necessary
- Grid establishment and use
- Image / type relationships
- Visual and organizational relationships between different pages

---

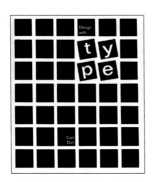

Carl Dair's 1967 Design with Type.

Kraf**twerk**

There is enough contrast between these typefaces to makes this look purposeful.

Kraft*werk*

The roman and italic forms of the same face are in concord with each other.

Kraftwerk

Awkward 'conflicting' relationship between Baskerville and Times Roman. The sizes and shapes of characters are too similar.

Structure in responsive layouts varies according to the changing layout that depends on the screen on which the page is being viewed. The possible uses of white space and choice of placement of elements on the page are of course reduced on smaller screens. This makes differences such as size (which is also more limited on a small screen), colour, typeface, etc., more important elements in the organization of type structure on a handheld device.

SEVEN CONTRASTS

Canadian designer Carl Dair wrote an influential book on typography in 1952, which has principles that continue to be useful. *Design with Type* takes an analytical approach to typography. Dair considers contrast, concord and conflict the factors that determine the success of a typographic design. Dair proposed a system of seven typographical contrasts that can be used to analyse and structure typography (see pages 82–83).

CONTRAST, CONCORD, CONFLICT

For contrast to be effective, it needs to be significant. Subtle differences between typographic parameters will result in what Dair calls conflict. If you juxtapose similar typefaces at the same size, the result will likely be that the faces are too different to have concord but too similar to have contrast. The same thing will occur if there are slightly different sizes or weights of the same typeface. Contrasts can be multiplied, as with the common example of a light serif face with a bold sans serif.

Concord is seen when contrasts are subtle and complementary. A common example of this is the relationship between a roman serif and its italic counterpart.

POSITION

Position of type on the page can be a strong differentiating and compositional element though usually a typographic contrast is also needed. This can be seen in the case of marginal heads or captions. A few words set in a margin appear in what is otherwise white space, so they draw attention, and become an element of composition. This is something that is more relevant to print and large screen design than design for small screens. The position of sidebars outside the main text grid, again with another type difference or background, also signals a different kind of text.

DESIGNING TEXT TYPE

Happily, there is no 'correct' typeface and setting. Otherwise, there would be a formula that would produce an ideal setting with an ideal typeface, which would make for a boring world that left no place for designers to make typographical decisions when it comes to text. However, there are rules of thumb and relative relationships that can be useful, which apply (mostly) equally to print and screen typography. For example, the following are good starting points for text:

Display type can be vertical and even crossed out — strengthening the meaning — while still being sufficiently legible, as shown by this cover from a Getty Research Institute title designed by Bruce Mau Design.

- The ideal average line length for long justified text is around 65 characters. Line lengths as short as 50 characters per line can work, though they will need more care if they are justified. Longer line lengths, up to 90 characters, can be quite readable if they are sufficiently leaded. Some suggest lines should be between two and three alphabets, which works out to between around 50 to 75 characters per line, with the midpoint being about 62 characters per line. Type on screen should be set flush left until better justification in css is developed.
- Good flush left type line lengths are similar to justified line lengths, though shorter lines argue in favour of flush left settings. Columns of fewer than 40 characters or so should be set flush left.
- Pages with multiple columns (perhaps obviously) suggest shorter line lengths.
- Increasing the number of characters per line suggests increasing leading; decreasing the number suggests reducing it.
- A larger page format suggests a larger text size, and a smaller page format a smaller size, whether in print or on screen.

Upside-down type can work well when it is not conveying language. Even If it shows meaningless words, it can distract, or even repulse, readers, as they try to read the upside-down type.

SEVEN TYPOGRAPHIC CONTRASTS

Carl Dair suggested that type can be in concord — that is, typographic elements are essentially the same in nature — as in a page of text, or they can contrast, when successful, in 'a unity of differences'. He then went on to describe the seven contrasts that he considered were relevant to analysis of typographic work.

Size

Aa

Size is a common organizer of type. Generally, bigger type is perceived as being more important, and the smallest as the least important, all other things being equal. Of course, this may not be true from the reader's point of view. For example, important clauses may be (perhaps deliberately!) buried in the small type in a contract. Size may be used as a purely visual element, as it is in drop caps, or in a chapter title, which visually divides a book into readable chunks. If the type is large but has little contrast with the background, whether because of its colour or weight, then it has less importance in the visual hierarchy. Size differences should be visually different to avoid a conflictual relationship.

Weight

Ss

Like size, contrast of weight should be significant. Weight contrast is often more effective between sans serif typefaces, because the difference in weight can be greater due to their structure. Bold versions of serif typefaces generally have thin strokes and serif weights that are similar in weight to the regular weight, while the heavy strokes are what gain weight.

Weight is often used to create hierarchical structure in typography. Weight can also be useful in text, especially when the reader may be scanning for a particular key word, such as in a printed piece that the reader is not reading continuously, but scanning for relevant words. Technical manuals often make use of this. For continuous reading, heavier weight text used for emphasis or to differentiate words will cause 'hot' spots that attract the eye, thereby disrupting the continuity of the reading experience.

Structure

RR

Structure is the word that Dair uses to describe the degree of contrast between strokes in the letter forms themselves. He differentiates between monoline and contrasting strokes, though the differences are on a continuum. The greatest difference is between a sans serif or an Egyptian (such as Rockwell) and a high-contrast typeface such as Bodoni. Shown here are Stone Sans and Stone Serif, two faces with similar weight and form intended to work together. Again, differences in structure should be clear, rather than subtle.

Form

Gg*g*

Dair refers to two kinds of contrast of form. One is the formal differences between letters in a typeface, for example, the linear nature of an M and curved nature of an O or the differences in form between upper- and lower-case letters. The second is differences between the formal characteristic between different typefaces, such as roman and italic versions of a face, which are subtle and work in concord with each other, and the differing formal characteristics of different faces, which should have significant contrast.

One of the most common uses of variation of form is the difference between roman and italic forms. Italics are an appropriate way of distinguishing type in text, because the visual density of an italic is similar to its roman version, so it indicates difference without strongly drawing the eye and thus interrupting the reading.

Italic can get overworked because it can be used for so much: it is used for emphasis, titles of publications from newspapers to books, other media (such as movies or television shows), foreign words (particularly Latin), as well as representing unspoken thoughts or events happening separately from a narrative.

Direction

Dair differentiates between direction contrast in display type in which letters or words contrast directionally with other elements on a page, and text direction, which he considers in terms of page layout. For example, narrow columns are vertical elements, while heavily leaded lines on a longer column create horizontal elements. As with all contrasts, contrast of direction should usually be distinctive but can sometimes be quite subtle, for example, if different type elements are radiating from a common centre, or otherwise set on a curve of some kind.

Texture

M M

Dair refers to texture as applying to relationship between letters, as a result of spacing and letter forms in display type, and the use of size, leading and typeface choice in text settings, and how such decisions result in visual texture. However, the texture of letters themselves is also worth considering, as the treatment of letterforms can provide effective contrast.

Colour

BB

Not to be confused with typographic colour, colour is a useful addition to the typographic tools to create visual contrast and interest. Dair was writing at a time when colour was expensive to print, and the internet did not yet exist, so he focuses on the addition of one or two colours. He suggests that coloured type should be used sparingly and be well-focused to be most effective. He also warns of the dangers of insufficient contrast between adjacent colours.

Organizational structure can be established using colour. Sometimes though, it works, at least visually, in the opposite way from that intended. On a white surface, black is the highest contrast colour. Using coloured type can work to emphasize, but it must be larger or bolder to function properly in terms of hierarchy of importance. You can sometimes see type of a light colour working at a large size, and not working at all at a small size (see page 106), to the point of being almost illegible, and to some extent, easy to miss. A bright colour, such as red, will work in terms of visibility but is less likely to be legible.

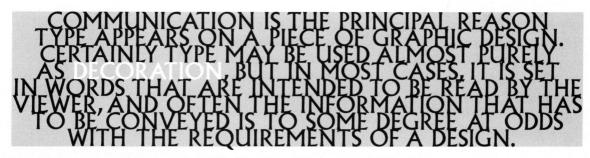

Although display and text typography have qualities of texture, type used principally for texture can be visually effective, evoking communication. Viewers see words and perhaps phrases but don't actually read it. The less legible word set in white, on the other hand, jumps out of the texture.

The subtle difference of direction between each letter is in concord. The effective contrast is that between the circular form of the text set on the circle and the vertical and horizontal forms of the large central letter.

- Even with a short line measure, the vertical space between x-height and baseline should be a minimum of about 1.5 times the x-height, though a larger x-height can mean that type can have a bit less relative vertical spacing.
- Overall, larger type should be set with tighter tracking and leading than smaller type.
- Word space (in text) should be about that of the full width (including side bearings) of a lower-case 'i' or the width of a counter space of a lower-case 'n'. Of course, this is only possible with non-justified type, because the word space will have to vary in justified type. In display type, the ideal word space will likely be somewhat less.
- Normally, a full page of text should have a maximum of around 45 lines.

Any of these propositions is worth challenging if you have good reasons. Readers are often tolerant of the breaking of at least some of these 'rules' for a short time, and can get used to their breach to the point of expecting them, with some exposure, if they find the content interesting. So while these generalizations are often useful, they are not absolute. Nevertheless, diverging from convention in text setting will probably act as an initial deterrent to readers, no matter how attractive the initial appearance might be.

FLUSH LEFT OR JUSTIFIED?

Flush left and justified type each have their advantages, but some designs are better suited to one or the other. Flush left is used for almost all text on the Web, and is often used in print.

FLUSH LEFT

Currently, HTML/CSS isn't well equipped for justified type, so flush left is the usual practice. In a print environment, it is an important design choice. As early as 1931, in his *Essay on Typography*, Eric Gill argued for flush left as being the best way to set text. The essence of his argument is that the ideal line length in terms of the number of words is 10 to 12 words (or an average of 50 to 60

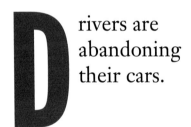

Drivers are abandoning their cars.

Type contrasts have to be handled carefully. A very big or otherwise differently treated capital on a word will not relate to the rest of the word. The first word of this block may be read as 'rivers' instead of 'Drivers'.

characters), and this results in too few word spaces to allow the line to be justified without sentences that suffer from what he calls the 'roughness, jerkiness, restlessness and spottiness', which can be a result of justified type.

Whatever the environment, flush left is usually the best choice when a narrow column is required. It avoids the problems with justified text, which increase proportionately as the number of characters per line is decreased, and are further worsened if the text includes many long words, which is likely to require a large number of hyphens. A narrow flush left column will also need a lot of hyphenation if there are many long words in the text, so the type of language being used is also a factor in deciding a good measure for text.

Flush left type also has the significant advantage in that it is easier to solve widows and orphans by subtly breaking lines to add a line, in a way that would cause visual problems, such as rivers or varying letterspacing, in a justified setting. It also makes a ragged bottom of multi-column pages seem more natural.

Finally, if you are setting text, particularly in a sans serif face, flush left will result in a more even typographical colour.

JUSTIFIED

Justified type makes rectangular blocks of text type, which can help with composition. It is also in concord with straight page edges and rectangular images. As long as the line length is sufficient, it is easier to set. However, for good text typography, narrow justified columns are a bad idea. While ragged type will usually need adjustment to be visually well set, justified type can often be set using hyphenation and justification parameters that need less intervention by the designer. Justified type is also slightly more compact. Its drawbacks are that it is prone to uneven colour and rivers due to the varying word space needed to make all lines the same length. It is also harder to solve widows and orphans in a justified setting. The fact that justified type is what readers are accustomed to in books and newspapers is also something to consider, though not a compelling reason to choose it.

When the dedicated computer system was no longer supported, maintaining the typographical quality of the series was a concern. The Postscript version of Eric Gill's Perpetua was a visually busier and less suitable typeface for text than the Alphatype system's text version that had been used before the desktop page layout systems and fonts. Traditionally, text faces were simpler in form, slightly wider set, and slightly heavier. This had been an inevitable consequence of cutting punches by hand at their actual size.

This setting, with about 30 characters per line, doesn't justify well at all. In some cases, there is as much space between adjacent words as there is between lines. This lacks rhythm and is difficult to read.

When the dedicated computer system was no longer supported, maintaining the typographical quality of the series was a concern. The Postscript version of Eric Gill's Perpetua was a visually busier and less suitable typeface for text than the Alphatype system's text version that had been used before the desktop page layout systems and fonts. Traditionally, text faces were simpler in form, slightly wider set, and slightly heavier. This had been an inevitable consequence of cutting punches by hand at their actual size.

The setting works much better flush left, though the rag is, as expected, a bit wild. This setting is too narrow for long text.

JUSTIFIED AND RAGGED TEXT

The narrower the column, the more we should consider flush left text. It will need more work to craft a good rag, but that will be easier than solving justification problems. It also makes it easier to solve widows, as flush left text doesn't have a hard right margin, so lines can be broken to bring down words without it being noticeable. Narrow columns are not well-suited to long text, especially if the text has many long words, which will result in too many hyphens.

Type design can draw attention to content, suggest something about the content, can help the reader navigate the material, and make the experience of reading more pleasant. These are all reflective of craft. The craft of the typographer is at first a visual one. A typographic layout in a script unknown to the reader may still attract attention, and the reader may have a positive experience looking at it. But in terms of communicating content, it will be useless. If the reader is able to engage with the content as language, they must be able to easily understand the relationships between typographic elements, and then be able to read the content in a coherent and useful way, without being distracted by characteristics of text that are unorthodox or inconsistent. There is a balance between the two, and that balance depends on the kind of reading that makes sense with the kind of reading that is expected. Certain kinds of design, such as magazines and many websites, need management of the alternating engagement between the visual and the textual content of a design. Publications such as books or any other example of material that is mainly textual, need focus on making the reading experience pleasant, and strong visual elements will only be distracting.

We have to be able to analyse our own typographic work. The connotations and intrinsic meaning are the subject of semiotics and other cultural considerations of our design. The effectiveness of communication can be determined by putting ourselves in the position of the viewer, and considering the stages of engagement. Dair's seven contrast model is useful for analyzing the aesthetic of typography, as well as the function of the contrasts in terms of what attracts attention and how information is ordered in terms of hierarchy. If we have addressed all these, our typography will be both effective and defensible (which shouldn't be underestimated, especially with client work, because if we can't communicate the value of our decisions, it is unlikely to be used).

Type design can draw attention to content, suggest something about the content, can help the reader navigate the material, and make the experience of reading more pleasant. These are all reflective of craft. The craft of the typographer is at first a visual one. A typographic layout in a script unknown to the reader may still attract attention, and the reader may have a positive experience looking at it. But in terms of communicating content, it will be useless. If the reader is able to engage with the content as language, they must be able to easily understand the relationships between typographic elements, and then be able to read the content in a coherent and useful way, without being distracted by characteristics of text that are unorthodox or inconsistent. There is a balance between the two, and that balance depends on the kind of reading that makes sense with the kind of reading that is expected. Certain kinds of design, such as magazines and many websites, need management of the alternating engagement between the visual and the textual content of a design. Publications such as books or any other example of material that is mainly textual, need focus on making the reading experience pleasant, and strong visual elements will only be distracting.

We have to be able to analyse our own typographic work. The connotations and intrinsic meaning are the subject of semiotics and other cultural considerations of our design. The effectiveness of communication can be determined by putting ourselves in the position of the viewer, and considering the stages of engagement. Dair's seven contrast model is useful for analyzing the aesthetic of typography, as well as the function of the contrasts in terms of what attracts attention and how information is ordered in terms of hierarchy. If we have addressed all these, our typography will be both effective and defensible (which shouldn't be underestimated, especially with client work, because if we can't communicate the value of our decisions, it is unlikely to be used).

This shows text as flowed in without intervention. The rag has an odd shape on the left column, and there is an egregious orphan at the top of the right column.

By adding some line breaks, and by adjusting word space, the rag is improved, and the widow solved. Although the average line length on the left column is less, it is not noticeable. Relatively time-consuming.

Type design can draw attention to content, suggest something about the content, can help the reader navigate the material, and make the experience of reading more pleasant. These are all reflective of craft. The craft of the typographer is at first a visual one. A typographic layout in a script unknown to the reader may still attract attention, and the reader may have a positive experience looking at it. But in terms of communicating content, it will be useless. If the reader is able to engage with the content as language, they must be able to easily understand the relationships between typographic elements, and then be able to read the content in a coherent and useful way, without being distracted by characteristics of text that are unorthodox or inconsistent. There is a balance between the two, and that balance depends on the kind of reading that makes sense with the kind of reading that is expected. Certain kinds of design, such as magazines and many websites, need management of the alternating engagement between the visual and the textual content of a design. Publications such as books or any other example of material that is mainly textual, need focus on making the reading experience pleasant, and strong visual elements will only be distracting.

We have to be able to analyse our own typographic work. The meanings constructed by the reader are the real meaning of our design. The likely effectiveness of our communication design can be estimated by putting ourselves in the position of the viewer and imagining the stages of engagement. If we have successfully analysed the content and analysed readers' likely relationship to that content, and then designed the typographic communication that both compels and facilitates that relationship, our typography will be both defensible (which shouldn't be underestimated, especially with client work, because if we can't communicate the value of our decisions, our design is unlikely to be used) and, more important, effective communication.

Type design can draw attention to content, suggest something about the content, can help the reader navigate the material, and make the experience of reading more pleasant. These are all reflective of craft. The craft of the typographer is at first a visual one. A typographic layout in a script unknown to the reader may still attract attention, and the reader may have a positive experience looking at it. But in terms of communicating content, it will be useless. If the reader is able to engage with the content as language, they must be able to easily understand the relationships between typographic elements, and then be able to read the content in a coherent and useful way, without being distracted by characteristics of text that are unorthodox or inconsistent. There is a balance between the two, and that balance depends on the kind of reading that makes sense with the kind of reading that is expected. Certain kinds of design, such as magazines and many websites, need management of the alternating engagement between the visual and the textual content of a design. Publications such as books or any other example of material that is mainly textual, need focus on making the reading experience pleasant, and strong visual elements will only be distracting.

We have to be able to analyse our own typographic work. The meanings constructed by the reader are the real meaning of our design. The likely effectiveness of our communication design can be estimated by putting ourselves in the position of the viewer and imagining the stages of engagement. If we have successfully analysed the content and analysed readers' likely relationship to that content, and then designed the typographic communication that both compels and facilitates that relationship, our typography will be both defensible (which shouldn't be underestimated, especially with client work, because if we can't communicate the value of our decisions, our design is unlikely to be used) and, more important, effective communication.

This shows text as flowed in with the default H&J settings in InDesign. There are distracting loose lines and an orphan.

Adjusting H&Js makes for better justification, and a slightly tighter fit. Word space is set to 85/100/130, letter spacing is set to −1/0/+3, and glyph scaling set to 99/100/101. Only minor adjustments were needed after the parameters were set up, even with this relatively narrow 50 character per line setting.

CONCLUSION

Typographic design can draw attention to content, can suggest something about the content, can help the reader navigate the material and make the experience of reading more pleasant.

The craft of the typographer is at first a visual one. A typographic layout in a script unknown to the reader may still attract attention, and the reader may have a positive experience looking at it. But in terms of communicating content, it will be useless.

To be able to engage with content as language, the reader must be able to easily understand the relationships between typographic elements, and then be able to read the content in a coherent and useful way, without being distracted by characteristics of text that are unorthodox or inconsistent. Certain kinds of design, such as magazines and many websites, need management of the alternating engagement between the visual and the textual content of a design. Other kinds of typography, such as books or any other mainly textual material, need to focus on making continuous reading easy. Strong visual elements will only be distracting.

We have to be able to analyse our own typographic work. The meanings constructed by the reader are the real meaning of our design. The likely effectiveness of our communication design can be estimated by putting ourselves in the position of the viewer and imagining the stages of engagement. If we have successfully analysed the content and analysed readers' likely relationship to that content, and then designed the typographic communication that both compels and helps that relationship, our typography will be both defensible (which shouldn't be underestimated, especially with client work, because if we can't communicate the value of our decisions, our design is unlikely to be used) and, more important, effective communication.

How do people read? How big should type be? What are the connotations of typefaces and how are they used in layouts? How readers engage with typography is, to a large degree, dependent on the characteristics of human vision and perceptual psychology. Even our physiology, such as our height, the length of our arms, and of course, the individual characteristics of our vision, affects how we interact with typography, as those physical attributes often influence or control the distance and angle from which we engage with type.

Biological and psychological dimensions of type

In most major traditions, type evolved slowly over time, and even the few original and invented scripts were influenced by existing scripts. The eye takes in the images of these scripts and sends them to the mind, where we make sense of them. As a result, reading is both a visual and a cognitive experience. We have to consider both elements to communicate using typography.

VISION AND ATTENTION

Things that all writing systems deal with are the qualities of light and reflection, the acuity of human vision, how the eye moves when gathering images, the size of the focal point of the lens and the distance of the viewer from the script. Writing systems also all visually represent oral language and evolved from the hand making marks on a surface. As a result, different writing systems have more in common with each other than they do differences.

How we look at graphic design in terms of composition and major elements is similar to how we look at the environment, and how we look at type is an adaptation of that. At first glance we decide whether what we see is interesting or relevant. If so, we continue to look at part of a scene (or photograph, or display typography), almost instantly make sense of it, then move our eyes to the next element. The human eye doesn't scan smoothly. It flicks from focal point to focal point. We don't actually look at a scene or object in its entirety. Instead, our minds construct an overall perception and understanding from what we perceive from each of the focal points.

READING

All human groups have spoken language. Written language has to be developed, and reading is an adaptation of how we see. As our eyes dart between the most important foci in our environment, so our eyes skip across text, reading groups of a few words at a time in sequence. Our eyes move in the direction of reading, fixating every few words, occasionally skipping back a bit, especially if we have difficulty understanding the text. These jumps are called 'saccades'. All competent readers read this way, though the length of saccades and the need to do backward saccades is a general indicator of a reader's skill and familiarity with the vocabulary and concepts of the content, as well as the typographical presentation. If we can read scripts that read from right to left, we of course reverse direction when reading them, and we look for orienting elements, such as subheads, on the right instead of the left.

So our eyes are see in discrete sequences, but, as separate images in film appear to show a continuous sequence, we have the illusion that reading and comprehension are a smooth and unified process.

Saccades are relevant to things like line length. If a line is too short, it forces the reader back to the beginning of the next line, making shorter saccades than normal. If the line is too long, it will take the eye beyond where peripheral vision is able to keep track of the beginning of the next line (though more leading will help), which can lead to doubling (starting the same line that has just been read), or skipping a line. Also, a result of line lengths that are too long is that the reader will feel that it is time to jump to the

Attention spans in print and on screen

Long type on screen is less likely to be thoroughly read than it is in print. In print, most of the time, the reader must make an effort to switch to other content. On screen, alternate content is easily accessed. This suggests that type on screen should be shorter and have more features that can recatch the reader's attention if lost.

The term 'saccades' was coined by French ophthalmologist Louis Emile Javal in the late 19th century to describe the quick jumps the eye makes between fixations where the eye registers what it is seeing. This diagram represents this in the reading process: the eye jumps from one point to the next, sometimes moving back, rather than moving smoothly over the text.

People read in much the same way as they look at the world in general. Their eyes jump from point to point in fixations of a fraction of a second. This is necessary, as the human eye's area of clear focus is a very narrow arc. When reading, these jumps, called saccades, are linear, mostly moving forward, occasionally moving backward to help the reader to understand and clarify.

People read in much the same way as they look at the world in
general. Their eyes jump from point to point in fixations of a fraction
of a second. This is necessary, as the human eye's area of clear focus is
a very narrow one. When reading, these jumps, called saccades, are
linear, mostly moving forward, occasionally moving backward to
help the reader to understand and clarify,

next line. Three or four saccadic jumps a line are what readers are
used to, and like so much in typography (particularly text), what
readers are used to is most effective. The importance of word shape
also becomes clear, as the saccades mean that we are not discerning every letter, relying largely instead on recognizing the shape
of words in peripheral vision.

We don't read everything completely (reading all the text we
see completely is impossible; the comment often seen on the
internet 'TL;DR' [Too long; didn't/don't read] is a response to
this). We look for interesting content, read it, but if the content
stops holding our interest, our eyes scan (or saccade) for something
else that is more interesting.

Keeping this mind is useful in informing how we use typography in design. Just because a reader might lose interest, it doesn't
mean we should give up in advance. We can anticipate this by
giving the reader various visible 'points of entry', such as subheads,
image captions, and pull quotes, which helps them to find relevant
points, and, we hope, re-engage with the text. On the other hand,
too many points of entry will work to distract the reader from the
text while they are reading it. So balance is important.

CONTEXT AND CONTENT

Contexts are important typographical considerations. This is obvious in the difference between type on billboards, say, and type in
dictionaries, but there are more subtle differences as well. We tend
to hold small books and devices, for example, closer to our eyes
than large books. We tend to look at laptops from a closer distance
than we do desktop screens. Posters and environmental type work
typographically one way from a distance and another way when
the viewer is closer.

The human eye has a narrow field of clear vision. When we first look at a design, our eyes dart from point to point, getting an overall impression. When we read text, our eyes skip from focal point to focal point.

Legibility?
What do you mean, legibility?
Do you mean:
1. easy to read fast,
2. easy to read at a distance,
3. easy to read in dim light,
4. easy to read when you haven't your glasses,
5. easy on the brain,
6. not tiring to the eyes,
7. possible to grasp in big gulps of meaning,
8. pleasant to read,
9. inviting to the eye, or
10. something else?

Irving C. Whittemore, *Print* magazine

Recognition legibility and reading legibility

Recognition can be important in the case where the viewer has expectations of what they will see. In the case where a driver wants to read what the name of the next town is, the greater legibility of the individual capital letters can be more useful.

In the case of a road sign indicating the exit for a town a driver wants to go to, even at the same size, the more recognizable word shape lowercase letters become more important.

Whether readers engage with typography as communication of language is fundamentally dependent on whether content is perceived as being relevant or interesting to them or not. However, much of typography presented to a reader is in a grey zone. If content is extremely interesting, people are likely to read it in spite of typographical obstacles. And no matter how attractive or legible the type is, if we are not interested in the content we won't read it. Typographic designers can entertain, encourage and facilitate. But they can't make people read.

LEGIBILITY AND READABILITY

Legibility (the ability of a person to visually discern different characters), is not the same thing as the more general term of readability, which is variously used to mean whether people find reading a given typeset text easy or enjoyable, to how well they remember what they have read, to describing the complexity of words and sentences in terms of language (which we can't do much about, unless we are writing the text). Readability is impossible to judge if you can't read the language.

Although phonographic systems such as the Roman alphabet and pictorially based script systems such as Chinese are conceptually different, in practice, English readers and Chinese readers read in much the same way, most of the time. We don't read letter by letter (or ideographic element by element); we recognize entire words and phrases rather than having to look and sound out each letter or element separately (unless, perhaps, we are children learning to read or are reading a foreign language that we have not mastered). We recognize many common words as single elements. We are fairly tolerant of variations; we can read a typeface we have never seen before without much trouble, and the occasional typographical error may pass unnoticed. (But not by everybody, and a noticed typo disrupts the reading process.)

We can appreciate the form of non-roman scripts, but we should be reluctant to use them in design, unless we are collaborating with a native speaker. Even designing in a roman script for a language we are not familiar with should be done with caution.

Examples of typefaces designed for legibility

ABCDEF   abcdefghijklmnopqrs   *DIN Mittelschrift*

ABCDEFG   abcdefghijklmnopqrs   *Frutiger Bold*

ABCDEFG abcdefghijklmnopqrs   *Interstate Bold*

ABCDEFG   abcdefghijklmnopqrs   *Tiresias*

ABCDEFG abcdefghijklmnopqrs   *Bell Centennial*

Examples of typefaces with legible characteristics

ABCDEFG abcdefghijklmnopqrs   *Helvetica Bold*

ABCDEFG abcdefghijklmnopqrs   *Univers 65*

ABCDEFG abcdefghijklmnopqrs   *Futura Bold*

Typefaces designed for legibility balance stroke and counter space evenly. As a result, they all have similar weights. They also have clearly differentiated forms and a moderate x-height. DIN was designed for industrial use in Germany in the late 1920s and is used for German highway signs. Frutiger was originally designed for signage and wayfinding in a Paris airport. Interstate is based on Highway Gothic B, a face designed for US highways in 1948. Tiresias was designed for people with impaired vision, and finally, Bell Centennial was designed for maximum legibility and economy in telephone directories.
Note that the three typefaces at the bottom are slightly less efficient in terms of total width.

PHYSIOLOGY OF LEGIBILITY

Legibility is a matter of physiology. The ability of the eye to tell the difference between different letters is at its base, and for most people, with normal or corrected vision, a typeface with normal weight, proportions and form will probably be comfortably legible if the x-height has an angular size of more than 15 minutes of arc (one-quarter of a degree), which equals approximately an x-height of four points at a distance of two feet or 50 centimetres, which equates to about 8-point type of a typical serif face, or 6½-point type of a typical sans serif typeface. If the reading distance is multiplied by some factor, the minimum size is increased by the

VERTICAL PROXIMITY

A common problem with vertical proximity of type occurs when subheads 'float' between the paragraph above and the one below, and heads that are followed too tightly, visually joining the last line and the following text.

GESTALT PRINCIPLES

In the 1920s, Germany psychologists developed a set of theories of visual perception known collectively as the Gestalt Principles of Perception. Although there is no direct evidence, it seems likely that they played some part in theorizing at the Bauhaus, which was founded in 1919. Gestalt principles and the Bauhaus have both been influential in graphic design ever since.

PROXIMITY

Proximity refers to visual elements that are close to each other being perceived as related. This is at the basis of typography: letters on their own rarely have meaning, and we read entire words in most cases, not the separate letters.
We understand items to be related to what they are close to.

SIMILARITY

A central element of typographic organization. Similarity of typographical treatment or location is perceived by the reader as indicating a relationship. Captions, subheads, pull quotes, sidebars, chapter titles, etc., are normally perceived as such because of typographic similarity with each other. The series of black dots on the right are perceived as being an R.

CLOSURE

Closure is related to continuity in that it relates to the mind's tendency to complete a path. As long as enough essential information is present, the mind supplies the missing pieces of an object. This figure is not a complete 'P' but we read it as such.

CONTINUITY

This works with visual typographic elements such as arrows, or other linear elements, where our eyes follow a direction until it is stopped by another visual element. In this case, our eye continues moving along the line to find the next word.

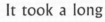

FIGURE / GROUND

The figure/ground relationship always applies to typography; on this page, the black type is on the white ground. This can be played with: in this case, the viewer can focus on either the white 'f' that can be seen on a red ground or the red 'i' on a white ground.

LEGIBILITY AND VISION

Legibility is not an absolute in terms of typographic form. It is a relationship between the viewer and the type that is affected by distance from the type, the eyesight of the viewer, and such factors as the contrast between the colour of type and the background.

vision vision
vision vision
vision vision
vision vision
vision **vision**
vision **vision**
vision **vision**
vision **vision**

In cases of marginal legibility, light faces tend to disappear, while the counters of bold faces fill in. A balance of stroke and counter gives the best legibility in such cases.

Spacing is important

Spacing is important

Spacing is important

Spacing is important

Those with poor central vision, such as that which can accompany macular degeneration, may benefit from increased spacing, which makes it easier to distinguish letter forms with peripheral vision. However, wide spacing will impair readability for those with 'normal' vision.

Smaller type needs more spacing for legibility and to balance with larger type. Here the smaller serif type is a version designed for captions that includes this characteristic, while the sans serif type has been tracked out to improve legibility.

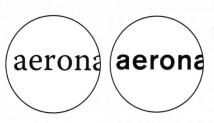

aeronautical

aeronautical

Strokes and counter spaces are sized at one minute of arc from the standard six-metre distance.

The whole letter is sized at five minutes of arc from the standard six-metre distance

The Snellen eye chart tests the limits of what is considered normal human vision. This image shows the limits of the eye in distinguishing between the shapes of the forms and the white spaces to identify the letter.

same factor. For example, if environmental type will be read from a distance of 50 metres, a reasonable minimum x-height would be 400 points (about five and a half inches, or 14 centimetres).

This approach is useful only for determining *minimum*, not optimum, practical type sizes. (A capital letter of 8.75 mm on a Snellen vision chart has an angular size of only five minutes of arc or one twelfth of a degree at a distance of 6 metres or 20 feet, but this is, by design, at the lowest limit of 'standard' human vision.)

People who have vision that needs mild correction will be able to read reasonably comfortably without correction by adjusting their distance from what they are reading, whether by moving the reading surface closer or farther from their eyes, in the case of books, magazines or screens, or by moving closer or farther from type in the environment.

As people age, their vision gets less flexible: as a result, older people are more likely to reduce their eyes' distance from reading material if they are short-sighted or hold reading material at arm's length if they are far-sighted (far-sightedness is the more common condition, which is why older people with otherwise good vision often need reading glasses).

The shape of letters themselves also influences legibility. Unusual letterforms will interfere with legibility, as will faces that are too light, too bold, unusually proportioned (which may make them harder to recognize) or unusually spaced.

Typefaces that are designed to be optimally legible tend to look similar: they have a relatively large x-height, and balance strokes and counters well.

Legibility of upper- and lower-case letters

It is claimed that lower-case letters are more legible than capitals, but it is more complex than this. At the same point size, capital letters are more legible simply because the forms are larger.

GENDARME gendarme

If the horizontal space used is the same, the lower-case letters are more legible: the forms are larger, and the ascenders and descenders help identify letters.

GENDARME gendarme

Typography Typography

Twenty-four-point Univers 53 appears much larger (and will be more easily read from a distance) than 24-point Univers 49, as the space taken up by the extended face is indeed much larger and more legible than that taken up by the condensed version. The x-height of the 49 is actually larger.

Display typography, images and composition of elements draw people into reading. Once people are immersed in reading, the goal is not to interrupt that process. Humans look for exceptions and differences from the surroundings, and are good at noticing them, which can amount to being distracted. So things that interfere with reading are themselves to be avoided.

This is where good text design (and good typesetting) come in. A suitable line length gives a predictable break and helps keep the reader oriented in terms of navigation from one line to the next. Appropriate leading is tight enough to avoid slowing the reader as they move between lines, and open enough that it is easy to distinguish between lines.

Uneven word spacing in justified type, or a very uneven or oddly shaped right edge with ragged type, will hinder reading.

Number of lines per page also affects readability. Somewhere between 30 and 45 lines is about right. On the short end of the range is better if you have room, and type on screen can be still shorter (or much longer on a scrolling page, but in such cases there should be visual interruptions that equate to a page length). For captions and other short elements where the text relates to an image, there is no minimum.

Readability is more complex and dependent on the individual than legibility. Readability suggests reasonable legibility, comfort of reading, the ability to move smoothly from one line to the next, the familiarity of the typeface, the quality of the setting of the type, whether it be fully justified or flush left, the number of characters per line, the leading, and even the content itself.

An unfamiliar vocabulary and subject matter will be harder to read. Practically, readability considerations include the quality of writing and the complexity of the text. Readability also depends on what the reader is used to. As Zuzana Licko wrote, 'We read best what we read most.' She was writing about typefaces and their treatment, but this includes the content as well. So in cases where readability of content is likely to be a problem, it suggests a need for more points of entry and making the text less visually dense.

DON'T SET TEXT TYPE TOO TIGHT OR TOO LOOSE

'Crowding' is a phenomenon in which nearby letters interfere with the recognition of a single letter, so text type should not be set too tight. On the other hand, we recognize words as a whole in many cases. Loose settings break words out into separate letters, and thus hinder word shape. The smaller the type, the more crowding becomes a problem, so smaller type should be set slightly looser (see page 202).

Zeitgeist
Zeitgeist

Although the Wittenberger Fraktur above is arguably less legible than the Janson below, they are both sufficiently legible in terms of readers being able to identify the forms.

The relative readability of each is dependent on what the reader is used to reading.

Parafoveal vision

Parafoveal vision is the part outside the central focus where we can see the letters surrounding what we are looking at, but not clearly. We use parafoveal vision during reading to fill in the gaps between the focuses of our saccades. This is where the shape of words become more important.

Simoncini Garamond is fairly typical Old Style typeface. Set at a size of 9 points, the type has an x-height of about 4 points, so would be a reasonable minimum for 'normal' reading.

Avant Garde 7 point type has an x-height of about 4 points, so would also be a reasonable minimum for 'normal' reading, though the very short ascenders and descenders make it appear slightly smaller. Avant Garde would be an unusual choice for text.

WEB TEXT LINES PER PAGE

Web text can scroll infinitely, so lines per page may not apply. In that case, putting in graphic or typographic breaks every 30 lines or so will help in avoiding tiring out the reader.

Legibility depends on context

Depending on the typeface, six-point type may be acceptably legible on an ingredients list on a food package or for a footnote. Thirty-six-point type may be too small for didactic text for works in an art gallery. Lighting, viewing angle, colour and materials, as well as typeface and size, affect legibility.

CONNOTATIONS OF TYPE

Connotations of type, which depend on the readers' experience and perceptions of type and what they associate with various kinds of typographic choices and treatments, are an important aspect of communication with the reader. Very dense and small type connotes difficult content, for example. Type that is larger than necessary may be perceived as either patronizing or communicating very simple content. Readers bring their past experience of typographic presentation of content to new typographic experiences. There are also visual qualities of type that have meaning. Type with soft or exaggerated features or air will suggest similar qualities about what it is expressing. Brightly coloured type suggests more energy than a calmer pastel colour. Large typefaces of the Modern classification, such as Didot or Bodoni, are associated with sophisticated clothing fashion because that's what they have been used for, but also because their elegance and refinement is something that is also associated with sophisticated clothing design.

CULTURE OF READERS

Readers are creatures of habit. For example, if your subject is law, and your audience is lawyers, what is the typographic form of what lawyers usually read in a professional context? If legal content looks like legal content, then it is likely to be taken seriously. This doesn't mean you should just follow previous designs, but you should relate the typography to the cultural expectations.

For another example, although most children have good eyesight, they (and buyers of children's books) expect large type. Readers of novels expect justified type and around 35 to 40 lines per page. Readers of newspapers expect narrow columns. Website users expect type to have a size of at least 14 pixels and have line spaces to indicate paragraph divisions.

Within these expectations, there is usually a place for typographic artistry, and always a place for typographic craft. Challenging readers' expectations can work well if thoughtfully done. Conventional doesn't mean good.

LAYOUT

How much readers engage with typography when encountering graphic design depends on several things, including the interests, vision and experience of the individual reader. Reader interaction with type can range from nothing more than a glance and then dismissal, to varying degrees of engagement in different parts of the work, to complete absorption in and mental engagement with the content.

The best typography in the world cannot make people read content that is of no interest to them. However, even the dullest material has some points that are potentially interesting. If the intention is to appeal to a wide range of people in terms of their likely interest in a subject, you must allow for a wide range of engagement. If your audience is a dedicated few serious scholars, then having several levels of engagement may imply frivolity and even put readers off.

Most of the time, at least in professional practice, you don't have control over the content of the design, but you can absolutely influence the degree to which a given reader might engage with the content, as well as influence *how* they engage with it.

There are some useful generalizations. First the viewer engages visually, or at what might be called a gross typographical level. This might be because of the appearance of the page format, or the structure, colour, composition or images, or large words. These might lead to an initial engagement with the content. Once the engagement has begun, the designer can help maintain it.

The most useful stance that designers can take is to put themselves in the position of the reader, and this is one of the pleasures of graphic design: the opportunity to learn what a group of people is used to seeing, how they think and what they are interested in. Again, this is not to say that our design should be constrained by previous work in a tradition. A new, intelligent and visually interesting way of presenting information is likely to be more engaging than a design that simply reproduces what has come before.

Weight Weight

Bold types can look smaller than lighter versions at the same point size, especially if they have the same widths, as in these Trade Gothic faces. This is because the size of the counters is smaller. It is most noticeable in typefaces in which the widths of both weights are the same.

Weight **Weight**

Some faces, such as Verdana, have a bold weight that are wider than the regular weight, which helps compensate for the effect of heavier weights appearing smaller, as wider typefaces appear larger.

Preattentive processing

Preattentive processing is a concept that comes from information design. It happens when we first look at a whole piece of design, and includes colours, composition, and large single words and short phrases. These basic features are seen before we actually pay attention, and then integrated into our overall understanding if we continue to engage with the piece.

In studies of readability, disfluency refers to the effect that making type less readable has on readers' ability to understand and remember content.

This shows the kind of choice of typeface and treatment of text used in disfluency studies. Both the typeface and the colour are intended to make reading more difficult.

In studies of readability, disfluency refers to the effect that making type less readable has on readers' ability to understand and remember content.

This shows a typeface called Sans Forgetica, designed to do the same thing. It relies heavily on aspects of Gestalt theories of perception.

Low resolution typography leads to a legibility paradox: the type above is likely to be more readable from a distance. From close, the eye focuses on the details. From a distance, it resolves into the whole.

Disfluency

Some studies suggest that if you can persuade readers to read less legible typography (for example, Impact rather than Times Roman), they will pay more attention to what they are reading and find content more persuasive than when it is presented in more reader-friendly settings. But the catch, of course, is that people are less likely to read such text in the first place. This phenomenon works in a controlled study when the subjects are assigned to read a text, but as any teacher knows, it is hard to make people read a text they are not inclined to read. So it is better to make text easy and inviting to read, unless you have a good reason to do otherwise.

GESTALT THEORIES OF PERCEPTION AND TYPE

Gestalt is German for 'shape', and in English the word is understood to mean 'an organized whole that is perceived as more than the sum of its parts'. The Gestalt principles are important because they deal with the (largely unconscious) participation of the viewer. Although we use these instinctively, being consciously aware of them can help us increase our typographical control of communication and viewer engagement. Some of the principles that are particularly relevant to typography are shown on page 94.

ENVIRONMENTAL TYPOGRAPHY

Typography in wayfinding and other environmental contexts needs attention to the physical position and needs of the viewer. It is often part of architectural design, and, sometimes unfortunately, left to architects, who may be unsophisticated in terms of typography. Though the basic typographical principles are the same, environmental typography is usually large and may depend on material qualities, often recessed or extruded from a surface, and made from various materials such as steel or other metal, concrete, plastic or even wood. Durability is particularly important for type exposed to the weather. It may be set into concrete, sandblasted, laser cut, cut with water jet, 3-D printed, etc. For less permanent applications, adhesive vinyl lettering is often used used.

VISUAL CONSIDERATIONS OF TYPE FORMS

Human perception influences how we see typographic forms. These aspects are difficult to quantify, and two people will see things in slightly different ways. There are general principles which apply though, and there is agreement on many basic typographic visual relationships.

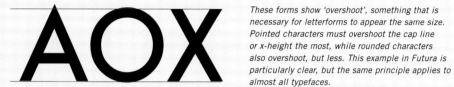

These forms show 'overshoot', something that is necessary for letterforms to appear the same size. Pointed characters must overshoot the cap line or x-height the most, while rounded characters also overshoot, but less. This example in Futura is particularly clear, but the same principle applies to almost all typefaces.

This Futura 'O' looks round, because it compensates for the human eye's tendency to see vertical lines as heavier than horizontal lines.

This is the same letter turned on its side. The variation in weight becomes much clearer.

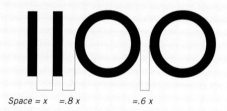

Space = x   =.8 x   =.6 x

To appear evenly spaced, round characters need less space around them. The ratios will be different for different typefaces.

ROX ROX

All caps faces made in wood type were often an exception. They often had no overshoot on the rounded characters, making them appear too small, though they are the same height.

Here the 'O' and 'R' on the left are from the historically accurate font Poplar. The same characters on the left have been adjusted to appear to be 'correct'.

Wrapping of public transportation with graphic vinyl sheeting is an increasingly common typographic sight.

. . . .

Cognitive dissonance

Readers' experience gives them an expectation of what the appearance of various kinds of content should be. If the appearance of typography does not resonate with their expectations, they may feel cognitive discomfort, which could lead them to avoid reading it. On the other hand, it might lead them to try to resolve the dissonance by reading the content. Using dissonance is something that is more likely to work with display type than text.

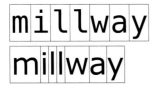

Although the balance of stroke and counterform is less than optimum in letters such as the 'm', and the 'i' and 'l' is surrounded by more than expected white space, and exaggerated serifs, the monospaced font shown on top may be more legible to those with vision impairments than is the conventionally legible forms and spacing shown on the bottom.

One aspect of environmental typography that is different from the self-contained nature of most printed or screen typography is its relationship to the visual environment and what it is trying to accomplish. It may be providing navigational information, or it may be intended to heighten or evoke an aesthetic experience connected to its surroundings.

It is important to know how people will encounter the typography. Do they approach from one angle or from all directions? Do they approach it from a distance, or do they see it coming around a corner? What are the possible light conditions? Will it have to endure vandalism or wear?

SUPERGRAPHICS

Large, often colourful, typography is much easier to design and prototype with architectural and image editing software than it was in the past. The ancestor of supergraphics is the advertising and commercial signage painted on buildings in the early and mid 20th century. As with architectural type and signage, supergraphics are experienced in a different way than an audience experiences printed books, magazines or websites. Because they are a significant part of the environment in which they exist, like physical architecture, they have to be well integrated into other features of the environment to be successful. This means thinking about the surrounding structures, colours and cultural features, as well the typographic work itself.

VISUAL DISABILITIES

With an aging population in much of the world, considering visual disabilities becomes more important. Older people tend to be far-sighted, but reading glasses will give most the ability to read normally sized text. However, older people are also more likely to have other impairments of vision which means that they may be able to read larger type more easily than smaller type. Because we are dealing with pathologies in these cases, which vary widely, increasing type size to some arbitrarily larger size will help relatively few readers. As a result, when designing print for an older audience, it is very helpful to make sure that the content is also available on the Web or on apps where it may be scaled to a larger size or read to the reader by computer software.

There is still a demand for large print materials though, and if a particular audience is used to reading large print, it should be used. Typographic rules apply: large print usually has fewer characters per line, so leading can be reduced. Large print is a case where particular attention should be paid to the legibility of typefaces, considering both the discerning of forms and the x-height.

Research has shown that those with problems with central vision (such as macular degeneration) are able to read monospace typefaces, such as Courier, in which all characters have the same width, more easily than the usual proportional typefaces.

This may be different characters formed to the same width have more different visual characteristics from each other than characters in proportional fonts. (For example the 'm' is likely to be quite dense, while the 'l' will have a lot of white space around it.) To some degree this increased legibility for some people may not be a characteristic of monospaced characters in particular but because the letters tend to be visually more widely spaced, making it easier to identify the characters even if they are not in sharp focus.

Trajan's column of 144 CE was built to celebrate Emperor Trajan's defeats of the army of Dacia in the area of the current Balkan states. The inscription, directly above the door, is carved on a 280 × 110 centimetres (49 × 109") marble panel that is perpendicular to the ground. The letters vary in size with the letters at the top being about 15 per cent taller than those at the bottom of the inscription, which is about 2.8 metres, or nine feet, above the viewer.

To help correct the distortion that would be caused by the relative position of the viewer and the letters, the letters are made larger the higher they are on the panel.

Accessibility

Electronic screens allow visually impaired people to read type, to choose which typeface to use, to resize it or have the computer read the text aloud. Accessibility can be further improved by using designers following the Web Content Accessibility Guidelines for type specifications and the Accessibility Standards for PDFs, which allow the computer to read document text and descriptions of images to the user. User-controlled type on screen enables users to make the type as legible as possible for their particular needs.

· ·

Font choice, fashion and social proof

Psychology applies to a designer's typographic design decisions. 'Social proof' influences our choices: if many other people behave in a certain way, we tend to believe it is the right thing to do. This helps explain fashions and fads in fonts and type treatment.

Dyslexia is a condition that can lead to people having difficulty in reading. The problem is not one of physiology but instead has to do with how vision is processed while reading.

Some research has been done on typefaces that help those who have trouble reading due to how they perceive letterforms. Comic Sans, though despised by graphic designers, has been found to be helpful for those who affected by certain kinds of dyslexia. New typefaces that address dyslexia have also been developed, and some studies show that they are helpful in some cases. In terms of treatment of text, it seems that more space between letters is helpful, though this might impede 'normal' readers.

This alphabet was designed to help those with certain kinds of dyslexia to read. It uses irregular letterforms to increase the difference between letters and adds weighting of the bottom of characters to strengthen the baseline, and help maintain the correct orientation of letters.

People with some kinds of dyslexia may be better able to read simply constructed typefaces that have more variations between letters than usual. The theory is that the subtle differences between letters help prevent the perception of letters flipping horizontally or vertically. This shows Dyslexie, designed specifically to address some of the problems of dyslexic readers.

This alphabet has been shown to help those with dyslexia to read better. It has similarities to the typeface above, and has been recommended to help some of those with dyslexia to read more easily.

The often-reviled Comic Sans, shown here, is recommended by the British Dyslexia Association as being a typeface that is comparatively easy for those with dyslexia to read. It shares some visual characteristics with the typeface shown above, especially if some tracking is added, in this case, 25 units.

Legibility in high-stakes circumstances

Legibility is sometimes evaluated in terms of speed and ease of reading, and this does lead to useful conclusions in many circumstances, as do studies of the relative identification and differentiation of letterforms. However, neither area focuses on the *avoidance* of misreading of words represented by those letters. The danger of errors can be the result of favourizing the ease of reading, in which we make presumptions about letters in our parafoveal vision. Common examples are highway signage and vehicle instrumentation.

The medical environment is a case in which the stakes and problems are different than they are in most legibility studies. In medicine, errors related to typography may lead to adverse, even fatal, consequences. This suggests different approaches than those used for general legibility and readability. Studies in disfluency (see page 100) may have some relevance here. One fairly widely accepted approach is that of 'Tallman' lettering, in which medicines with similar names have part of their names capitalized and, sometimes, bolded. This is intended to reduce 'at a glance' legibility and emphasize the difference between words. An example is cyclo**SERINE** and cyclo**SPORINE**. Does it work? Study results have been mixed.

ITALIC VERSUS BOLD FOR TEXT EMPHASIS

Weight is useful for headings. It is also useful if you want a word to jump out of the text, in order to make it easy to find. For the same reason, it is not as good as italic if you want to differentiate a word only when the reader comes naturally to it. The reader's eye tends to go straight to bolded words.

Much of the vocabulary of modern typography is derived from the letterpress printing that was the main method of reproducing typography for 400 years after its introduction, although the technology has changed completely. Some of the words, such as *ascender, descender, ligatures, paragraph indent*, are as logically relevant as they ever were. Others, such as *leading*, come from the strips of metal that were inserted to vertically space lines. Other words that have been retained are *em* and *en* spaces and dashes, which refer not directly to letterforms but to the sizes of the spaces and dashes. Even terms such as *type size* are derived from the height of the metal piece of type upon which the character appeared.

Italic emphasis works better for continuous reading.

Much of the vocabulary of modern typography is derived from the letterpress printing that was the main method of reproducing typography for 400 years after its introduction, although the technology has changed completely. Some of the words, such as **ascender, descender, ligatures**, and **paragraph indent**, are as logically relevant as they ever were. Others, such as **leading**, come from the strips of metal that were inserted to vertically space lines. Other words that have been retained are **em** and **en** spaces and dashes, which refer not directly to letterforms but to the sizes of the spaces and dashes. Even terms such as **type size** are derived from the height of the metal piece of type upon which the character appeared.

Bold works better for skimming for particular words of interest.

EMPHASIS IN SOME OTHER SCRIPTS

事業是幹出來的，不是吹出來的。

Emphasis in Asian languages is usually indicated with points or hollow points above or below the characters. Chinese and Korean are shown here.

한글의 본 이름은 훈민정음이다.

أنا الذي يجب أن أشكرك (أنت).

Arabic often uses parentheses for visual emphasis, though bold, underlines and slanted letters are sometimes seen.

COLOURED TYPE

Coloured type of relatively low contrast may work at large sizes but be too weak at small sizes. The colour should be adjusted to make the colours visually balanced. There is no formula that works; it depends on the colour, size and style of type.

Letters

Letters are a lot like people: they come in all shapes and sizes, with different personalities and charms and foibles, but all have the same basic reason and purpose for existence.

— CARL DAIR

Although the type on this example is all the same tint, the larger type appears darker than the smaller type.

Letters

Letters are a lot like people: they come in all shapes and sizes, with different personalities and charms and foibles, but all have the same basic reason and purpose for existence.

— CARL DAIR

The larger type is set at a tint of 60 per cent, while the smaller type is set at 77 per cent tint to make them appear more consistent.

Letters
Letters
Letters

Although these are all the same tint, the lighter weight type also appears to be lighter in colour.

60% tint used for large type

77% tint used for text type

CONCLUSION

Typography serves as a way of visually calling out to an audience, as well as organizing and presenting content. Any typographic elements serve all these purposes, though not at the same time. Like spoken language, typography communicates best when there isn't too much irrelevant noise, and when the content is presented in an interesting way. In the case of typography, the parallels are visual: engage the reader and once the reader has begun to read the text, avoid visual noise and make sure that the type is legible and well-organized.

Outside of school or personal practice, the designer seldom has control over the content: sometimes uninteresting or unclear text is the raw material we are given to work with. How the material is presented is the focus of the designer and affects not only whether the potential reader engages but also how they engage.

The visual rhetoric of display type is as important as legibility. Even fairly unorthodox typefaces are likely to be sufficiently legible in display type, so legibility can be sacrificed to visual effect.

Text type, on the other hand, should always be moved in the direction of clarity and accessibility.

As with graphic design in general, the designer's own senses and experience are good guides to making typographic decisions. However, the designer will benefit from research to better understand the different requirements of different audiences if they are not designing for an audience very much like themselves. Consideration of how people read and how vision works will probably reinforce the lessons of the designer's own experience. The basic psychology of perception is similarly universal, but again, keeping it in mind will help typographic designers to check the validity of their own assumptions.

. . . .

Chinese script legibility

Chinese poem set in the original and an English translation:

床前明月光，
疑是地上霜。
举头望明月，
低头思故乡。

Moonlight reflects off the front of my bed.

Could it actually be the frost on the ground?

I look up to view the bright moon,

And look down to reminisce about my home town.

Although the more complex Chinese characters (which can have up to 52 strokes) must be bigger to have the same legibility as roman script, the greater spatial efficiency of Chinese language and script means that it still takes up a smaller area.

. . . .

Visual noise

A significant difference between visual noise and aural noise is that aural noise is forced on you because your ears are not directional. Visual noise, which can be image or typographic, can be ignored by not looking at it. So a page can have a lot going on, but if the text itself is free of visual interference, reading is not necessarily affected, though distraction is still possible.

Writing systems and typography depend on a mutual understanding of systems and organizational structures between the creator and the reader. An ability to deal with these systems, organizations and classifications becomes even more important with modern technology, and an ability to logically and efficiently manage systems is increasingly a part of a successful design project.

Systems of organization

Any but the simplest communication is a matter of organization. Grammar and syntax organize language. It is the structure of language that gives it meaning. The same is true of visual communication. In the case of typography, the organization of shapes defines letters, the organization of letters defines words, and the order of words defines meaning. This visual organization extends beyond representation of words. A designer's typographic decisions organize complex language into hierarchies, and visually define types of information. They propose the relationship of different kinds of information to the reader and often influence the reader's decision about what and how he or she wants to read.

    We learn some visual language structures at an early age. First we learn the alphabet and how the letters represent the sounds of language, that word spaces define the extent of words, that capital letters and periods mark the beginning and ends of sentences, that large letters alone at the top of a page give the title of a piece of writing, etc. As we grow older, our understanding of conventions of how words are visually presented grows more sophisticated and open to challenge. As a communication designer, the typographer should have the most sophisticated view of all.

Writing systems may be completely different, yet their visual structures may be in some ways analogous.

LETTERS, WORDS, PARAGRAPHS

What makes one phonetic script different from another is the form of the characters and the sound each element represents. What makes one roman typeface recognizable and different from others roman faces is the way the features of the essential shapes they share are constructed.

STRUCTURE AT THE LETTER LEVEL

A normal roman typeface has a common underlying structure: consistent weight, x-height, ascender and descender heights, serif style, angle of stress and modulation. This applied to writing and was translated into printing. In early serif type, it was the result of using a flat-nib pen held at a consistent angle, and a drawn baseline, and a drawn or imaginary 'mean line' to establish the x-height, as well as ascender, descender and cap lines. The pen held at a constant angle gave a natural consistency between parts of strokes drawn at the same angle. A later example is that of Modern typefaces, influenced by a split-nib pen and the practice of engraving.

STRUCTURE AT THE WORD, SENTENCE AND PARAGRAPH LEVELS

Non-alphabetic visual markers, such as periods, commas, question marks, indents, italics, etc., enhance communication of language. Punctuation usually represents the diction that one would use in reading the text aloud, or in one's head, but sometimes it helps structure and clarify the communication of complex thoughts, that, being written and edited before being seen (or spoken), tend to be of a higher degree of complexity than we normally encounter in spoken language. Though punctuation is usually the writer's or editor's responsibility, how it is treated is the designer's job. The punctuation within a typeface is a factor in typeface choice. How paragraphs are indicated, such as space between paragraphs, or the use and size of a paragraph indent, are typographic, not editorial, decisions. If the indication is too weak, the text will appear too dense and unbroken. If the divisions are visually obtrusive, the paragraphs will stop seeming to be part of a coherent text and instead appear to be individual blocks of content.

The triangular stylus pressed into clay is the modular basis of cuneiform. The stylus might be considered an ancestor of moveable type, with a single form being used to create the full range of characters.

Nicolas Jenson's 1475 type, influenced by humanist manuscript styles written by a flat-nib pen that was held at an angle of about 30 degrees from the horizontal. The N is an exception. If it were consistent, the vertical strokes would have the same weight as the I and the T. Visually, this would make the middle of the N appear weak.

TYPEFACE STRUCTURE

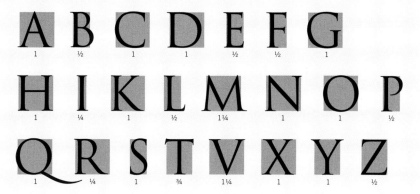

The image above shows the proportions of Roman inscriptional capitals, also known as square capitals. Most are designed with relation to an approximate square. A is shown on a square.

Majuscules moved towards more consistent widths as typefaces evolved over time.

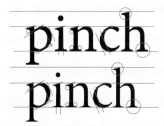

These two versions of the Minion typeface are structurally similar, though the weights are different. The display version below is slightly lighter and narrower than the text version, with thinner serifs, more contrast, smaller x-height and the spacing between letters is tighter.

These two versions of News Gothic show similar differences. The version on the bottom, intended for larger sizes, has more contrast between thick and thin strokes, is narrower, has more complex shapes, increased angles between intersecting strokes, and is tighter.

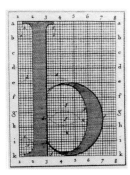

This 'b' from the Romain du Roi of 1692 shows an early application of a grid to typeface design.

Oakland

Zuzana Licko of Emigre designed the Oakland family (later incorporated into the Lo-Res family) in 1985. This face, Oakland Eighteen, is based on a grid 18 pixels high. Conceptually, it's similar to cuneiform.

Similarly, unusually formed characters, too little or too much space between words, or punctuation that is too weak (periods and commas that may be confused, or apostrophes and quotation marks that may be not be seen) will also interfere with reading.

Although there was a trend away from strict adherence to the pen stroke in letter constructions as metal type evolved, alphabets generally continued to have a fairly coherent internal structure, in that the strokes and curves that make up the characters are consistent (see page 246). However, the idea of structure as an explicit aspect of letterforms came back strongly with the representation of letterforms on screen, first as system fonts, then as representations of printed letters with bitmaps. As screen resolution and rendering technologies improved, the influence of technical limitations has quickly diminished, to the point today where forms of most kind are well represented by the high resolution of modern screens and printers.

Grids have been explicitly applied to letterforms themselves. Louis Simonneau's 1692 engravings for the committee-designed Romain du Roi used a grid to rationalize the letterforms. Gridded type forms returned with Russian constructivism, and later in de Stijl, and was revisited with the development of the computer, where the gridded nature of the screen influenced the work of designers such as Wim Crouwel (see page 114) and Zuzana Licko of Emigre.

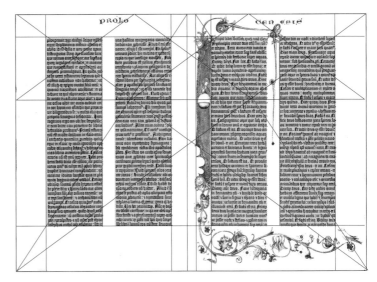

The text of Gutenberg's Bible of the 1450s is highly structured, with the lines defining the page block. The graphic elements, added afterward by hand, are less structured.

The mechanisms of the printing press made the characters themselves into the smallest modular elements, and made the vertical and horizontal line a stronger organizing principle, while the forms themselves diverged from the structural influence of handwriting with a flat-nibbed pen.

While grids have always been part of formal writing, more graphic typographic and other elements have consistently broken out of the constraints. If we look at the illuminated capitals that we see in Gutenberg's Bible, the decorated letterforms avoid the text and the edge of the page but are otherwise unconstrained.

There is a trend away from a fixed programmatic approach, amplified by the changeable nature of current typographic media. Now both the letterforms and their visual character can be easily modified an almost unlimited amount, taking reliance away from organizational structures. However, while technology can change suddenly, the basic forms and conventions evolve very slowly.

PAGE GRIDS AND OTHER FORMS OF ORGANIZATION

The page grid is often what we think of when the word 'structure' comes up in typography. However, other elements also structure the information in a similar way to the grid. A usable hierarchy and a logical way of presenting information to readers is dependent on the way that information is located on a page, screen or other context, as well as how it is presented in terms of size, colour, typeface or other typographical parameter. These visual elements structure the content in the same way that a grid does.

The designer's choice of page size in physical media is both important in itself, and in how it affects the page's relationship with structures and elements on the page. The page size influences the type sizes, and determines how complex the page design can be. Electronic media screens, of course, have a fixed maximum size, though depending on the device the format may be changed by rotating it, and the user often has a choice of which device to use to view a given typographic work. The design of the typographic experience in these cases falls not only to the designer but also the users themselves.

....

Technology of production influences type character structure

The cuneiform system of writing used the impression of a single triangular stylus as a modular element to compose characters. In the Islamic tradition, characters are composed according to multiple nib widths. Blackletter and early roman typefaces reflect the influence of a flat-nib pen. Typefaces of the Modern classification reflect both the aesthetic of engraving and the structures produced by the split nib, rather than the flat nib. The sans serif characters of the late 19th century reflect the aesthetic of machine tools.

VRBANI

This engraved lettering from 1677 anticipates the contrast, stress and modelling of the Modern typefaces of Didot and Bodoni (of 100 years later) more than it reflects the typefaces of its own time.

....

Underlying grid structures

Although the presence of a consistent grid is recognized by the reader, the underlying structure of a page is not. Much theorizing has been done about both page size and the relationship of the text block to it. The Golden Ratio, in which the relationship between the sides is 1:1.618, or the European standard paper size, where the relationship is 1:1.414 (the relationship between 1 and $\sqrt{2}$) are often cited. Examples of writing on this are Jan Tschichold's *The Form of the Book*, which looks at classical structures, and Josef Müller-Brockmann's *The Grid*, which considers the modernist grid. However, the designer's eye is a more useful guide in establishing a grid and other relationships than a theoretically based geometry.

Josef Müller-Brockmann's book, written in 1961 a time when the International Typographic Style was being disseminated from Switzerland to the rest of the world.

Wim Crouwel's 1968 Vormgevers poster anticipates the bitmap fonts that were ubiquitous on desktop computer screens fifteen years later.

Moving to within the page or screen, the main defining structures are the page format and the typographic grid and text baseline grid which in turn structure the page content. The typographic grid is not only part of the method of design, or a reflection of a particular design methodology, but a bridge between the intention of the designer and the experience of the reader/user. The grid is one of the most versatile and potentially complex aspects of page organization and is worth the most attention.

However, even Josef Müller-Brockmann, who was one of the most eloquent supporters of the typographic grid, recognized that the grid was not an end in itself, writing: 'The grid system is an aid, not a guarantee. It permits a number of possible uses and each designer can look for a solution appropriate to his [*sic*] personal style.' Adhering to a grid is not always necessary or even desirable. A grid can (but doesn't have to) constrain design. A grid is not a law; sometimes it is irrelevant, sometimes it just makes sense to ignore it, but having one means it is available for when it is useful.

The fact that a page on screen is controlled by the screen size, and that the user has the ability to change the size of the window and the typographic elements, and may choose whether to look at a device in landscape or portrait orientation. This means that designing a page structure must anticipate this (see Chapter 10).

Grids are also part of a cultural system that results from the evolution of writing and printing. As with most cultural systems, the most successful ones connected with writing and printing are those that resonate with our senses and perceptions. This includes the way that we physically read, both in terms of the relationship of our vision to typography in different environments and our relationship with typography in the environment, where we may be using type for navigation as well as for textual and connotative information. Finally, our vision/brain systems, and how we take in and interpret visual information, apply to typography as much as they do to other kinds of visual design (see Chapter 5).

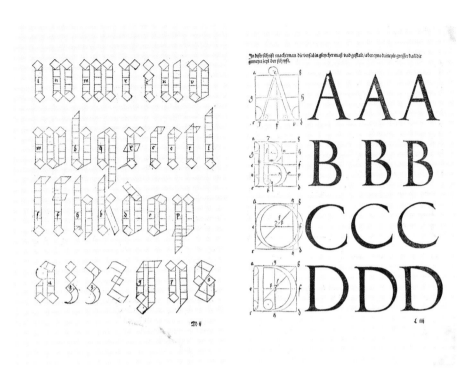

Albrecht Dürer, in a 1525 book on measurement, analysed both blackletter and roman type in terms of geometry; he was less successful with the roman type, as roman forms are more optically than geometrically structured.

The Bauhaus interest in simplified modern forms led to Paul Renner's late-1920s drawings for Futura, which was composed of geometric primitives. These forms were visually corrected by the Bauer foundry. The kind of lack of refinement of the original Futura forms has become something of a current style in typeface design.

A difference between Renner's original drawings and a galley proof produced at the Bauer foundry is shown in this comparison of the 'b'. The bowl is no longer a circle, but thins to avoid the excessive density where stem and bowl join.

The use of paste-up and photo-engraving let the Italian Futurist Filippo Marinetti make an almost complete departure from the grid. Only the letterpress material at the top and bottom, and bottom right of the page are horizontal and aligned at the left and right margins. This 1915 event poster integrates hand lettering, letterpress type and pasted-up images of letterpress type.

Jan Tschichold was an early proponent of the formal and complex grid, anticipating the International Typographic Style of the 1950s and 1960s (grid lines added).

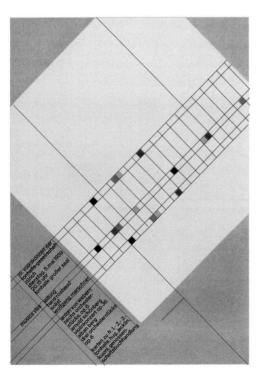

The grid reached it most influential point with the complex grids of the International Typographic Style, exemplified in this 1958 poster by Josef Müller-Brockmann (grid lines added).

The grid serves three main purposes. The first is helping define the visual character of a page. Adherence to a grid affects the appearance of a page, which in turn affects the degree to which a viewer wants to further interact with it. The second purpose is to present and organize the typography, and any other visual material in a page or series of pages. The third is to supply a system to the designer so it isn't necessary to decide the exact position of every item on the page. A grid offers a finite number of possibilities to choose from. In a collaborative project, with many designers working on the same project, a grid becomes a necessity.

In the case of the grid of a design that presents linear textual material (such as a novel), which demands a consistent and predictable approach, the structure will probably be simple, and, once established, will not need much more thought. Once the reader has decided to read the book (a decision likely itself affected by the typography), the function of the structure is simply to present a consistent and pleasurable reading experience.

A grid becomes more actively helpful for both designers and readers when the content is not entirely linear, as in a design with many different sections and authors that must still maintain visual unity such as a magazine or complex website. A grid provides a systematic approach to the decisions regarding placement of type and other elements, while allowing for visual variety.

This is useful, as it provides 'defaults' that the designer can adhere to, and also provides a way for the reader to better control their own reading experience. It is a tool, though, and shouldn't be an invariable structure that limits the creativity of the designer.

For long text, the designer is best to stick closely to a standard columnar grid. This may be a single column, which is typical for books such as novels and non-fiction, or several columns such as those found in print magazines and newspapers that focus on long reading. *New Yorker* magazine is an example, where the writing is presented on a consistent (though verging on being uncomfortably narrow) column width, or newspapers with typically five (for

THE BASELINE GRID

The root of the page grid is the dominant baseline grid; the starting point of the baseline grid and the last baseline in a text frame should be considered in designing a page grid. The beginning of the baseline grid can be adjusted to work with the desired page grid. Text frames can have custom baseline grids for setting text styles with different leading than the document baseline grid.

Different voices

Structuring different kinds of content can be done dramatically or subtly. In a newspaper, for example, essays can be distinguished subtly; set in the same typeface and size as the news, but in a wider measure and a different justification, such as flush left, for example, while the news stories are set in narrow justified columns. This keeps the voice similar but recognizably different. Using a dramatically different size, typeface, weight, or colour implies a more distinct voice or type of content.

GRIDS AND COLLABORATION

In a case in which many people work on the same project (such as a magazine) or a document where the same type of content is necessarily spread over many pages, a grid is indispensable.

*The images and pull quotes have little
relationship to the text grid, which, except
for the pull quotes' incursion, is applied
strictly to the text.*

tabloids) or six (for broadsheets) columns. Websites may have as many as twelve columns for horizontal computer screens, and as few as one for devices.

One good reason for adhering to a consistent grid for text is that a good line length is inextricably related to its leading. Another reason is that text is generally all the same 'voice', and a different measure implies different content. Changing the width or location of text on the page is a useful tool to indicate some kind of change of content or voice.

Changing grid relationships for the *same* kind of content works the other way: it disrupts reading and weakens the coherence of the material. As with most rules, this one is sometimes broken for good aesthetic reasons, but making layout decisions for purely aesthetic reasons means you are subordinating the content to the page design. A piece of good writing (or very interesting content) can survive this, but if the reader is less engaged with the content, such aesthetic decisions can lead to him or her abandoning the project of reading the material, which suggests a failure of the typography. Putting pull quotes all the way across a column of text is a typical example of this: it may look good, but it risks losing the reader by interrupting the flow of reading.

For graphic typography (headlines, decks, pull quotes) and captions, it often makes sense to break the adherence to the grid, because such elements are generally short, easily read and have visual and compositional functions, which may not benefit from a strong relationship to the grid. For captions in particular, the relationship to the image they refer to is more important than their relationship to the grid.

There may be material that is relevant to the main text content but not part of it. This may be primarily visual, as with graphs or other visual representations of information, or typographic, such as sidebars or marginal notes, which contain information that supports the principal content. These may or may not have a strong relationship to the grid.

TYPES OF DOCUMENT GRID

Because most contexts for grids are more or less rectangular, both in print and on screen, the rectangle has a strong influence. Grids tend to relate to the page edges, so the horizontal and vertical are most common orientations. This is reinforced by software defaults.

SINGLE-COLUMN GRIDS

The most basic typographic grid is the single-column grid used for extended reading, for example, a novel. Normally, all elements on the page, such as the running heads and folios as well as the text block, are in the same location, with the frequent exception of chapter title pages on which the text generally starts lower on the page, and running heads are almost always absent.

ASYMMETRIC GRIDS

Often used in books and posters, the asymmetric grid is useful if you want to have marginal material appearing in the same relation to the text. It can also be useful for things like poetry books, as poems with short lines are mixed, and an asymmetric grid strengthens the visual relationship with the left edge of the page, and so makes the book seem more balanced.

MULTIPLE-COLUMN GRIDS

Next higher in complexity are multiple-column grids (usually of the same width), which are typical of magazines and newspapers. In practice, they often include some horizontal elements, such as hang lines, or guides that show fractions of the page such as halves, quarters, or thirds, or smaller divisions.

They may have columns of different widths, as this book does, where marginal text and images are controlled by a column that is narrower than that which controls the page block.

MODULAR GRIDS

Yet more complex in structure are modular grids. They are particularly suitable for pages with images that need vertical separation. They are usually constructed with the baseline grid of the principal text of a piece as their foundation. Like multiple column grids, they may be of varying complexity. The 'classic' modular grid has vertical and horizontal distances between each division or 'zone'. However, a modular grid may have no vertical distance between zones, and less often, no horizontal distance either, if images have no space between them.

COMPOUND GRIDS

Compound grids include more than one grid system. They are, in practice, usually multiples of divisions of the lowest common denominator, dividing a page into two and three columns, for example (a six-column grid divided in thirds or in half, depending on, or something with greater complexity, such as Karl Gerstner's grid for *Capital* magazine (see page 123). Compound grids are common in magazines, where features, for example, may be on a different grid from columns or listings. The advantage, as always with complexity, is that a compound grid gives more flexibility within its structure. The disadvantage is that it gives the designer more decisions to make and more options to choose from.

ORGANIC GRIDS

Sometimes elements placed intuitively on a page serve as the basis of organizing structure. This can be a useful approach to a single work such as a poster or web page, but it is not likely to be useful as an underlying element for a book or series system.

THREE-DIMENSIONAL GRIDS

Three-dimensional grids can be graphically suggested on a page or simulated on a computer screen. These can both be visually striking as well as useful for organizing complex information. They can also, as Müller-Brockmann demonstrated in his book *Grid Systems*, be used in actual three-dimensional environments.

Sidebars should be treated differently enough that the reader can tell the difference from the main text, though they operate at a similar level of hierarchy. This suggests a different typeface, with a similar or slightly smaller x-height, so the auxiliary text does not dominate the page because of its relative novelty in comparison to the principal text.

Type whose main function is to communicate language should generally closely adhere to a grid, with that adherence being strongest with text type, and able to be looser with more graphic type.

Other organizing elements

The grid is, of course, not the only aspect of typographic organization. Colours, type sizes, typefaces, type orientation or other type treatments also can serve as both tools to devise a system of organization, and for the reader to understand the visual vocabulary of a design. We often see this in practice with sidebars, captions, annotations, pull quotes or other elements that the reader engages with in different ways. When designing for screen, the use of rollovers, links, and animations add to the possibilities for structuring information and the reader's experience. In any medium, some typographic treatments deal with hierarchy, others with order of reading, others with signalling different types of information.

The grid system is an aid, not a guarantee.

Josef Müller-Brockmann, *Grid Systems in Graphic Design*

The experience of any typographic design by a reader is to some degree a learned one. The learning may take place almost instantly, with a novel, for example, as the reader adjusts to the typeface, size, leading, line length and other aspects.

For a design with many different elements, it will likely take a bit longer for the reader to understand the typographical organization and internal structure of a document. If the design is not effective (or the content not interesting), readers may not put in the effort to understand the system, and they may move their attention elsewhere. The more engaging the content, the more the reader will be willing to spend time learning an unfamiliar system. Still, bad typography can discourage readers from even very engaging content.

PAGE DIMENSIONS AND GRIDS

The most basic aspect of page organization is the page or screen area itself. The size and proportions should of course suit the content, though a large website, book series or magazine may mean that a designer has to work within pre-established specifications no matter what the content is.

Ideally though, a designer will have the freedom to choose the size, format and the relationship of page elements to the page itself. Even if the page format is set, there are many possible ways that the 'live' area can be divided. Sometimes the grid can be dispensed with, or be formed organically from typographical or other elements, particularly with posters or other single page elements. A grid that suits one part of a document or screen presentation may not suit other parts. In magazines or complex websites, it has long been common to have more than one 'standard' grid. There might, for example, be a two-column, three-column and five-column grid depending on the section of a magazine or website. There might be a seven-column grid that is divided differently in different places, again depending on the section. The more complex the structure, the more valuable software features are, with tools such as style sheets, master page elements and snap-to-grid in print, and efficient use of css and JavaScript libraries on the Web.

TYPOGRAPHIC BASELINE GRID

Sometimes grids are designed first, with the text being designed to fit the grid. This is particularly true when images dominate, or when a particular page or screen format is needed. When text dominates, a grid may be formed from the bottom up. That is to say, the text setting and leading grid are established first, and then multiples of the leading are used to establish page proportions, margins and the relationship to images and other elements, often using the kinds of ratios and structures discussed below.

GRID STRUCTURES

Underlying page layout systems have a long history that predates the mechanical constraints of moveable type systems, which themselves had structures that are the result of the mechanical nature

TEXT STRUCTURE AND STYLE SHEETS

Paragraph and character style sheets are equivalent to page grids applied to text: style sheets help give clear division between different text treatments and functions the same way that grid gives clear suggestions to location of elements. Like the grid, the style sheet can be ignored for good reason, particularly for type that functions graphically.

. . . .

Baseline grids

The baseline type grid is a common foundation of the page grid, but as there may be many different baselines on a page, the relationship may be less clear.

of the system. Medieval grids tended to use simple geometry as underlying principles, while Renaissance grids were often based on more sophisticated geometric relationships, most notably the golden ratio or 'divine proportion', as Leonardo da Vinci called it, of 1:1.618. Other relationships that are used are 1:1.414 which is the square root of 2 (and is the proportion of European standard paper sizes), ratios such as 3:2, 5:3, 4:7 and even musical relationships such the relationship between perfect fifths, minor thirds, etc.

These proportions may be useful as inspiration, but adhering to some kind of strict geometrically derived grid is unlikely to be noticed or appreciated by the reader. The eye of the designer is usually a better guide than sticking to theorized proportions.

The grid reached its most influential point in the 1960s and is still indispensable to graphic designers today, particularly in things like books, magazines and websites. Still, just as the designer's eye is the best judge in establishing a grid, the designer may at times choose to ignore the grid that he or she has established.

A development of the 'new typography' of the early 20th century described and promoted in Jan Tschichold's book, *Die Neue Typographie*, the International Typographic Style, also known as Swiss Style, was developed in Switzerland in the late 1950s and

The nine-volume Polyglot Bible, printed by Christophe Plantin in Antwerp between 1568 and 1572, needed a grid to organize the five languages it included. Because of the varying lengths of translations, the vertical divisions were changed from spread to spread.

early 1960s, by designers such as Müller-Brockmann, Armin Hoffman, Max Bill and others (somewhat ironically, at a time when Tschichold had long since recanted the dogmatic pronouncements of *Die Neue Typographie*). The Swiss Style was a strong design influence around the world and continues to influence typographic design, sometimes directly, and sometimes in work that reacts to or is actively against the influence of the grid on design.

Tschichold was a proponent of form following function but also of function following, at least to a certain degree, form: for example, he suggested that standardized paper sizes should be accepted as a foundational frame for typographic design.

THE CURRENT CONTEXT

Computer screens have fixed dimensions. Books and other printed materials can be of all kinds of sizes, but a given screen is always the same size, and in the case of desktop or laptop machines, has the same orientation. So the structure of pages on such machines must work within this constraint. Generally, the smaller the format, the simpler the grid will have to be.

Designers new to typography are often inclined to accept default decisions made by the programmers of software. They may be satisfied with default 12-point or 16-pixel type and are even more likely to be satisfied with the 20 per cent autoleading that is the typical default setting for text in most programs. He or she may even be satisfied with whatever margins are the default in a page layout program. Some of these are generally rectified quickly, as instructors, peers and the student's own observation and aesthetic sense come into play.

However, the decisions made by the programmers of the software we use also affect page structure subtly, just as they do other aspects of typography produced on the computer, and these may bring an unwanted influence on even the most advanced typographer when setting up a grid or other typographic choice. We probably won't use the default settings, but they are often a starting point, and so affect where we end up.

Karl Gerstner used the square as the basis for the complex grid of Capital magazine.

JAN TSCHICHOLD

DIE NEUE TYPOGRAPHIE

EIN HANDBUCH FÜR ZEITGEMÄSS SCHAFFENDE

BERLIN **1928**

VERLAG DES BILDUNGSVERBANDES DER DEUTSCHEN BUCHDRUCKER

Title page from Jan Tschichold's influential book that formed the foundation of the Swiss International Style of the 1960s.

Page layout options for publications

- Size and shape of text panel
- Width of the measure
- Number of lines per page
- Size of margins and gutters
- Position of blocks per page and per spread
- Position, size and treatment of irregular elements such as drop caps, pull quotes, heads, etc.
- Position, size and treatment of running heads/feet/folios

Text options

- Choice of typeface
- Size of type
- Alignment
- Leading
- Minor adjustment of tracking or word space

Other things to think about in print projects

Amount of text and available space. How much room you have available/ have to fill.

Type of binding. Spreads in samples and on screen are misleading as the page division is just a black line, not a physical reality. Perfect binding needs wider margins at the spine, because the book doesn't lie open as sewn books do.

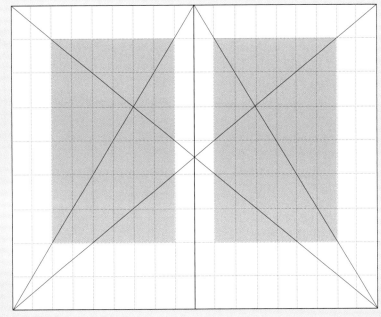

Page grid based on the Golden Ratio of 1:1.618.

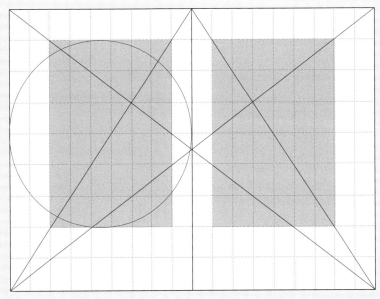

Van der Graaf canon, derived from J.A. Van der Graaf's study of medieval manuscripts in the 1940s. Page proportion 2:3.

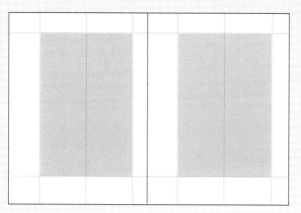

Asymmetrical text grid, suitable for text of varying line lengths such as poetry.

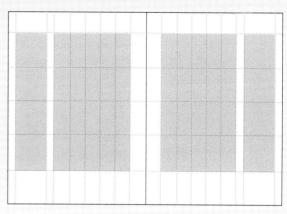

Symmetrical grid with space for marginal materials.

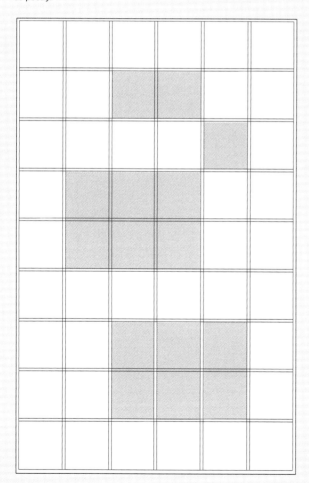

Modular grid appropriate for text and images.

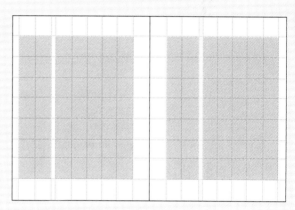

Asymmetrical grid with space for marginal materials.

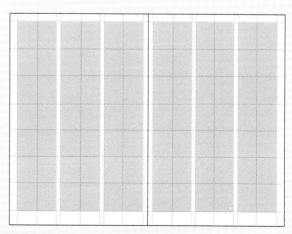

Three-column grid typical of some magazines, though other grids may apply to different parts of a magazine.

WEBSITE PAGE GRIDS

Website grids can be complex, but increasingly, web pages are read on small screens as more people access sites by smartphone rather than desktop and laptop computers. Current devices often have very high resolutions. However, human vision has to be taken into account on phones, because their dimensions are often about 5 × 7 inches, so while the resolution of type may be high, the type can be too small for human eyes. Web pages are typically smaller than the largest screens, so may have a maximum width smaller than a large screen.

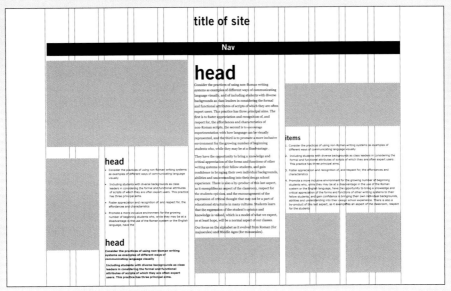

Desktop

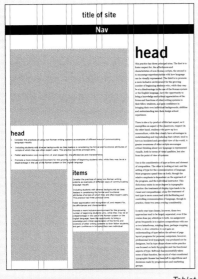

Tablet

Phone

The grid is necessarily simpler on a smaller screen. White space is a useful organizational and compositional element on a large screen but less useful on a small screen. The differences between different sizes will also be less on a small screen.

Even that most basic of useful grids, the baseline grid, can work against us. Having a software baseline grid controlling the text positioning allows for consistent leading and location of text on a page. However, it may make us want to adhere to the grid even when it doesn't contribute to the design. A document baseline grid usually makes sense for the most common text style in a document, but in some cases ignoring the grid makes for better type.

Smaller text will visually integrate better with the main text if it has less leading. For example, if the text of a book is 11/14 point, a block extract might be best at 10/13, though the grid will prefer 10/14, even if it results in slightly varying spaces above and below the extract. Narrower settings will also need less leading. An image caption is likely to both be set smaller and with a narrower measure, making an optimum leading still less (see pages 131 and 208).

The existence of the baseline grid and the ability to lock to it invites designers to stick to the grid even in those circumstances where it is not typographically ideal. As with all features devised by the writers of software, the baseline is most useful when subject to question. In print, software features that allow the locking of the first line of a paragraph to a grid are often useful for type that doesn't work with a document baseline.

Baseline grid increments

Sometimes, if the leading of the dominant text is (for example) 14 points, it may be useful to make the software baseline grid half that, so a baseline of 7 points. This is very helpful if you are using half line spaces to divide paragraphs. Occasionally, splitting the baseline grid again and using a grid of 3.5 points may make sense, though it can start to get confusing to use.

Software tends to influence work in a way that leads to unquestioned typographic relationships. Most software begins with type that is horizontal, with conventional kerning, and other defaults. The more the influence of those defaults are recognized, the better the typographer can challenge them.

....

Baselines in CSS

Using baselines for structure is more challenging on websites, as the type is centred on the line height, and is not attached to a baseline as it is in page layout software. As a result, the relationship between different sizes of type on adjacent lines may not work as expected.

PARAGRAPH INDENTS

Don't use an indent unless it's needed to indicate that a new paragraph is starting. Indents should not be used after any kind of heading.

Don't use paragraph spaces and paragraph indents. One or the other is enough.

**We read best what
we read most.**

Zuzana Licko

The system for writing Arabic is modular,
based on the width of a flat nib.

The Carolingian writing reforms of the
early 800s introduced ascender, x-height,
baselines and descender lines to help
standardize writing.

GRID AS STYLE

The degree to which typography is structured varies. The grid (or
lack thereof), its complexity, how it is used, and how closely it is
adhered to is part of typographic style.

The avant-garde movements of the early 20th century often
made a particular point of rejecting grid structures or at least
questioning the traditional page structures that the grid represents.
The Futurist design of Filippo Marinetti subverted the conventional typographical grid when using metal type and, with the
photoengraving that led to his most memorable work, ignored it.

Grids exemplified the modernist belief in rationality and the
idea that there was a 'right' way to do things. The Swiss style was
particularly apt in Switzerland, where the frequent necessity to use
the three Swiss official languages (German, French and Italian) on
the same design presented complex organizational problems.

Josef Müller-Brockmann's *Grid systems in graphic design* and
Karl Gerstner's *Designing Programmes* are foundational examples
of the systematic approach to page layout.

WHAT KIND OF GRID?

A grid should be as complex as necessary but no more complex
than that. Too simple leads to lack of versatility; too complex
increases the number of design decisions that must be made and
thus makes the process of design more time-consuming and may
lead to an incoherent visual effect, unclear organization or other
problems. Better to have a slightly too complex a grid than not
complex enough, because a complex grid does not force complexity, and if there are varying degrees of complexity on similarly
structured pages (as there often are), parts of a complex grid can
be helpful in structuring simpler pages.

The grid should be used as a tool to organize page elements,
not as a restrictive framework. However, the choice of grid is likely
to have an influence on a design, as its purpose, at least in part, is
to aid in decision-making, so it is an aid to the designer in the
process of layout. It also has (perhaps obviously) the function of
providing the reader or user of the design a set of tools that lets
them understand a typographic structure. A modular grid helps if
there are many images. A columnar grid (with some horizontal
divisions if necessary) works for pages with mainly text.

TRADITIONAL TYPE SIZES

The structure of the traditional type size system loosely relates to percentages between the sizes. Clearly, increasing 5-point type by one point changes it by 20 per cent, a significant and useful difference. Increasing 60-point type by one point changes the size by less than 2 per cent. Having a system like this avoids unproductive time spent considering imperceptible differences in size.

6 point   The size of type should increase proportionally to maintain a consistent visual differences between siz

7 point   The size of type should increase proportionally to maintain a consistent visual differenc

8 point   The size of type should increase proportionally to maintain a consistent visua

9 point   The size of type should increase proportionally to maintain a consistent v

10 point   The size of type should increase proportionally to maintain a co

12 point   The size of type should increase proportionally to main

14 point   The size of type should increase proportionally t

16 point   The size of type should increase proportio

18 point   The size of type should increase prop

26 point   The size of type should increase

30 point   The size of type should in

36 point   The size of type shou

42 point   The size of type sh

48 point   The size of type

60 point   The size of ty

72 point   The size of

Print and screen sizes

The point used traditionally in print is about $\frac{1}{72}$ inch. The CSS pixel is a relative measurement that equals about $\frac{1}{96}$ inch at a distance of 28 inches, or about three quarters of the size of a traditional point. This means that 14 pixel screen type is approximately equivalent to $10\frac{1}{2}$ point type in print. Of course, in both environments, one typeface at 14 pixels is likely to appear larger or smaller than another, depending on x-height and character width. Different cuts of Garamond Premier Pro have been used at appropriate sizes (see page 160).

The character on the left shows the letter's vector form while the one the right shows how it was rasterized, before antialiasing was developed, on early 72 dpi computer screens at a size of 11 points. Smaller than this, the type was not readable on screen. This character of early screens was the inspiration for the Oakland font on page 112.

LOCKING TO BASELINE GRID IS GOOD, BUT BE CAREFUL...

In a collaborative project with a designer in another city, I was responsible for the typography for a very large book. We settled on a 22-point baseline grid. I prepared galley files with the type locked to a 22-point grid and sent them to the designer. As he did not normally use baseline grids himself, when he flowed my type into his image document, it locked to the 12-point default grid, so the type was all on a 24-point leading. Given the amount of work it would have taken to lay out the file again, and given that the client had approved it (they had also approved the 22-point leaded galleys, but hadn't noticed the change), we decided to let sleeping dogs lie.

The invention of moveable type was a mechanizing of the writing process — turning it into a set of steps that required equipment and technical expertise to mass produce printed pages. It was not that someone who was untrained or badly trained couldn't set type; there was nothing conceptually difficult about it. However, an untrained person was unlikely to do it well, both in terms of typographical choices and technical execution. Modern drawing and page layout software have changed how this manifests itself, but the essence of the effect of lack of training remains: the work of an untrained person may be sufficient to produce adequate typography, but it is unlikely to be done efficiently or well.

One of the problems of modern page layout software is that there are many ways to achieve an intended appearance. It is easy to place elements on a page without having an underlying system. One may have the aesthetic training, but without a good knowledge of systems, the software system included, anything beyond the simplest project is likely to be less than optimum in terms of both consistency and adaptability to change. The larger and more complex the project, the more important the understanding and employment of systems becomes.

In the days before the desktop computer, typographic execution was usually separated from the design process. The production of type was done by different people, in different places and with different technologies, than was the creation of design. Designers might hand-letter display type, or use press-down type, but text type, and most often, display type, was produced by a type supplier. Only those designers who worked for a printer would have access to the production of typography and those other technical aspects of design that are now the province of software.

Currently, the designer usually executes the typography, and doing this efficiently and well means separating the tasks of typography tasks from the tasks of design. Trying to design and execute the typography simultaneously will probably lead to a bad job of both, as it is impossible to give proper attention to two tasks at the same time. Multitasking, whether by humans or computers, is in reality rapid task-switching. Executing design and, in particular,

istory is closely tied to economics, because recorded history is largely the study of writing, and writing was developed and spread because of economic reasons.

Writing was first developed to store records of possessions, debts and taxes, and was spread in the course of trading activities. The development of the printing press, at least in Europe, is inextricably related to the birth of industrial economies, and printing led to the modern age of technical growth and consumer-driven economies. This history can be seen even in the basic character set of modern type fonts. In addition to the alphabet and numerical figures, and the kind of legal characters that define economic as well as other relationships, fonts also include characters that represent currency. And, of course, like many of our activities, most of typography is driven by economics.

Even the most informal of economies is driven by visual representations of language, whether handwritten script, black-and-white laser prints, or colour prints from small printing businesses.

Most typography is driven by economics, from the sale of font and page layout software licences, to the practice of typography, which is usually involved in economic promotion, as in advertising and company websites, or in the production of goods that use typography, such as books and magazines, or to identify and give information on or about goods or services for sale.

The leading for the large text is 12.5 points, the text on the bottom of the page 10-point, and the caption to the left of the image has 7-point leading. For a design like this, the baseline grid should be set for the dominant text, so 12.5. Consider locking the first line of the other styles to the grid, though if the images are not always on the baseline grid, captions may be better controlled with a text wrap on the image (not actual size).

COMPOUND GRID

Compound grids are often used in magazines and websites. This shows a traditional compound grid, with an overlay of a two-column and three-column grid. A similar effect could be produced with a twelve-column grid, but such a grid gives less clear guidance. Note that headline and deck, as graphic elements, could work well with less relationship to the grid, as could the captions.

Chinatown

Culturally distinct neighbourhoods and business areas are an area of relief from the ubiquity of international retail shops that make the commercial landscape of cities all over the world increasingly bland and homogeneous. In many cities, the Chinatown is the oldest and most enduring of ethnic neighbourhoods. | ANGELA NOUSSIS

Diverse business areas are an area of relief from the ubiquity of international retail shops that make the commercial landscape of cities all over the world increasingly bland and homogeneous. For the last 30 years the fastest growing immigrant communities including those from China are in the suburbs. The Chinese districts in city centres are under threat. In Toronto there are two Chinese business areas. One is on the verge of disappearing. The other is thriving.

The first Chinatown in Toronto grew up around Elizabeth and Dundas Street. It slowly migrated west, but traces of it still remain at the original location. Many of the earliest inhabitants came from Toi San county of Guangdong province in Southern China.

Toronto's Old Chinatown is one of the largest in North America. Its main intersection is Dundas Street West and Spadina Avenue, and extends north and east. Once almost entirely populated by immigrants from South and Southeast China, it has had an influx of mainland Chinese, as well as a significant Vietnamese population.

The street is busy, with active trade at stores and pop-up street vendors, as well as malls on the west side of Spadina south of Dundas. One of them, Dragon City, has a reasonably-priced restaurant with lots of natural light windows, quite unusual in Chinatown, where restaurants tend to be in large rooms with windows on one side of the room, often obscured.

Although Chinatown has fewer Chinese residents, as north Toronto, Richmond Hill, and other suburbs have attracted many people, west Chinatown is still a popular destination for those wanting the cheap and exotic vegetables that are still available in the bustling supermarkets that continue to do good business. This one reason for the famously horrendous traffic in Chinatown. It's also a great place to get cheap haircuts.

New communities of Chinese immigrants in suburban areas also drew wealth and professional immigrants away from downtown. Although these areas have many Chinese businesses and areas with almost entirely Chinese businesses, they are not Chinatowns in the sense of those found in city centres: they are a suburban phenomenon, where residential areas are not integrated with businesses, and the automobile is the most common connection between where people live and where they buy or otherwise carry on commercial activities. Unlike those newer developments in the suburbs, Chinatown's economy relies heavily on tourism and Chinese seniors.

As many younger, higher-income immigrants settled elsewhere in the city or suburbs, those left living in the district are typically from older generations who depend on downtown's dense concentration of services and accessibility to public transportation. Nevertheless the businesses on Dundas and Spadina are still a destination for both Chinese and other citizens of Toronto.

In the early 21st century, downtown neighbourhoods became more attractive to urban professionals and young people who work in the city core. Chinatown's proximity to the University of Toronto, Ryerson University and OCAD University, leading to some gentrification of surrounding areas and potentially changing the face of old Chinatown.

The Chinatown centred around Broadview and Gerrard, east if the Don Valley Parkway, is a different story. Anchored by grocery stores that are doing good business, many smaller stores are shuttered. It is no harder to reach than west Chinatown from the suburbs, but there is no doubt that the smaller resident Chinese population of the area makes it more difficult for businesses catering to a clientele with a Chinese background.

The history of Toronto's Chinatown is both a history of racism and a history of acceptance. The first settler from China was Sam Ching, who opened a laundry in 1878. He was soon followed by others, who also often opened laundries. This competition was not welcomed by laundries run by Europeans, who militated for a tax on new laundries.

Traditional Chinese foods and medicines bring customers from all over Toronto and surrounding municipalities.

唐人街

Signage in Chinatown reflects not only the script, but other visual and cultural aspects. There is a predominance of red and yellow, colours that connote good luck and prosperity (with the yellow representing gold).

20 MARCH 25

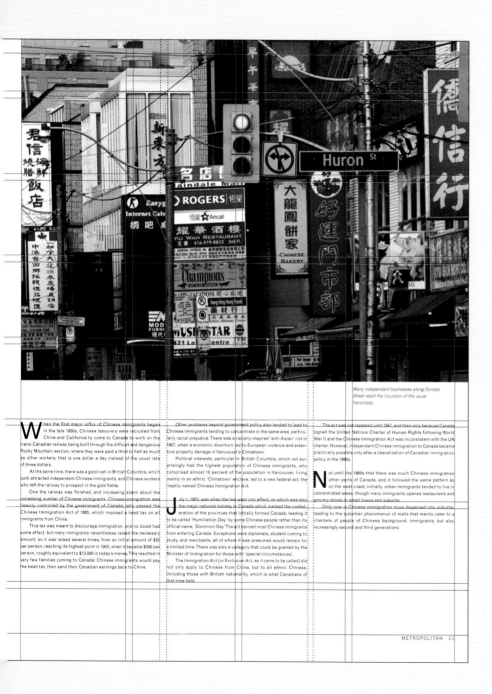

Many independent businesses along Dundas Street resist the incursion of the usual franchises.

When the first major influx of Chinese immigrants began in the late 1800s, Chinese labourers were recruited from China and California to come to Canada to work on the trans-Canadian railway being built through the difficult and dangerous Rocky Mountain section, where they were paid a third to half as much as other workers, that is one dollar a day instead of the usual rate of three dollars.

At the same time, there was a gold rush in British Columbia, which both attracted independent Chinese immigrants, and Chinese workers who left the railway to prospect in the gold fields.

One the railway was finished, and increasing alarm about the increasing number of Chinese immigrants, Chinese immigration was heavily controlled by the government of Canada, who passed the Chinese Immigration Act of 1885, which imposed a head tax on all immigrants from China.

This tax was meant to discourage immigration, and no doubt had some effect, but many immigrants nevertheless raised the necessary amount, so it was raised several times, from an initial amount of $50 per person, reaching its highest point in 1903, when it became $500 per person, roughly equivalent to $13,000 in today's money. This resulted in very few families coming to Canada; Chinese immigrants would pay the head tax, then send their Canadian earnings back to China.

Other problems beyond government policy also tended to lead to Chinese immigrants tending to concentrate in the same area, particularly racial prejudice. There was a racially-inspired 'anti-Asian' riot in 1907, when a economic downturn led to European violence and extensive property damage in Vancouver's Chinatown.

Political interests, particular in British Columbia, which not surprisingly had the highest population of Chinese immigrants, who comprised almost 10 percent of the population in Vancouver, living mainly in an ethnic 'Chinatown' enclave, led to a new federal act, the inaptly-named Chinese Immigration Act.

July 1, 1923, was when the law went into effect, on which was also the major national holiday in Canada which marked the confederation of the provinces that initially formed Canada, leading it to be called 'Humiliation Day' by some Chinese people rather than its official name, 'Dominion Day' The act banned most Chinese immigrants from entering Canada. Exceptions were diplomats, student coming to study, and merchants, all of whom it was presumed would remain for a limited time. There was also a category that could be granted by the Minister of Immigration for those with 'special circumstances'.

The Immigration Act (or Exclusion Act, as it came to be called) did not only apply to Chinese from China, but to all ethnic Chinese, including those with British nationality, which is what Canadians of that time held.

The act was not repealed until 1947, and then only because Canada signed the United Nations Charter of Human Rights following World War II and the Chinese Immigration Act was inconsistent with the UN charter. However, independent Chinese immigration to Canada became practically possible only after a liberalization of Canadian immigration policy in the 1960s.

Not until the 1960s that there was much Chinese immigration other parts of Canada, and it followed the same pattern as on the west coast; initially, urban immigrants tended to live in concentrated areas, though many immigrants opened restaurants and grocery stores in small towns and suburbs.

Only now is Chinese immigration more dispersed into suburbs, leading to the suburban phenomenon of malls that mainly cater to a clientele of people of Chinese background, immigrants, but also increasingly second and third generations typography need focused attention over time. For many designers, it is typographic detail that suffers at the expense of the overall design, unless they take off their creative and compositionally focused hats, and put on their craft and detail-oriented hats.

This applies to on-screen design as much or more than it does to print. Those who train as web designers sometimes tend to be the reverse of print designers: they focus on and understand the technical systems but pay less attention to the visual and communicative systems that are the actual carriers of information, often because technology is where their education is focused.

Typographic designers in print and web

Making a division between 'print designer' and 'web designer' is misleading. Communication designers in any medium use typography. Most graphic designers are educated to some degree in print and screen design, and design for screen is an increasing part of design practice. Furthermore, there are different kinds of screen design, ranging from highly interactive systems, to complex information systems, to screen interpretations of traditional magazines and newspapers. In any medium, the understanding of how typography works is essential to the professional designer.

Karl Gerstner:
Designing Programmes

Programme as morphology
Programme as logic
Programme as grid
Programme as photography
Programme as literature
Programme as music

Programme as typeface
Programme as typography
Programme as picture
Programme as method

Arthur Niggli Ltd.

Karl Gerstner's Designing Programmes, *originally published in 1964, twenty years before the desktop computer, anticipates the importance of systems in contemporary typographic practice.*

METRICS

Although font metrics might be thought of as a subset of form, the decisions that are associated with the structural dimensions of a typeface design are a significant part of how a typeface appears and its suitability for a given purpose.

A typeface with a large x-height is very different in appearance from a typeface with a small x-height at the same point size. Likewise a typeface with a narrow set width is perceived as different from one with a wide set width. One thing that is constant is that the overall size of letters is the main factor in how large they appear. This is most often noticed in the x-height, but it also applies to wider characters (which look larger) and narrow characters (which look smaller). Even changing the tracking changes the way the typeface appears and works. Tight type looks smaller, up to a point. Tracking type out makes it look slightly larger until it visually breaks up into separate letters. It is easy to make type less readable by increasing or decreasing the tracking too much.

CONCLUSION

Thinking about structures has always been part of a graphic designer's practice. The designer works not only with the structures of a page, but also in the cultural, linguistic, visual and hierarchic structures of visual communication. In current practice, technical typographic structures have become more important to design practice than they used to be. The graphic designer now is in control of technological systems that in the past were either executed by others, or did not yet exist.

Professional designers are largely at the mercy of the economic and political structures in which they work. Before the Industrial Revolution, the typographic designer produced works mainly for an economic and cultural elite. Typographic design was usually within a well-established and slowly evolving typographic tradition, with typeface designers making only incremental changes and refinements. Not until the Industrial Revolution did the changing economic and cultural structures lead to radical change and invention in typeface design, with attracting attention and promoting consumption being the principal aims.

Although the practice and technologies of design have changed continually from Gutenberg onwards, the biggest single change, affecting both the creation of design and its audience, has been the desktop computer and design software. While there have been individuals in the past who worked in all aspects of the production of typography, they were rare until the desktop computer and page layout programs. These programs have made possible technical and visual innovations that would formerly have been impossible, letting the designer produce almost any typographic effect imaginable. At the same time, these changes have put the responsibility of what used to be the duties of others into the designer's hands.

If I was influenced by anything, it was architecture: structure having to do with logic. If you don't do it right, the whole thing is going to cave in. In a certain sense, you can carry that to graphic design. Fortunately, however, nobody is going to die if you do it wrong.

Paul Rand

Hyde

The Makeup of the Marquise

is pictured through artful allusion as both artist and artwork. For the moment, I will merely point out that the similarities between the two images lend an allegorical tinge to the later painting, endowing it with a further connotative resonance as an image that has to do with representing the practice of painting itself.

The implied point of view in *Madame de Pompadour at Her Toilette* invite a reading along these line, not least of all because it is quire different from Boucher's earlier treatments of this kind of subject. For instance, in *Morning, Lady at Her Toilette*, which survives only in an engraving by Gilles Edme Petit (fig. 15), there is a more spatially convincing distance between viewer and image. Seen from farther away, more of the woman' body is visible. The dressing table is shown from the side, perpendicular to the picture plane, and it is articulated by a terminal edge char parallels the surface of the canvas, reiterating the distinctions between here and there. *Morning* maintains clear divisions between a constrained pictorial space and the viewer's pace—between inside and outside, proximity and distance—through the inviolability of toilette so-called fourth wall. The viewer' perspective in the engraving is comparable to the place usually assigned to the male suitor in depictions of women at their toilettes during this period, as in Jean François de Troy's *A Lady Showing a Bracelet Miniature to Her Suitor* (fig. 16).[36]

If the spatial organization of *Morning* is structured by distance, the portrait of Pompadour at her toilette conveys an effect of proximity-an effect that is characterized by the size of the figure relative to the picture itself, the cropped edges of the composition (which would have been even more pronounced in its rectangular format), and the partial view of the tabletop as it slope toward the picture plane, leaving the viewer no logical place to be when looking at it. No doubt this effect is exaggerated by the final alterations to the painting that extended the table. Yet even without them, the picture posies an impossibly close vantage point for the spectator: we see as if situated on the tabletop itself. But our vantage point need not be understood exclusively as a fiction of Boucher's painterly imagination if we regard this image as his voyeuristic portrayal of Pompadour's own reflection in a mirror; that is, if we regard it not as his portrait of Pompadour but as a painting of her mirrored reflection.

In the oil sketch of Pompadour standing before her dressing table (see fig. 13), Boucher effectively represents the very viewing structure I am suggesting here: Pompadour and the toilette table, with its smaller free-standing mirror, arc positioned before another large mirror fit into the boiserie of the wall. This sketch invites us to imagine that Pompadour has just been looking at herself in the toilette mirror, from which she now turns away. But in that imagined regard of a moment earlier, she would have seen herself reflected not only in the toilette mirror but also in the wall mirror, where she would have seen the back edge of the psyche-glass, and herself looking into it. (The same sort of vermeil-framed mirror was, by the way, originally in *Madame de Pompadour at Her Toilette* but was changed to the simple lacquered

Fig. 15. Gilles Edme Petit (French, 1694–1760), after François Boucher
Morning. Lady at Her Toilet, etching after lost painting of 1734, 31.8 x 21.6 cm (12½ x 8½) New York, Metropolitan Museum of Art

118

Fig. 16. Jean François de Troy (French, 1679–1752)
A Lady Showing a Bracelet Miniature to Her Suitor, ca. 1734, oil on canvas, 64.77 x 45. 72 cm (26½ x 8 in.) Kansas City, Nelson-Atkins Museum of Art

119

This design for a book series, based on the type baseline grid, allows for either text or art on a page. Because the series is focused on artworks, which generally should not be cropped, the grid allows for one dimension of the image, usually the bottom, to float, so the original proportions can be preserved. The captions always appear in the same place at the bottom of the page, which speeds up decision-making and formatting.

A graph-paper-style grid can be useful for a generally unstructured page. The page edges are probably more or less square, and this kind of grid helps avoid having elements that are almost, but not quite, lined up, something that is visually disturbing.

The layout with narrow columns on the left has gutters one times the leading, while the one on the right has a gutter three times the leading.

HOW WIDE SHOULD GUTTERS BETWEEN COLUMNS BE?

The default gutter width in page layout software is generally one pica. The best size depends on the setting. It shouldn't be too narrow, because we will risk having the reader read right across the gap. It shouldn't be too wide, because it will imply that the two columns are not related. A rule of thumb is one times the leading of the text as a minimum, and three times the leading as a maximum. There may be exceptions, particularly on the wider side.

A single letter can become a bold and welcome medium of typographic planning.

Herbert Bayer

The designer is now often solely responsible for managing the technical systems of typographic production. These tasks need a systematic approach and organization which is completely different from the design function. Technical skill has become part of what makes a good designer of typographic work, unless you are in the unlikely position of having a typographic expert you can assign execution of your work to. You might have something close if you are designing front ends for websites, but the coder is unlikely to be a good typographer.

Visual communication designers consequently need to think beyond the visual structures of grid and hierarchy, and also give thought to the organizational structure of the production of each design project.

Given the inevitable limitations of time, more efficient use of software means less time in production, allowing more time for the design process. Furthermore, making good use of the available systems helps permit both more efficient global changes and alterations to a design and less likelihood of introducing errors or inconsistencies when these changes are made.

Working on screen design may or may not include coding the design, but just like printing, the designer must understand the affordances of the technology to be able to work with coders, and understand the new visual and typographic conventions that are evolving with the technology.

Today, the graphic designer needs mastery of systems and technology, as well as culture and visual form.

ORGANIC GRID USE

A grid can be treated as a strict framework, or as a guide, with decisions made more intuitively. The grid can also be derived from an initial intuitive placement of an element.

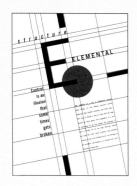

The example on the left above sticks strictly to the grid. On the right, the grid influences but does not control the page.

This organic grid is derived from the arbitrary placement of the large 'E'. It, and divisions derived from it, are the underlying structure for the other typographic elements of the composition. As here, organic grids tend to focus on the visual elements of typography. This kind of placement is unusual on screens but entirely possible in HTML5.

Type is first a symbol of language. When we see type, we recognize it as a representation of words before we read it. Even scripts we aren't familiar with are recognizable as language. Literacy has meant different things in different cultures. In its earliest forms, reading was an esoteric and often secret skill. Over time, literacy became available to other parts of the population and became an essential part of national identity, society and culture.

7

Type as culture and symbol

Although type choices may or may not be consciously based on historical or cultural reasons, they are unavoidably influenced by them. Designers who understand typographic culture and history will have more control over their typography. It is also useful to be able to discuss choices from these angles to help others recognize the suitability of typographic decisions beyond those of subjective personal taste. As well as the choice of typeface, type treatment is also subject to visual style, and that style is inextricably linked with what is appropriate at any given time, or in different contexts. Also, in an environment where cultural backgrounds are increasingly diverse, the designer must recognize that different typefaces and uses of type may evoke different expectations of and approaches to content depending on the readership.

Type is one of the few areas in the profession of graphic design in which a designer can be a demonstrated cultural (as well as a technical) expert. Unlike colour or layout, which are to some degree subjective, there are, as in grammar, generally accepted typographic principles and knowledge that, when mastered, not only improve design but demonstrate the designer's expertise to others, which helps foster respect for that designer's more subjective decisions. Although typography is influenced by style, the fundamentals of good typographical practice change little. The designer who can articulate these can help clients (and instructors!) recognize the suitability or unsuitability of typographical choices beyond personal opinion.

The use of Cree syllabics on a library in downtown Toronto acts as a typographic architectural acknowledgement of indigenous peoples' relationship to the land, whether or not the viewer can read it.

Holy Bible
Outlaws
Examiner

Blackletter and Fraktur types retain many and sometimes conflicting associations: the Christian establishment, Nazism, authoritative information, tattoos, heavy metal music.

American modernism

Although Helvetica was essentially a formalization of Akzidenz Grotesk, a typeface designed in the late 1800s, its wide use in business and government applications is largely due to its successful promotion by Linotype in the USA. It retains its connotations of the corporate establishment.

Auriol

This 1901 Art Nouveau typeface was inspired by the calligraphic Japanese script that often appeared on the Japanese woodblock prints that influenced European lithographic art at the time.

CULTURAL EXPERTISE RELIES ON CULTURAL EXPERIENCE

If we haven't grown up in East Asia, we may not be able to tell the difference between Chinese, Korean and Japanese writing systems, or the difference between Thai, Cambodian and Burmese scripts. To someone who doesn't read those languages, these scripts are principally form, though we recognize them as communication of language that we don't understand.

We should be cautious if asked to design with typography of foreign languages, especially non-Latin scripts, unless we are collaborating with a designer with knowledge of the relevant cultural typographic system. Even Latin scripts have to be used carefully if we are dealing with languages we don't know, as we won't be familiar with the connotations of typefaces and typographical conventions in those languages. And if we don't understand the content, we can't properly design it.

On the other hand, principles of organization — such as the theories of Gestalt perception and logical relationships discussed in Chapter Five — apply to all human perception. Also, the culture of the internet is to some degree international, so some aspects are shared with all internet users no matter what their language is.

Cultures are not only national and linguistic. Different professions, subcultures and communities of interest are accustomed to different ways of having typographic content presented to them. For example, appropriate typography for an engineering journal is likely to be different from that for a craft hobbyist's newsletter. Familiarity, if not immersion, with the culture of the audience is needed to design effectively.

TYPOGRAPHY AND CULTURAL INFLUENCE

Cultures constantly borrow elements of visual communication from each other. While script and typographic conventions are resistant to evolution in terms of form and usage, they are visually influenced from the outside. In the 1600s, the Dutch exported their blackletter-influenced roman types to the rest of Europe, and these typefaces affected the Venetian-influenced romans that had dominated most of Europe. In the Art Nouveau period of the late 1800s, for example, lithographic practice was influenced by Japanese woodblock prints, which had influence on lettering and some typefaces, notably Auriol.

With the internet, visual cultures influence each other to an even greater degree than they did in the past. Typographical conventions in other cultures may give us ideas that we would not otherwise come to. Although the alphabet in some sense has at times been imposed through its history, it has also been eagerly adopted, as it has been quickly recognized as a useful technology by cultures that are introduced to it. Currently, the history of colonialism and American cultural hegemony mean that most pervasive influence is Euro-American, but this is likely to change as other parts of the world gain influence.

This tendency for boundaries between typographic and other design cultures to disappear also implies that the designers will have less of a command of what might historically have been their own culture.

abcdefg ABCD

The rationalist Modern typeface is a logical conclusion of the characteristics of the first Roman typefaces: their stress was close to vertical, the Modern is completely vertical. They had thicker and thinner strokes, the Modern attempts to have either thick or thin, with abrupt modulation between the two.

Exhibitions are light buildings, quickly assembled and quickly disassembled: l a b o - r a t o r i e s for i n d u s t r i a l building.
One wanted to build in iron because stone, as a material, was far too heavy and expensive: "With iron, the various parts of the construction could be fabricated in the many separate workshops." Beyond this, iron had the advantage "of giving the building a s p e c i a l character, highly appropriate to its purpose." (See *Monographie. Palais et constructions diverses de l'exposition universelle de 1878, exécutées par l'administration*, p. 7.)
The h i s t o r y of e x h i b i t i o n s b e c o m e s the h i s t o r y of i r o n c o n s t r u c - tion. Following the first tentative efforts of 1851 (London) and 1855 (Paris), it happened almost regularly that previously untried solutions on which a group of constructors was working were realized for the first time. Immediately thereafter, they left their stamp on life to the broadest extent. Often it was a matter of a daring and even dubious way of building (Eiffel Tower) into the unknown.[48]
Exhibitions not only summarized the results of the development but they also anticipated it.

What might look like bad typography to the contemporary reader because of its uneven typographic colour was accepted practice in Germany in the early 20th Century, when spaced text was used to indicate emphasis; the Fraktur traditionally used had no italic or equivalent. Spacing for emphasis seems unintuitive, as the spaced text is visually less intense than normal spacing because of weaker typographic colour. As shown in this English language facsimile which maintains this convention, italic was used for publication titles.

Cultural influence occurs in other script traditions as well. Arabic writing styles traditionally have complex structures. When typographic technology was introduced from Europe, the structure of Arabic typefaces began, in terms of vertical metrics and variation, to be simplified, influenced by the simpler European type structures.

Changes in economic culture are also influential. During the Industrial Revolution, new and inventive typefaces were created that reflected the culture of inventiveness and excess of Victorian era capitalism. Instead of the slow evolution of an established craft, type designers both invented new typefaces, and imitated others' typographic creations. The development of electrotyping meant that foundries could not only imitate typefaces, they could actually copy them, foreshadowing digital font piracy. The culture of capitalism was reflected in typographic practice.

THE EUROPEAN TRADITION

In the European tradition, what we call 'roman' type was formed by the joining of Roman capitals with the script favoured by humanist writers of the 1400s, which imitated the historical Carolingian minuscule that had been developed around 800 CE.

Blackletter, the other dominant major style of the Renaissance, is based on the narrow, darker and more angular style that had evolved from the Carolingian minuscule in the period between 800 and 1400 CE, largely within the culture of the church.

From the beginning of typography in Europe, the style of type had communicated a philosophical cultural attitude: the choice of whether to use blackletter or roman faces in the early Renaissance was initially a consciously philosophical design decision by the humanist subculture, because blackletter connoted the church establishment, while the humanist script connoted a more open and human-centred approach to knowledge. At the same time, there was a cultural geographic aspect to typographic choices, as parts of Europe, most notably Germany, held on to blackletter forms of text, while in southern Europe, particularly the Italian peninsula, the Roman style dominated. The relationship between typefaces and current philosophical outlook recurs over time, as Robert Bringhurst discusses in *Elements of Typographic Style*.

The popularity of Roman type coincided with the explosion in the number of presses. This meant that Roman text was what became familiar to most of the new readers who were exposed to the increase in available reading material. However, even where Roman text was the dominant style, blackletter continued to be used as a signifier of authority.

This distinction between different type styles and their associations with cultures is clear, but similar distinctions are found between the more subtle and not-so-subtle variations in current typographic practice. Largely through association, some type styles carry meaning, which can change over time.

CONNOTATIONS OF TYPE

How type is used and treated also has cultural meaning for the reader. This applies both to display type and to a lesser extent, text. With display type, in addition to the form of the typeface, any textural treatment of the type, colour and alterations to the forms of the letters affect readers' perceptions.

The connotations of display type depend on the relationship of its appearance with the words it is representing, though what the typeface has become associated with in the reader's experience is also important. Formal script type implies a particular kind of sophistication, a childish script suggest content about or for children, etc. For example, Helvetica (and similar faces) have visual qualities that suggest precision and organization. But, because of how they have been used, they also have connotations of modernism and the voice of corporations.

The treatment of display type also has connotative qualities beyond its form. Colour, graphic treatments and typographic qualities such as size and weigh also carry connotations. With text, the typeface may communicate something, but the appearance of the block of text and use of white space are even more important in signalling particular kinds of content and evoking expectations of the content.

. . . .

Humanists

The Humanists were a network of scholars associated with the Roman Catholic church in the 1400s, who looked to classical Greek and Roman principles of observation and philosophical development instead of the focus on dogma and religious tradition of the mainstream church. This extended to their writing style, in which influential Humanists imitated the form of Greek and Roman scripts copied during the Carolingian Renaissance of 400 years earlier.

Formal and cursive Chinese characters, showing the tendency for people to write quickly and carelessly. The same factor led to roman minuscule letters and italic letterforms. Some Simplified Chinese characters are influenced by cursive versions of traditional formal characters.

Technology
Helvetica

Technology
Template Gothic

Technology
OCRA

TECHNOLOGY
Neuland

Technology
De Vinne

Helvetica has connotations of the establishment, modernism and the rightness of technology. Template Gothic might suggest the 1990s and a challenge to faith in technology. OCRA is a more straight-faced reference to technology with a suggestion of the basic elements of it. Neuland is either playing against type or suggests primitive technology. The De Vinne invokes technology of the 1800s.

The good type-designer… realizes that, for a new [text] font to be successful, it has to be so good that only very few recognize its novelty.

Stanley Morison, *First Principles of Typography*

The connotations of text type are more dependent on how it is laid out and otherwise treated in its entirety. It is true that the initial experience of reading may be affected by the appearance of the typeface. For example, we can argue that old style typefaces have a more human voice than sans serif faces. However, this is part of the first impression and disappears in the act of reading, at which point legibility, readability and content take over.

TEXT TREATMENT CONNOTATIONS

Even with exactly the same typeface, readers will react differently to different treatments of the type. Leading, tracking, type size, measure and text layout affect how readers perceive content. Dense type with a long line length and little leading is not only harder to read, it carries the connotation of being harder to read. This might put a reader off or, conversely, give a desired impression of seriousness and importance. A lighter type block, resulting from more-than-average leading and a short line length, suggests text that is less serious, but it might be more inviting to the casual reader. It also can look as if the designer is trying to stretch content. Type in a children's book connotes simple, easy reading; multiple narrow columns suggest newspapers and thus current information, and so on. Layout, size and leading affect the perceptions, expectations and experience of the reader more than the choice of typeface.

The form of text type should be unnoticed

If a text typeface is distinctive enough to draw attention to itself while being read, it will detract from the reading. We can't look at a typeface and read content at the same time.

Though the Web has been around for only 35 years rather than the 600 years since the beginning of printing in the early Renaissance, it already has established conventions that have evolved. These originate in part from preceding technologies and conventions, in part from the different nature of the medium itself, and finally, in part from active evolution that has arisen from within the medium. A web page today doesn't look much like one from 1986. For an obvious example, the link underlined in blue was a standard on the early Web but would seem odd or perhaps consciously 'retro' today. Certain menu items, such as the magnifying glass, the settings icon or the collapsed menu item (see page 32), have become part of the visual language of internet users.

TYPE FORMS EVOLVE SLOWLY

As we have seen, letterforms and associated conventions are conservative and evolve slowly. With high literacy rates all over the world, the increasing number of users with experience and expectations of typographic communication is slowing the evolution even more. Although how type is used changes, the appearance of good typographic practice is similar across cultures and media. Principles of hierarchy, the importance of size and other indicators of the structure of information also change little, though there are more ways of employing them on a computer screen, and the possible structural complexity of the information is, of course, greater.

There are exceptions to the conservatism of typographical convention. The use of common initialisms, such as WTF and YOLO, and abbreviated or informal spelling are a result of the advent of more or less real-time personal typographic communication, first on email, and now with text messaging. Emojis are also a relatively new and widely adopted development. It will be interesting to see if these new conventions find their way into more formal typographic practice. So far, there has been little sign of this happening.

Another change, more immediately relevant to typographic design practice, is the availability of web fonts starting around 2010. Previous to this, designers were limited to a few typefaces for text that were resident on all users' computers (see page 216). Other typefaces could only exist as image files on a website, unless the font was installed on the user's computer. Now there are many good high-quality fonts available, and with the increasingly high resolution of computer and device screens, and better control of typographic parameters in CSS, excellent typography is possible.

Types do have essential qualities, romantic, documentary, poetic, realistic, efficient and so on, which are capable of reflecting an author's intention.

Carl Dair, *Design with Type*

. . . .

Tschichold on the zeitgeist

In 1928, Jan Tschichold suggested in his book, *Die Neue Typographie*, that sans serif type was 'the only one in spiritual accordance' with the early modernist times in which he wrote. He also believed that asymmetric typographic layouts similarly reflected the times. However, in later life he regretted his uncompromising attitude, recognizing that the content and reader are the most important influences on the design.

. . . .

Paralinguistics / paratypography

Paralinguistics explains how the way things are said can affect the way we hear what is being said. This applies to typography in the same way: the visual qualities of type affect the interpretation of the words that are set.

Style is the adaptation of the forms of function and display to the spirit (and hence to the taste) of the times.

Karl Gerstner, *Designing Programmes*

TYPEFACE OVERUSE

Many of the versions of Times Roman are excellent typefaces. But the fact that it was a default typeface for early laser printers and for Adobe InDesign led to a rejection by typographic designers. Now, with many typefaces available, and the default font for InDesign now being Minion (also an excellent typeface), Times has been rehabilitated. For the same reason, though, designers now tend to avoid Minion. The same applies to the use of Myriad, the default font for Illustrator: using Myriad currently often looks like a mistake when it turns up in logos and signage.

REFERENCE, HOMAGE, FASHION, APPROPRIATION, PLAGIARISM

Typography, like spoken language, is by its nature imitative. The letters we use are necessarily essentially the same as those that came before in order for us to understand them. This can lead to taking from the past, particularly in 'postmodern' design, as in Paula Scher's controversial Swatch ads of the mid-1980s, which were a more or less literal copy of Herbert Matter's Swiss tourism ads of the mid-1930s. This kind of revival is part of graphic design practice, in which the past always informs the present, but it suggests we need to give some thought to the differences between reference, homage, appropriation and plagiarism. The availability of easily copied images on the internet increases the need for this.

The flow of cultural influences works in all directions with typography, as well as other aspects of culture. Depending on the relationships between the cultural-political entities involved, it may be considered imposition, or adoption or appropriation. Today it is almost impossible to entirely associate current graphic styles with a political or cultural location beyond the actual language used. The hegemony of Anglophone culture has resulted in Roman characters (often English words) frequently appearing in design intended for non-English speaking audiences, while Chinese, Japanese and other scripts are seen in Western graphics. Tattoos are a common example of individuals' adoption of other scripts.

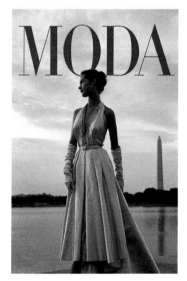 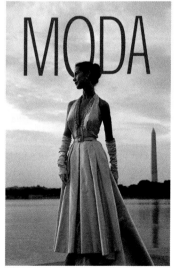

The Modern typefaces, particularly Didot and Bodoni, have had a very long run evoking high fashion. There is no reason why other faces should not be used if they can evoke the same feeling. Cooper Black would not work, but the Grotesque Light Condensed has an appropriate appearance and has the benefit of originality.

The access to other's typographic traditions can simultaneously both enrich our work, showing respect for other cultures or put us in danger of parody, cultural appropriation or theft. This takes ethical consideration.

The history of typeface design in particular has been a history of conscious imitation, with refinement being the goal; Garamond's typefaces of the mid-1500s in Paris were based on the typefaces Francesco Griffo designed and made for Aldus Manutius in Venice, while Griffo's faces were refinements of Jenson's work of the late 1400s. Baskerville was trying to perfect Caslon's work, and Bodoni was influenced by Baskerville's work. The idea of originality in typography is a product of the Industrial Revolution.

So it can be hard to distinguish between innovation and imitation: all typography is by necessity derivative to some degree. Typography is a tool of designers that depends on the experience and expectations of the reader to work effectively as communication. References and homage are often a part of that. Others' use of type will influence our work, but in the end, the original qualities of how we use type is what makes our work our own.

FASHIONS IN TYPOGRAPHY

Like many other aspects of human culture, typography is also susceptible to fashion. The professional designer must be consciously aware of typographic fashion in order to work either with it or against it. It cannot be ignored.

Innovation in the choice and style of setting of display type (for example, the tight setting of advertising type in the 1970s and 80s, postmodern and grunge typography, the changing popularity of various typefaces), all are at first revolutionary, then fashionable, then derivative and boring, and then may gain a sort of echo fashionability as nostalgic or referential.

Typography that makes little sense now might be absolutely appropriate ten years from now. However, the typographer works in, and mainly for, the present. The kind of design we are working on determines how relevant current fashion is. Unavoidably though, fashion will be present, because typographic design inevitably reflects its time.

Akzidenz Grotesk
Gill Sans
Futura
Helvetica
Avant Garde
Meta
Gotham
Circular

All the sans serif typefaces above are currently used, but their characters reflect the design fashions and culture of their times, and their popularity changes over time. Typefaces that become very popular generally have a strong reaction against their use for a time after they fall out of favour.

. . . .

Type and philosophies

Current philosophical outlooks often influence and are reflected by typographic fashion for both layout and typefaces. From humanist writing to the wide leading and white space of the late Enlightenment to the first flush of 1800s consumerism, to the influence of modernism on typography, notably exemplified by Jan Tschichold's *The New Typography*, Walter Benjamin's *Art in the Age of Mechanical Reproduction*, and the writings of postmodernist philosophers such as Roland Barthes, Jean Baudrillard, Pierre Bourdieu and Jacques Derrida.

DIFFERENT READERS, DIFFERENT TYPOGRAPHY

Each of these pages has the same content the differences between them are the typefaces, the grid used and the composition and treatment of elements. Each suggests a different kind of reading.

SOME DISPLAY TYPE FASHIONS OF THE 20th CENTURY

Typefaces as well as the way they are set are subject to fashion; the styles reproduce typical characteristics of fashionable typographic practice at various times in the 20th century. Not all type followed these fashions. Typography for advertising and marketing materials tends to follow fashion more than editorial design.

TYPES OF FASHION

Beginning of the 20th Century: centred type and derivations of the Modern typeface.

TYPES OF FASHION

The New Typography of the 1920s was the basis of the International Typographic Style of the 1960s.

Types of fashion

1950s and 60s: hand lettering was common and it influenced typographic form.

Types of Fashion

1970s and 80s: tight, bold settings with slightly exaggerated type forms.

tYp-es OF fash-iOn

Late 1980s to mid-1990s: desktop computers led designers to experiment and challenge convention.

TYPES OF FASHION

Early and mid-1990s: use of newly available software effects.

TYPOGRAPHY AS PERSONAL IDENTITY

Brand typography, special interest websites, newspapers and magazines often represent particular cultural and social groups, and constitute part of the reader's cultural identity. Newspapers use typography to literally express their content but also to signal what their content is and how they deal with it. The newspaper that one chooses is still a signal of the social and political identity of the reader.

The Toronto Sun appeals to a conservative and anti-government readership. The typographic approach is deliberately unsophisticated, and on the front page, typographic content, apart from headlines and teasers, is absent. The advertising on the bottom panel is aim at the presumed tastes and concern with cost of a considerable part of the readership.

Toronto's Globe and Mail appeals to and represents an educated and privileged demographic. Editorials tend to towards a slightly right-of-centre political position. Typographically, it is relatively sophisticated, with flush left text, some attention to white space, and showing the use of a drop cap on an editorial story. The advertisement on the bottom reflects the concern with money, an expected attribute of many of its readers.

The Toronto Star is aimed at a middle class, and editorially supports a centrist political party. The typographic design is less refined than the Globe's, and follows a traditional model of justified text columns and has a slightly sensationalist style of headlines both in content and presentation. It is also traditional in that it is strong in investigative journalism. The advertisement on the bottom for a private school addresses a likely aspiration of the demographic.

SOME SCRIPTS

Although most of the readers of this book likely work mainly with the Roman alphabet, much of the world uses other scripts. Some of the visual principles apply to all scripts. But there are differences, and considering today's diverse audiences, graphic designers should have some familiarity with other scripts. Below is a look at the basic characteristics of some of them.

Grafisch ontwerper

Roman alphabet, descended via Greek from Phoenician script, is an alphabetic system based on characters taken from Egyptian hieroglyphs (around 1500 BCE).

平面设计

Simplified Chinese. Twentieth century reform of traditional Chinese script. Influenced by cursive forms and simplified complex elements. Used principally in mainland China. Usually set left to right, may be set in any direction. Characters are composed of one or more of 214 radicals or basic elements.

平面設計

Traditional Chinese, evolved over 4000 years. Now used mainly in Hong Kong (China), Taiwan (China) and overseas. Usually set left to right, may be set in any direction. As with Simplified characters, all characters are the same width. Simpler characters were not changed in Simplified Chinese, as the two characters on the left show.

التصميم الجرافيكي

Arabic, an abugida (or alphasyllabary) in which short vowels are indicated by diacritics. Evolved from Phoenician. Written right to left. Highly calligraphic, with ligatures and initial, medial and final forms of letters. Persian script is a variation.

ビジネスのための書道
Katakana　Hiragana　Kanji

Japanese, uses Kanji, evolved from traditional Chinese. Includes two syllabic systems: Katakana (used mainly to write words of foreign derivation) and Hiragana. Now usually written left to right, traditionally written in vertical columns, right to left.

графический дизайнер

Cyrillic alphabet, evolved from Greek script, by way of the Byzantine empire, with added characters from the invented Glagolitic script. Written left to right.

thiết kế đồ họa

Vietnamese alphabet, an adaptation of the Roman alphabet, a result of both European colonialism and the unsuitability of the Chinese characters, which had been used previously, to the Vietnamese language. Written left to right.

గ్రాఫిక్ డిజైన్

Telugu script, an abugida in which vowels are independent forms at the beginning or ends of words, otherwise indicated by elements added vertically to consonant letterforms. Descended from Brahmic around 500 CE. Written left to right.

그래픽 디자인

Korean alphabet, devised in the 1400s to replace an adaptation of Chinese characters to write the Korean language. It is a 'featural' alphabet: the forms are related to the sounds of speech and the position of the mouth in making them, thereby giving a clue to the pronunciation in the form of the letters.

ᒉ"ᐃᐳ ᒪᔦᑏᐄᐧ

Canadian Aboriginal Syllabics, used to write several First Nations languages. Invented in the 1840s by Mistanaskowew, a Cree speaker and James Evans, a missionary. An abugida (influenced by Devanagari syllabics) with the orientation of characters indicating different vowels. Inspired by Sequoyah's Cherokee syllabary.

การออกแบบกราฟิก

Thai abugida, evolved from Brahmic script via Old Khmer. No word spaces are used (though lines must be broken at a word division).

FASHION AND BANALITY

The difference between what is fashionable, and thus contemporary, and what is banal, because it looks like what everyone else is doing, is a fine line, and what is fashionable today is bound to be boring tomorrow. Looking at historical typographic trends or look back at the typography that has won awards every year makes this clear. Trends begin with innovation, then become commonplace, and then dated. Graphic design award juries tend to look for work that balances originality with stylishness.

Focusing on fashion with layout and typeface choice instead of communicating content will probably result in ineffective communication. However, it is also a reality that we are embedded in a culture or cultures. There is no way to avoid reflecting our cultural surroundings. So if we want to make typographic design functionally and aesthetically effective, we should focus on those aspects. The contemporary element will be there anyway.

In the treatment of text, of course, there is no way to avoid convention. Trying to avoid it completely will likely end in work that may be formally interesting but poor at communicating. Typography inevitably copies from the past and present culture: you can't design a 'better' alphabet, because the letters have to be recognizably based on existing accepted letterforms, or they will be meaningless. Though this hasn't stopped people from trying.

Humans are adaptable, though, and novelty does draw attention. The goal is to balance originality, appropriateness and readability. Differences between layout and display type treatment can and will vary widely between designers and still function well. Treatment of text will also vary, but less so than the more visual aspects of type. Innovative treatment of page layout and display type can draw readers in. Text that is typographically unconventional is more likely to be talked about than read.

IMITATION / INSPIRATION

Copying contemporary typography can be perceived as derivative, inspiration from the past can be perceived as creative.

New approaches to alphabets

Herbert Bayer and Jan Tschichold both proposed new approaches to alphabets, dispensing with caps (suggesting that the two-case system is unnecessary) and trying to make phonetic aspects clearer.

the quick brown fox jumps
over the lazy dog

The Irish playwright George Bernard Shaw left £500 in his will to fund the devising of a new alphabet that would accurately describe the forty phonemes of the English language. The Shavian alphabet was completed by Kingsley Read.

The image above shows Systemschrift, a 1927 typeface designed by Kurt Schwitters. A single case face, in which Schwitters sized letters in accordance with the sounds they represent, hence the larger vowels.

Image from The Scarecrow, a typographic children's story entitled The Scarecrow by Schwitters, Kätte Steinitz and Theo van Doesburg, 1925. This shows elements of Dada and Constructivism.

. . . .

Ideological alignment

Centred type implies support of the status quo, through the inevitability of horizontal the horizontal placement of each line and literal visual balance. Asymmetric type challenges this and suggests agency on the part of the designer, and a modernist emphasis on form following function. This was the thinking in the early 20th century, and it still makes logical sense. But culture is stronger. By the end of the century, modernist asymmetric design had become conventional, so the ideological message of asymmetry lost its meaning.

Display type offers much more latitude for experimentation and individuality, so appearing to reproduce a contemporary designer's visual typographic style is likely to be criticized. This is not necessarily fair, because, as previously stated, fashion is an unavoidable reality of design, no matter how much one might try to avoid it, and more than one designer at a time is likely to come up with the same conceptual and aesthetic ideas. Surface similarity doesn't always mean imitation.

Being too fashionable may lead you to be thought of as more of a stylist than a designer. Again, focusing on the purpose of the design is a good way to develop effective display typography. Imitating typographic fashions from the past, somewhat ironically, can be perceived as innovation in the present.

THE READER

We can classify readers, but any time we categorize, the categories are generalizations and thus inaccurate. Nevertheless, classifications can be useful, as long as we don't believe they are an accurate representation of reality. It is relatively easy to design for our own demographic, but in many cases we are designing for a wide range of people or at least an audience different from ourselves. We have to ask what the anticipated readers are likely to find interesting, how they might expect the kind of content they are reading to be presented typographically, and how the readers will approach the content. This doesn't mean that we have to simply present what readers expect to see, but we do have to take our original approaches to content in a way that engages, not alienates, our reader.

CONCLUSION

Typography signals its content and its originating culture. Much of graphic communication, particularly that which communicates and reflects contemporary cultures or subcultures, reflects the time and society from which it originates, in typeface choice, layout and relationships with images, as well, of course, as the choice of images themselves. Most typographic works capture moments in time and place but will in the future become representative of a past, and the aesthetics and cultures of that time.

More purely typographical works, such as books of text, are more conservative: the pages of a novel published a hundred years ago is likely to look, typographically, much like a novel of today.

Display type, on the other hand, changes quickly; the advertising typography of only twenty years ago is noticeably different from the advertising typography of today. Newspaper layouts similarly evolve, though more slowly. Newspaper text typography changes more slowly yet.

The internet is where the biggest and fastest changes have taken place. The availability of real choices in typefaces and improved control means that good typographic design is now possible, and the capabilities of HTML5 give options that are beyond what is possible in print. Nevertheless, what makes good type in print is in most ways what makes good type on the internet.

You're always a child of your time, and you cannot step out of that.

Wim Crouwel, in *Helvetica*

This interesting, if typographically confused, restaurant sign has too many conflicting typefaces and styles. The main restaurant name, set in a typeface based on Irish religious uncial writing of the Middle Ages, doesn't make sense in historical terms. Visually, though, the uncial's connotations of handcraft are not inappropriate.

Using lettering with a monowidth feeling works for the Romanized name and description of the restaurant, and it resonates well with the uniform width of the Japanese characters. Only the Helvetica at the bottom rings a false note.

In the past, there were relatively few typefaces available, of which most were likely to be of high quality, as the cost of producing a new typeface was considerable. The foundries would not spend the resources to produce a font that was not well executed. Now that anyone can design, produce and distribute a typeface, the overall quality has gone down as the number of typefaces has gone up, though there are many foundries that produce high-quality typefaces. Choosing which typeface to use has become more difficult because of the ever-increasing number of choices. The designer should evaluate typefaces carefully in whatever context they are being used to make sure that all necessary and desired features are present.

Typefaces

Over the last two hundred years, the Roman alphabet has diverged into many variations of visual detail that remain more or less unchanged in their essential forms. The Industrial Revolution, the continuing importance of advertising in Western economies and cultures, as well as the development of the desktop computer which first proliferated in the Western European and North American markets has led to there being more versions of roman typefaces (that is, more fonts) than there are in other typographic traditions.

A BRIEF HISTORY OF THE ROMAN TYPEFACE

From their adoption for printing in Europe in the 1400s until the typographic explosion of the Industrial Revolution in the 1800s, roman typefaces were almost always incremental evolutions of previous forms.

The contemporary lower-case Roman alphabet evolved from the humanist writing style of the 1400s used in Venice and elsewhere in what is now Italy. The roman typeface of the late 1400s is an adaptation of this style and changed little in its translation from a style of handwriting to inked metal forms. Roman typefaces have continued to evolve their appearance over time, reflecting new philosophies and technologies, but the basic forms have remained constant.

The italic version of the Roman face descended from a more cursively influenced form of that same style of writing, and continued to evolve in concert with its roman equivalents.

1470 Venetian Humanist

1500 Venetian Old Style

1530 French Old Style

1670 Dutch Old Style

1720 English Old Style

1757 Transitional

1790 Modern

1805 **Fat face**

1810 **Clarendon/Egyptian**

1815 **Sans serif**

Some of the notable developments beginning from the first humanist models. Significantly, as shown here, these all exist as currently available (and widely used) digital fonts.

157

THE 18th-CENTURY EXPLOSION OF TYPE STYLES

The Victorian era introduced many new forms of metal and wood type in an effort to make advertising stand out in a competitive environment. These included new letter proportions and new serif styles. Condensed forms were popular, because more large letters could fit in a horizontal space. Below are some contemporary versions.

Iota

Fat faces *One of the first of the Victorian advertising styles, with the hairline serifs and abrupt modulation between thick and thin strokes of Modern faces but a greatly increased weight of thick strokes.*

Iota

Latins *Defined by their pointed and triangular serifs.*

Iota

Clarendons *The Clarendon approach was also based on Modern faces, but it took the strategy of thickening all strokes and bracketing the serifs.*

IOTA

Tuscans *Ornate, complex and pointed serif forms.*

Iota

Sans serifs *The sans serif fonts dispensed with the serifs and made all strokes equally heavy.*

Iota

French Clarendons *This name was given to Clarendon-style typefaces with reverse stress; the horizontal strokes are thicker than the vertical strokes, which is the opposite of usual structures.*

SOME DISPLAY FACE EXAMPLES

These are a few examples of typefaces either more suitable or only suitable for display or very short text.

Grotesque Extra Condensed

Grotesque Extra Condensed has a good texture, is legible, and because it isn't associated with anything in particular, it is versatile.

Kaufman

Script faces can be used for small amounts of text but are more useful for display type. Different script faces have strong and very different connotations.

Blackoak

Blackoak is based on a Victorian wood style. Interesting but much too distinctive to use a lot. It can be a strong graphic element in a composition.

Arnold Böcklin

Some display typefaces are evocative of a time. This has such strong Art Nouveau qualities that it is unlikely to be useful for many purposes.

Helvetica Thin

The same form as Helvetica, too light (and tightly spaced) for a text face, best used large.

Rotis

The various cuts of Rotis are too distinctive to be good for long reading.

Univers 53

Too wide for anything but display or very small display/text applications.

ITC Bodoni 72

Shown here is a 'book' version (though its '72' name suggests that it should be used at 72 point), but is much too light, tightly spaced and narrow to work as a text face. Other Bodonis should also be used with caution.

Roman type evolved slowly and steadily, with a few clear points of change. The evolution of Dutch Old Style in the 1600s was significant, as the roman style gained some of the darkness, verticality and high contrast of the blackletter style, of which a modern example is Janson. The 18th Century Enlightenment led to a more rational and abstracted version of roman type, exemplified by the Romain du Roi typeface and notably, Baskerville in the 1700s, and ending with the high-contrast, vertically-stressed Modern typefaces, such as Didot and Bodoni at the end of the 1700s.

With the move away from an economy of demand—where there wasn't much production (beyond the basic staples), and only the rich had discretionary income—to an economy of supply when the problem became one of getting people to consume everything being produced, the focus on text typefaces ended for a time. Attention switched to advertising display typefaces.

Visual invention became important as advertising became widespread, and each advertisement tried to shout down its neighbour. The increase in printing capacity of the new steam-powered presses also led type foundries to persuade printers to buy an ever-increasing number of typefaces for all the advertising that filled printed material and dominated urban public space. During this time, little attention was paid to text faces, which in most cases were variations on the Modern typeface of the late 1700s and early 1800s.

Following the invention of the Linotype and Monotype typesetting machines (which were most valuable for the time they saved in setting text material) in the early 20th century, there arose a financial incentive to develop and market a wider variety of text faces for the growing market for reading materials. The largest source of inspiration for these was the past. Typefaces that had been forgotten by all but historians of typography and scripts were revived. New variations based on or influenced by historical models were also developed. As well, new typefaces founded on original principles and concepts were commissioned by type foundries. For the first time in history, designers and printers had a wide choice of text typefaces to choose from.

NOT CURSIVE
more cursive
more cursive

The history of the drive to write faster, resulting in with simpler, more cursive forms, is embodied in Roman typefaces. Minuscules are a formalization of Roman majuscules, while italic are a faster and simpler to write version of the minuscules. Shown above is Matthew Carter's Charter.

abc

Bodoni, 1800

abc

Scotch Roman, 1813

abc

Century Expanded, 1900

Text typefaces didn't develop much during the 18th century, mostly being slightly more developed versions of the Modern face known as Scotch Modern. These contemporary versions, based on typefaces almost a century apart, all show the same vertical orientation and high contrast.

Taken from the 1828 Bruce Foundry, New York, this is an example of a highly decorated typeface intended for advertising.

A COMPLETE SERIF FAMILY

Garamond Premier Pro has a wide range of different cuts that reflect how type was designed and created before the pantograph allowed scaling of a single size of type. Forms that were created by hand were necessarily smaller and simpler at small sizes than they could be at larger sizes. This worked well with human vision, which sees the smaller and simpler form better at small sizes. Few jobs need all the available cuts of this Garamond, but the availability of all the different cuts is useful, especially if the whole job will be set in typefaces from the one family. Now, many text typefaces have four scalable cuts: roman, italic, bold and bold italic. Italics to match romans began in the 1500s, with Garamond. Bold and bold italic versions began at the end of the 1800s, associated with the development of the Linotype and Monotype mechanical typesetting machines.

Garamond Premier Pro (Adobe)

Large use

Plantagenet
Light Display

Plantagenet
Display

Plantagenet
Medium Display

Plantagenet
Semibold Display

Plantagenet
Bold Display

Text use

Plantagenet
Regular

Plantagenet
Medium

Plantagenet
Semibold

Plantagenet
Bold

Medium large use

Plantagenet
Subhead

Plantagenet
Medium Subhead

Plantagenet
Semibold Subhead

Plantagenet
Bold Subhead

Small use

Plantagenet
Caption

Plantagenet
Medium Caption

Plantagenet
Semibold Caption

Plantagenet
Bold Caption

TYPE CLASSIFICATIONS

Systems of classification can be useful for mentally organizing typefaces, for discussing them with others, and as a way of considering and evaluating how well a typeface works in a given context.

Most designers are taught the basic historical type classifications of serif type such as Blackletter, Old Style, Transitional, Egyptian, and of sans serif such as Grotesque, Humanist, Geometric and Neo-Grotesque. The Vox-ATypI system, which blends historical reference and formal descriptions, was created by Maximilien Vox, and revised and adopted by the Association Typographique Internationale (ATypI) in the mid-20th century. It works adequately for the Roman type tradition (though is dismissive of other traditions, in that they are covered with the single category 'non-Latin'). It is useful when discussing type with others who are familiar with this widely used system, so it makes sense to be familiar with it. But it is not the only way to organize Roman typefaces.

Robert Bringhurst, in his book *Elements of Typographic Style*, suggests categorizing typefaces in art-historical terms, with Roman faces being characterized as Renaissance, Baroque, Neoclassical and Romantic. Garamond and Baskerville (for example) are classified respectively as Renaissance and Neoclassical. This might be considered a modified historical system and is only relevant to the European tradition.

The scholar Catherine Dixon devised a type classification system that puts much more emphasis on the formal characteristics of typefaces, and less on their history, giving a more objective and versatile system.

An approach that deals exclusively with form is the PANOSE system, developed in 1985 but which appears to be dormant today. It was devised as way to help software find the most similar available typeface to replace a typeface not loaded on the computer. It was something like a sophisticated and automated font stack in CSS. It focused on Roman script, though many of the descriptions could be applied to other writing systems.

The PANOSE system quantifies the appearance of typefaces. It proposed that type foundries assign digits to fifteen parameters that describe visual features of a typeface. It was intended to help computer software substitute a missing font with the most similar

Should it be my good f
this indulgence, I wou'd u
to perfect an Edition of th
Elegance and Correctne

Even what seems a small difference in approach to type can be rejected by readers. The Transitional typeface of John Baskerville of the mid-1700s was something of a typographical scandal, though it is, to our eyes, a slightly abstracted version of the Dutch Old Style typeface. It was condemned as being painful to read to the extent that it would damage reader's eyes. The Modern typeface, which was (and sometimes still is) criticized as being unreadable, was in many ways a logical extrapolation of Baskerville's face.

Difference of x-height of otherwise similar forms makes a big difference to how typefaces appear.

Difference of x-height of otherwise similar forms makes a big difference to how typefaces appear.

The difference between 14-point Kabel, a face that adheres closely to the original Rudolf Koch face, and a 14-point 1970s ITC interpretation of Kabel with a very large x-height. Though the forms of the letters are otherwise similar, the effect of changing the x-height makes them visually much different from each other.

EXTENDED TYPEFACE FAMILIES

Adrian Frutiger's Univers (1957) was one of the first organized extended typeface families. Otl Aicher's Rotis (1988) is one of the first type families with a range between serif and sans serif versions. The variable font format has the potential to extend this approach.

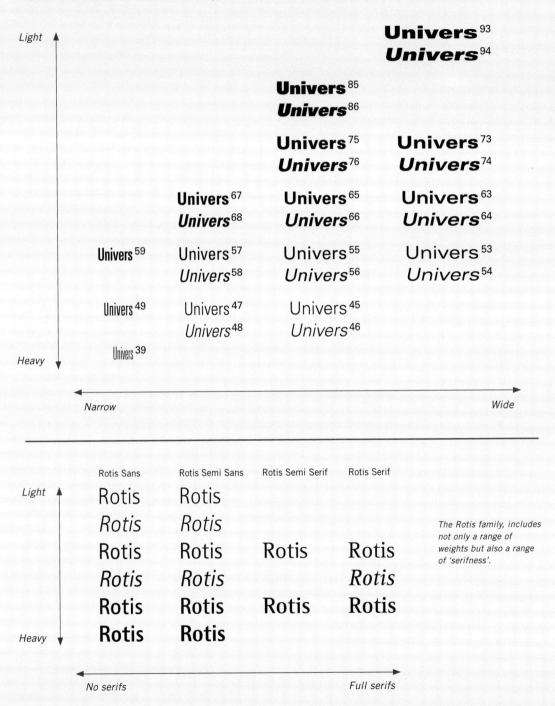

The Rotis family, includes not only a range of weights but also a range of 'serifness'.

ADJUSTING SERIF VERSUS SANS SERIF TYPE

Although sans serif typefaces can be excellent for text, they often do not work as well as serif typefaces when intercharacter space is adjusted. In this comparison, otherwise identical setting in terms of average characters per line, the sans serif setting shows more obvious problems with typographic colour due to varying word and letter space, something that the serifs in the bottom setting help conceal. The sans serif works better in the flush left setting, but again, tracking to adjust the rag or to tighten text is more noticeable.

The principles of graphic design are often summarized by such words such as: balance, rhythm, emphasis and unity, which apply to the arrangement and treatment of elements on a page. The elements of design are commonly summarized as line, shape, texture, space, size, value and colour. Although type is undoubtedly subject to these factors, just as any element on a page, its main function, which supersedes strictly design considerations, is to convey some kind of linguistic content to the reader.

The function of type is the principal reason it appears in graphic design. Certainly type may be used almost purely as decoration, but in most cases, it is set in words that are intended to be read by the viewer, and often the information that has to be conveyed is to some degree at odds

Variations in word and letter space are more visible in sans serif typefaces, especially in this setting of Avenir, because the roundness of the characters makes the varying distances more obvious.

The principles of graphic design are often summarized by such words such as: balance, rhythm, emphasis and unity, which apply to the arrangement and treatment of elements on a page. The elements of design are commonly summarized as line, shape, texture, space, size, value and colour. Although type is undoubtedly subject to these factors, just as any element on a page, its main function, which supersedes strictly design considerations, is to convey some kind of linguistic content to the reader.

The function of type is the principal reason it appears in graphic design. Certainly type may be used almost purely as decoration, but in most cases, it is set in words that are intended to be read by the viewer, and often the information that has to be conveyed is to some degree at odds with the

The greater complexity and serifs of this setting of Sabon to some extent disguises the variations in space between words and letters.

The principles of graphic design are often summarized by such words such as: balance, rhythm, emphasis and unity, which apply to the arrangement and treatment of elements on a page. The elements of design are commonly summarized as line, shape, texture, space, size, value and colour. Although type is undoubtedly subject to these factors, just as any element on a page, its main function, which supersedes strictly design considerations, is to convey some kind of linguistic content to the reader.

The function of type is the principal reason it appears in graphic design. Certainly type may be used almost purely as decoration, but in most cases, it is set in words that are intended to be read by the viewer, and often the information that has to be conveyed is to some degree at

If there is no adjustment to the rag, the sans serif font works well for this flush left text setting. However, adjustments to tracking and spacing will be more visible, as they are above.

The principles of graphic design are often summarized by such words such as: balance, rhythm, emphasis and unity, which apply to the arrangement and treatment of elements on a page. The elements of design are commonly summarized as line, shape, texture, space, size, value and colour. Although type is undoubtedly subject to these factors, just as any element on a page, its main function, which supersedes strictly design considerations, is to convey some kind of linguistic content to the reader.

The function of type is the principal reason it appears in graphic design. Certainly type may be used almost purely as decoration, but in most cases, it is set in words that are intended to be read by the viewer, and often the information that has to be conveyed is to some degree at

The serif type also makes it easier to imperceptibly adjust the rag with subtle adjustments to tracking and word spacing.

ITC Bodoni
ITC Bodoni
ITC Bodoni

Three versions of Bodoni, named Six, Twelve and Seventy Two, based on the characteristics of Giambattista Bodoni's typefaces designed for large and small use. The middle version is an interpolation between the top and bottom versions.

Times Roman

Old Style or Transitional? It can be, and is, categorized differently by different people. Its serifs and contrast support the argument for Transitional, while its oblique stress is an Old Style characteristic.

Mayo
Mayo

Both these typefaces are clearly Modern serifs, but their visual quality is very different.

one available on the system being used. The first digit describes serif style, the second weight, and so on (see page 171). These fifteen numbers can give a useful description of the appearance of a typeface. The PANOSE table of a font is not easy to access, though it can be seen using FontForge or other type editor.

Smaller foundries often do not complete the PANOSE table, and it is not used by most current software, so its practical use is increasingly limited.

While useful conceptually, PANOSE (or any other system) can't completely describe a typeface. Rates of change of stroke weight, or degrees of variation are at best comparative, not quantitative. And such things as ink traps, for example, are not accounted for.

Dutch typographer Gerrit Noordzij applied his handwriting classification system to typography based on the calligraphic style or medium that is at the base of the typeface design. For example, typefaces until the Transitional classification largely reflect the appearance of the flat nib pen while Modern typefaces reflect the split nib pen as well as engraving techniques.

While Vox-ATypI is useful for organizing roman typefaces according to historical chronology, PANOSE is potentially useful as a way of categorizing typefaces by form, and Bringhurst's and Noordzij's systems give insight into the aesthetic and material origins of a typeface, these systems of organization are not much help in assisting the designer to choose a typeface.

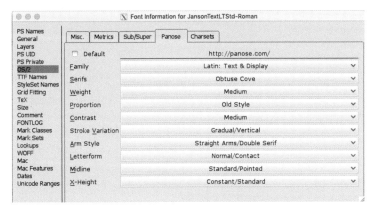

The PANOSE description of a font shown in the open source font editor, FontForge.

They do not really address the aesthetic aspects of a typeface in a given context or the connotations (for a given audience) that a particular face might have, nor whether the face works with other elements on the page: some designs have light images that would make a heavy face inappropriate, others need a visually strong typeface to balance with other elements.

For your own practice, it is helpful to keep a list or chart of typefaces used for different projects and purposes. Instead of categories, it often makes sense to think of typefaces as being on various continua (see page 166). Classifications are useful, but always open to question. To communicate with others, you do need to use a system that others use. Type identification sites such as Identifont.com work (when they do) with formal characteristics.

Classification systems give little help in deciding what a good font for a given purpose is. For example, Modern 20 is a Modern serif, just as Bodoni is, but they are very different in their visual effect and where one is suitable, the other probably will not be. The more accurate a classification is, the fewer typefaces it will include.

CONTEXTS

The suitability of a typeface depends on its context. For example, for books we need type that is readable, familiar, resonates with the content, and that works, visually, at arm's length. Conversely, for signage and wayfinding use, we need type that is large enough, very legible and that works aesthetically with the surroundings.

> **Wayfinding**
>
> Wayfinding needs to be visible both in terms of lines of sight, that is, it must be noticeable and identifiable, and the designer must consider how the viewer will encounter it in terms of possible different distances and angles.

For contexts in which the appearance of a typeface is important, such as visual identities, wordmarks or display type, high legibility is less important than the visual forms of the letters. The Nike logo is an extreme example of this: it is not legible in the

> Type is saying things to us all the time. Typefaces express a mood, an atmosphere. They give words a certain colouring.
>
> Rick Poynor, in *Helvetica*

. . . .

VOX-ATypI
Typeface classifications

1 Classicals
  1.1 Humanist
  1.2 Garalde
  1.3 Transitional

2 Moderns
  2.1 Didone
  2.2 Mechanistic
  2.3 Lineal
    2.3.1 Grotesque
    2.3.2 Neo-Grotesque
    2.3.3 Geometric
    2.3.4 Humanist

3 Calligraphics
  3.1 Glyphic
  3.2 Script
  3.3 Graphic
  3.4 Blackletter
  3.5 Gaelic

4 Non-Latin

CLASSIFYING TYPEFACES: FUNCTIONAL

The more ways you have to think about type, the more confidently you can choose a typeface for a given purpose. Below is not a definitive system but can provide suggestions and help you defend your typographic choices. Typefaces existing on continua of relativity. It is useful to think of them this way instead of categories with firm distinctions being drawn between them.

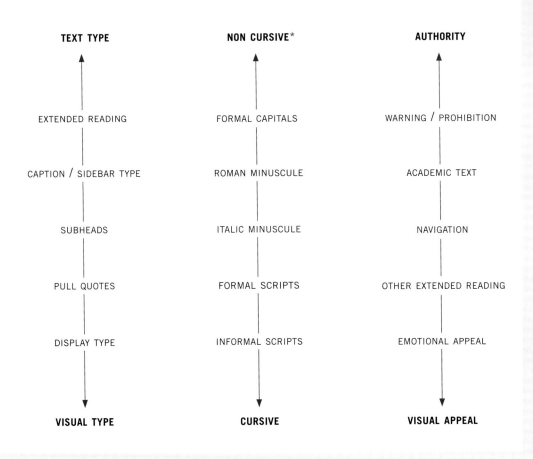

EXAMPLES OF CONTINUA OF FUNCTIONAL TYPOGRAPHIC ATTRIBUTES

TEXT TYPE	NON CURSIVE*	AUTHORITY
EXTENDED READING	FORMAL CAPITALS	WARNING / PROHIBITION
CAPTION / SIDEBAR TYPE	ROMAN MINUSCULE	ACADEMIC TEXT
SUBHEADS	ITALIC MINUSCULE	NAVIGATION
PULL QUOTES	FORMAL SCRIPTS	OTHER EXTENDED READING
DISPLAY TYPE	INFORMAL SCRIPTS	EMOTIONAL APPEAL
VISUAL TYPE	**CURSIVE**	**VISUAL APPEAL**

Although 'cursive' implies joined text, the drive behind cursive writing is speed. Quickly written majuscule forms led to Roman minuscule forms, while quickly written forms of minuscule led to italic forms.

CLASSIFYING TYPEFACES: VISUAL

This table focuses on the visible attributes of typefaces rather than their aesthetics or suitability for a purpose. Effective text faces will generally gravitate towards the middle column (though exceptions are always worth considering). Any visual attribute may work for a display typeface if it suits the design context.

CONTINUA OF VISUAL TYPOGRAPHIC ATTRIBUTES

C Light	C Medium	C Bold
O Vertical stress	O Oblique stress	O Reverse stress
P Formal	*p* Formal / cursive	*p* Cursive
R High contrast	R Moderate contrast	R Low contrast
d Large x-height	d Moderate x-height	d Small x-height
M Narrow	M Normal width	M Wide
O Abrupt modulation	O Moderate modulation	O Gentle modulation
A More connotation	A Some connotation	A Less connotation
B Simple	B Moderately complex	B Highly complex
S High sharpness	S Moderate sharpness	S Low sharpness
H Heavy serif weight	H Moderate serif weight	H Light serif weight

← *Moderate* →

'What does Bringhurst say?', is a common question asked by designers trying to settle a point of difference. This doesn't mean he is always right, but his opinion is usually taken seriously.

The most popular typefaces are the easiest to read; their popularity has made them disappear from conscious cognition. It becomes impossible to tell if they are easy to read because they are commonly used or if they are commonly used because they are easy to read.

Zuzana Licko

usual sense, but because of its familiarity, is legible as a typographic wordmark. The Coca-Cola logo is far from being optimally legible in terms of rendering the letters 'coca-cola', but is distinctive and instantly recognizable. It is very old-fashioned in its form, a stylized version of Spenserian script, the form of handwriting taught in schools in the USA when the company was founded in 1886 (only two years after the introduction of the Linotype machine!). The era is also a context: although its iconicity is valuable, the Coca-Cola wordmark would not be a likely logo for a start-up company today.

Text typefaces should of course be first legible, but the appearance of the text (rather than the appearance of the forms of the characters), and how the setting contributes to the overall composition of the page should resonate with both the nature of the content and the reading experience, which is influenced by the reader's previous relationship with and perception of text type.

PERSONAL TYPEFACE CLASSIFICATIONS

We all have our own ways of thinking about typefaces that are helpful in making type decisions. They may even be effective when discussing typographic matters with other designers.

For example, a typeface may be described by a designer as too 'serious' or 'technical' or 'frivolous' or 'aggressive' or 'boring' for a given application and other designers will understand, even if they don't necessarily agree. Or a typeface may be considered 'friendly', 'anarchic' or 'too pretty' or something like that. It may have too much 'sparkle', caused by small elements such as thin serifs or high contrast between thick or thin strokes. Or it may appear too heavy, giving too dark a typographic colour for a given setting or relationship with images. Or it may look too similar or otherwise clash visually with a typographic or other element that is part of the overall work. But on the whole, the character and overall appearance of the type and experience of reading is much more important than the visual appearance of the individual letterforms.

The look of the letterforms is much more important in display type. Letterforms function differently in large and small contexts.

Surprisingly, this is something that even experienced designers may lose sight of.

Different functions: different typefaces

I have seen a respected designer with many years' experience choose a typeface for text just because he liked the loop on the face's 'g'. This decision would make sense for display use (it was a very nice loop!) but not for text. There are many aspects of a typeface that are more important than the features of a single letter, such as overall typographic appearance, typographic colour and legibility, availability of necessary weights and styles, alternate characters such as old style figures and small caps. The appearance of the loop on the 'g' in a text setting is something that would be barely recognizable even if you were looking directly at it, and would make no impact at all on the subconscious level of someone in the process of reading. And if you did notice the 'g' every time you saw it, you wouldn't be reading: you'd be looking at letters.

TYPEFACE LEGIBILITY

Type must be *sufficiently* legible in display and *very* legible in text functions. Obsessing about 'optimum' legibility is only relevant if we are dealing with street or highway signs or some other case where the user may be operating on the borders of legibility. Text type must be legible enough to be easily readable. Anything more is irrelevant. For people with impaired vision, optimum legibility may become significant. In most cases, this is best addressed by increasing the size of a reasonably legible typeface or in the case of screen type, facilitating the user's control over the appearance of the type, rather than trying to optimize the letterforms themselves, which will likely bring only an imperceptible improvement. Any typeface with normal proportions and weight should be legible enough, leaving a lot of latitude for typeface choice.

If optimum legibility were crucial, there wouldn't be nearly as many text typefaces used: we'd all use the most legible ones.

Sometimes typefaces with large x-heights are considered to be more legible, and they are, at a comparable point size. But if typefaces are compared at the same x-height, the differences in legibility tend to disappear (see page 175).

TEXT FACE CHOICE IS NOT AS IMPORTANT AS YOU MIGHT THINK

What you do with the typeface is more important. Things to think about when designing text for a given context, in usual order of importance:

1 Size
2 Line length
3 Leading
4 Typographic colour
5 Availability of cuts and alternates
6 Tracking and word space settings
7 The appearance of the letterforms and other glyphs (given a reasonable width and weight)

Don't spend time on the last item at the expense of the first six.

Caslon Regular
Caslon Bold

n **n**

Bold versions of Roman typefaces generally have thickened vertical strokes, while the thin strokes and serifs remain close to the regular weight.

TRACKING: DIFFERENT TYPEFACES

Most typefaces are designed to be properly spaced at text sizes, and this should be adjusted with caution, though a slight amount of added tracking can help small type. Some typefaces are exceptions, as is the case with the Helvetica Neue shown below, in which the spacing is better suited to larger display type.

Helvetica Neue Light with 0 tracking is unusually tight and needs loosening up to work as text.

Tightening up a typeface can make it more suitable for a display setting. Loosening it can make it more suitable for text. But overdoing tracking can make type fall apart into a sprinkling of letters instead of readable words.

For text, the 50 unit (50/1000 em) tracking in the example shown is better for reading.

Tightening up a typeface can make it more suitable for a display setting. Loosening it can make it more suitable for text. But overdoing tracking can make type fall apart into a sprinkling of letters instead of readable words.

At 100 unit tracking, the text is starting to break apart into separate letters. Loose tracking can be somewhat mitigated by increasing the leading.

Tightening up a typeface can make it more suitable for a display setting. Loosening it can make it more suitable for text. But overdoing tracking can make type fall apart into a sprinkling of letters instead of readable words.

This is a setting of Horley, with the same tracking as the Helvetica Neue above. The 0 tracking is okay, the 50 track of the middle setting is much too loose, and the 100 track on the bottom verges on being unreadable.

Tightening up a typeface can make it more suitable for a display setting. Loosening it can make it more suitable for text. But overdoing tracking can make type fall apart into a sprinkling of letters instead of readable words.

Tightening up a typeface can make it more suitable for a display setting. Loosening it can make it more suitable for text. But overdoing tracking can make type fall apart into a sprinkling of letters instead of readable words.

Tightening up a typeface can make it more suitable for a display setting. Loosening it can make it more suitable for text. But overdoing tracking can make type fall apart into a sprinkling of letters instead of readable words.

PANOSE CLASSIFICATION SYSTEM

Janson Text

	2	3	6	2	6	5	6	2	3	3
	Family Kind	Serif Style	Weight	Proportion	Contrast	Stroke Variation	Arm Style	Letterform	Midline	X-height
0	Any	Any	Any	Any	Any	Any	Any	Any	Any	Any
1	No Fit	No Fit	No Fit	No Fit	No Fit	No Fit	No Fit	No Fit	No Fit	No Fit
2	Latin Text	Cove	Very Light	Old Style	None	No Variation	Straight Arms/ Horizontal	Normal/ Contact	Standard/ Trimmed	Constant/ Small
3	Latin Handwritten	Obtuse Cove	Light	Modern	Very Low	Gradual/ Diagonal	Straight Arms/ Wedge	Normal/ Weighted	Standard/ Pointed	Constant/ Standard
4	Latin Decorative	Square Cove	Thin	Even Width	Low	Gradual/ Transitional	Straight Arms/ Vertical	Normal/ Boxed	Standard/ Serifed	Constant/ Large
5	Latin Symbol	Obtuse Square Cove	Book	Extended	Medium Low	Gradual/ Vertical	Straight Arms/ Single Serif	Normal/ Flattened	High/Trimmed	Ducking/ Small
6		Square	Medium	Condensed	Medium	Gradual/ Horizontal	Straight Arms/ Double Serif	Normal/ Rounded	High/Pointed	Ducking/ Standard
7		Thin	Demi	Very Extended	Medium High	Rapid/Vertical	Non-straight Arms/Horizontal	Normal/ Off-Centre	High/Serifed	Ducking/ Large
8		Oval	Bold	Very Condensed	High	Instant/Vertical	Non-straight Arms/Wedge	Normal/ Square	Constant/ Trimmed	
9		Exaggerated	Heavy	Monospaced	Very High	Instant/ Horizontal	Non-straight Arms/Vertical	Oblique/ Contact	Constant/ Pointed	
10		Triangle	Black				Non-straight Arms/ Single Serif	Oblique/ Weighted	Constant/ Serifed	
11		Normal Sans	Extra Black				Non-straight Arms/ Double Serif	Oblique/ Boxed	Low/Trimmed	
12		Obtuse Sans						Oblique/ Flattened	Low/Pointed	
13		Perpendicular Sans						Oblique/ Rounded	Low/Serifed	
14		Flared						Oblique/ Off-Centre		
15		Rounded						Oblique/ Square		

The PANOSE Typeface Classification Number allows a very complete description of the appearance of Roman typefaces. It has been used by some applications to match unavailable fonts with a close match. This shows PANOSE 1, Development was started on PANOSE 2, but it hasn't been publicly implemented and seems to have been abandoned.

Family Kind *defines whether a typeface is Roman or not.*

Serif Style *describes the appearance of the serifs used in a font design. Serif and sans serif faces are classified within this digit.*

Weight *classifies the appearance of a font's stem thickness in relation to its height.*

Proportion *describes the relative proportions of the characters in the font.*

Contrast *describes the ratio between the thickest and narrowest points on the letter 'O'.*

Stroke Variation *describes the rate of transition of stroke thickness changes on rounded glyphs.*

Arm Style *describes diagonal stems and the termination of open rounded letterforms.*

Letterform *differentiates between vertical and oblique fonts and describes the roundness of the character shapes.*

Midline *describes the placement of the midline and the treatment of diagonal stem apexes.*

X-height *describes the relative height of lower-case characters and the treatment of upper-case glyphs with diacritical marks. (Ducking refers to the rare practice of designing accented capitals that are smaller than regular caps.)*

....

**Relative advantages of
sans serif and serif text**

SANS SERIF

- more possibilities in terms of weight
  and widths
- higher legibility, particularly at medium
  weights, display settings
- aligns well to screen pixel grids

SERIF

- more familiar to readers
- adjustments to letter and word space
  are less obvious
- may be better for reading because
  characters are more distinctive in
  parafoveal vision
- more opportunity for refined typography
  in terms of alternate characters

legible
legible

*Plantin, above, will hold up better than
Times Roman, below, in difficult conditions
such as on a photograph. Plantin is also well
suited for small type.*

PAIRING TYPEFACES

**Finding typefaces that work well
together is a case of trying things
out. Using Carl Dair's seven contrasts
as a tool for selecting typeface and
analysing pairing is a good start.
Definite rules for pairing are too
restrictive.**

CHOOSING TYPEFACES

Choosing a display typeface is about how it looks: how well it resonates with the content and how well its characteristics work visually in terms of composition. The essential questions are about how it works: is it readable, does it set well in the design's alignment and characters per line, does it have the glyphs needed for the design, does it have enough weights for the design, does the copy fit well in the space assigned to it?

CHOOSING A TYPEFACE FOR TEXT

Typefaces for text should be chosen for their effectiveness in communicating the content. This includes their legibility and readability, and their appropriateness to the content. Having your own way of classifying and choosing typefaces (while still being conversant with the common historical classifications) can make your work better, from the point of view of communication and aesthetics, and easier to defend and present to clients or other critics.

There are questions you can ask yourself that may help you decide if a typeface is suitable for text.

First, can you actually use it? If the license for a type family is expensive, and you or your client can't afford it, there's not much point in specifying it for a client job, even if it does just 'happen' to be on your computer. Work that goes out in public with an unlicensed font could draw unwelcome legal attention and costs.

Second, does it have the necessary features (such as small caps and old style numbers, if you need them), and is it technically good in terms of letter form, spacing and kerning? If a typeface is too tight or too loose, you can track it out or in. But if it has some characteristics you don't like now, you could well hate them before the project is finished.

Third, how well does it work for the job? This includes how well it visually resonates with the meaning and voice of content; type colour; its aesthetic qualities as a block on the page; efficiency, meaning how much text can fit comfortably in a limited amount of space; how easy it is to read at the size and in the context it is being used in. If it is going to be read on devices, how does it work on screens?

If a typeface isn't too dark or light, or too wide or too narrow, doesn't have technical problems or odd characteristics, and has every needed glyph, this is better than choosing an otherwise 'perfect' typographical form that poses readability problems or missing features.

On the whole, for extended reading, a font that is unremarkable is best. Something of average weight and width, and easily recognizable letterforms, will do the job. If you have more text than space, something slightly narrower can help. If, on the other hand, you need to fill space, something wider might work better. Don't let typefaces with large x-heights mislead you though; a typeface with a large x-height will take up more horizontal space but will also appear bigger.

Some faces are more suited to having more or less leading without the type looking forced, which can help with fitting text to a given amount of space. Testing the typography in its design context is the only way to be sure. Often changing the size and leading is enough to make a setting work, rather than changing the typeface itself.

Under adverse conditions (for example, low contrast, type on image, small sizes, etc.), some typefaces are better than others. Monotype's Plantin is a good example; it was developed for printing newspapers in the early 20th century, when type was usually smaller than it is today and when printing was often variable in ink coverage. Its cut reflects the characteristics of typefaces that were historically used for text until the late 1700s: large x-height, relatively low contrast, clear contrast between counters and strokes, and large punctuation. Typefaces that have these characteristics are worth considering when choosing a text face that will be knocked out of a coloured background, or printed or displayed on an image.

Using a small number of typefaces for most of your work (particularly text work) also makes sense. The more you work with a face, the better you know its idiosyncrasies and how to use it well. Many designers tend to go back to the same typefaces, from Josef Müller-Brockmann and Wolfgang Weingart's preference for Akzidenz Grotesk, to Massimo Vignelli, who liked to stick (most

Punctuation size

A seemingly minor consideration is punctuation size. Punctuation should be larger at small sizes, and a typeface that has small periods or very narrow commas or quotation marks should be rejected for text settings.

multi-
multi–

Monotype News Gothic has a hyphen that is too short for text. Bembo's hyphen might be considered too long, especially for large type. Size of punctuation is something that should be considered when choosing a text typeface.

Relying on a few typefaces for text in different projects can make sense. Working with a typeface is a learning process, and the more you work with one, the better you understand how to get the best out of it.

RIOSA
RIOSA

Perpetua Titling, shown first above, is a majuscule-only typeface which has the characteristics of a display face: it is lighter, more refined and more condensed than the Perpetua Regular which is shown second.

graphic

The rough outline of Bernhard Antiqua of 1912 shows both the idiosyncratic hand-painted form of early 20th-century advertising lettering and an early example of a type design with a deliberate distressed effect. It would be hard to fit coherently into any but the broadest classifications (e.g. 'novelty' or 'graphic'), but its specific visual attributes can be easily described.

of the time) to versions of Helvetica, Bodoni, Garamond and Century Expanded, to Timothy Sweeney who used only Adobe Garamond for his journal *Quarterly Concern*, to Experimental Jetset's predilection for Helvetica. Not all designers work this way. However, many have a few text typefaces that they prefer to use, even if they do not use them exclusively, and that selection is likely to change over time.

Some advanced type students lack confidence in their ability to choose typefaces, especially for text. It is sometimes more useful to think of it as being more important to avoid choosing a bad or under-featured typeface, rather than aiming to choose the perfect one. Doing a good job with whatever you have chosen as text face (as long as it doesn't *not* work) is more important than the choice of typeface. How well it works is more important than how it looks.

CHOOSING DISPLAY TYPE

Display type depends on the visual quality of its forms. Display type is (usually) large. Thus, it is both visually dominant and usually has only a few words. So the reader is both more struck by its visual aspects and is more willing to read it, even if it might be considerably less than optimally legible. For an absurd example, people will cheerfully read a few words in Mistral (see page 176), but are unlikely to read a couple of hundred words of Mistral text. Less obviously, this extends to more conservative typefaces that are not always suitable for text use. Bauer Bodoni, for example, makes a good display face but needs great care to work successful as a text typeface.

The same thing applies to all cap settings or type with very tight leading. They can work very well in display type but should never be used for text.

Many contemporary computer text faces, being completely scalable, are designed as a compromise between what would be ideal for text and what would be ideal for display.

They tend to lean towards being designed to look good at display size, on a foundry website or in print, which is the way that many designers see, and then choose, typefaces.

TEXT TYPEFACE X-HEIGHT COMPARISON

Although the length of an alphabet varies between different typefaces, if the x-heights are matched, there is much less difference. Below are some common typefaces, showing the length of the lower-case alphabet at 12 points, then set at the same x-height, showing that there is less difference between typefaces than it might initially seem, once they are matched visually. With the sans serif fonts, there is more variation in width, but it is clear that the narrower faces appear smaller.

All typeface showings in this column are 12 point	Showings in this column are adjusted to 5 point x-height	
abcdefghijklmnopqrstuvwxyz	abcdefghijklmnopqrstuvwxyz	Perpetua
abcdefghijklmnopqrstuvwxyz	abcdefghijklmnopqrstuvwxyz	Garamond (Adobe)
abcdefghijklmnopqrstuvwxyz	abcdefghijklmnopqrstuvwxyz	Joanna
abcdefghijklmnopqrstuvwxyz	abcdefghijklmnopqrstuvwxyz	Caslon (Adobe)
abcdefghijklmnopqrstuvwxyz	abcdefghijklmnopqrstuvwxyz	Bembo
abcdefghijklmnopqrstuvwxyz	abcdefghijklmnopqrstuvwxyz	Baskerville
abcdefghijklmnopqrstuvwxyz	abcdefghijklmnopqrstuvwxyz	Goudy Old Style
abcdefghijklmnopqrstuvwxyz	abcdefghijklmnopqrstuvwxyz	Electra
abcdefghijklmnopqrstuvwxyz	abcdefghijklmnopqrstuvwxyz	Janson
abcdefghijklmnopqrstuvwxyz	abcdefghijklmnopqrstuvwxyz	Times New Roman
abcdefghijklmnopqrstuvwxyz	abcdefghijklmnopqrstuvwxyz	Palatino
abcdefghijklmnopqrstuvwxyz	abcdefghijklmnopqrstuvwxyz	Trump Medieval
abcdefghijklmnopqrstuvwxyz	abcdefghijklmnopqrstuvwxyz	Scala Sans
abcdefghijklmnopqrstuvwxyz	abcdefghijklmnopqrstuvwxyz	News Gothic (Adobe)
abcdefghijklmnopqrstuvwxyz	abcdefghijklmnopqrstuvwxyz	Akzidenz Grotesk
abcdefghijklmnopqrstuvwxyz	abcdefghijklmnopqrstuvwxyz	Folio
abcdefghijklmnopqrstuvwxyz	abcdefghijklmnopqrstuvwxyz	Trade Gothic
abcdefghijklmnopqrstuvwxyz	abcdefghijklmnopqrstuvwxyz	Helvetica
abcdefghijklmnopqrstuvwxyz	abcdefghijklmnopqrstuvwxyz	News Gothic (Monotype)

A few type families make the distinction between display and text cuts along the lines of the hand cut/type foundry division of the past, with display, text and caption or web versions (see page 160).

Most of the thousands of typefaces available are intended for display, and no one would normally use them for text. As Walter Tracy suggests in his book *Letters of Credit*, while a display face probably won't work for text, a text face can be used for display.

Legibility

Legibility is like the power of an automobile: you need enough power to operate with other traffic and no more. Type must be legible enough to read comfortably, but most of the time, any more than that won't help the reader. Thus many typefaces are sufficiently legible, but they tend to be 'normal' in terms of weight, set width and overall form.

TYPE CHOICE AS STYLE

Some designers and typography teachers would suggest that style should be avoided, arguing that choice of typeface (as well as other typographic choices) should be based entirely on rational reasons, taking a modernist 'form follows function' approach.

However, attention to style when choosing a typeface and its setting is valid and rational; type style may be a transient part of visual culture compared to the basic form of the alphabet, but it is still part of both the designer's and the readers' culture.

In fact, it is not possible to avoid the perception of style. For example, Helvetica was promoted as a rational and connotation-free typeface, but because of how it was and is used, over time it acquired a perceived connection with large corporations and governments. This is more significant in typefaces serving a display function, but still holds to some degree for text faces. Type choice may situate a work in the larger culture, whether by convention, by which a typeface contributes to the expectations of a reader, or by reference, when a typeface's associations are used to some kind of original purpose.

> Have no
> fear of
> perfection
> –
> you'll never
> reach it.
> –
> Salvador
> Dali

> **Have no
> fear of
> perfection
> –
> you'll never
> reach it.
> –
> Salvador
> Dali**

Even with virtually the same setting, the style of these two typefaces gives a distinct flavour to the two versions of this quote. The version on the left implies a thoughtful irony, the one on the right suggests a more humorous tone.

Mistral

Designed by Roger Excoffon in 1953, the evocative but rather unreadable Mistral has continued, for some reason, to be a favourite among travel agencies.

Choc

Another enduring and popular brush style face is Excoffon's Choc.

TYPE TREATMENT CONNOTATIONS

Different reactions can be provoked by different treatments of the same typeface, whether by position or treatment of the forms themselves. Dense type with a long line length, little leading and little white space is not just hard to read, it carries the connotation of being hard to read. Light type, with more-than-average leading and a short line length suggests text that is less serious. Type in a children's book looks like children's book type, text books look like text books, medical websites look like medical websites, and so on. Readers' perceptions are formed by their reading experiences. You can push things with an aesthetic at odds with readers' expectations, or even give one kind of content the appearance of another, but it should be part of a deliberate and well-considered approach to communicate what the author and designer intend.

MIXING TYPEFACES

You will often see the suggestion, sometimes stated as a rule, that you should use no more than two or perhaps three typefaces in a design. This 'rule' is often broken in magazines and other such documents. Using many different typefaces is also a characteristic of Industrial Revolution advertising styles, which inspires some typographic designs. Whether or not to mix several typefaces depends on the typographic project. Mixing several faces in a typographic wordmark is unlikely to be a good idea, but it may make sense for a complex typographic system for a magazine.

Using several typefaces in web design brings another consideration: having several fonts on a web page will make it slower to load, which matters to users with slower connections.

Because some faces work better for text and others better as display, sometimes using different text faces for different purposes in the same project can make sense. For example, one of the many versions of Bodoni intended for text might make a good display type. So Bodoni as display and Baskerville as text could be a good combination on a page: both have vertical axes and give a light and refined impression, but Baskerville (presuming it is based on a text cut of Baskerville, as most are, with Baskerville Old Face, based on a large display cut, being a common exception) has less contrast,

Choc, a French advertising typeface, sometimes shows up in Chinese restaurant signage.

Art history

This unusual and unrefined type style helped identify and unify a series of books produced by the Getty Center, while the interior of the books was set in Sabon, a classic version of the 16th century Claude Garamond designed typeface. Developed by Bruce Mau Design.

Caption
Display

Two different cuts of the same type family, (Warnock) that would work well at different sizes don't work when set together at the same size.

Head

This Baskerville text works with the head above, which is set in Bauer Bodoni. If they were the same size they would clash visually.

Head

This Times text works with the head above, which is set in Janson. If they were the same size they would clash visually.

> **Text types when enlarged can be used for headings. Display types, if reduced, cannot be used for text setting.**
>
> Walter Tracy, *Letters of Credit*

less 'sparkly' serifs, and a much gentler modulation between thick and thin parts of strokes. On the other hand, Baskerville could work well for both text and heads.

Using similar typefaces together will only work if the typefaces are at different sizes. Setting Bodoni and Baskerville, or Janson and Times, together at the same size will be visually disturbing.

The 'rule' would be better stated, 'Don't use more faces than necessary.' Using many typefaces for no good reason is a mistake. If you do have a good reason, then go ahead. But if you are using several typefaces, they should be distinctly different, whether in terms of form, size or treatment.

DISPLAY TYPEFACES AND TYPOGRAPHY

Display typefaces have characteristics that make them appropriate mainly for large, primarily visual, uses. Unlike text type, the visual quality of the letterforms of a display setting are often as important as what the words mean. In some cases the type might be nearly illegible and still work. Some of the things that have to be considered in text are not very important in display type.

Does the appearance of the typeface resonate with the subject? Do the typeface and setting work in terms of composition? Is the spacing of letters and words working well in terms of both communication and composition? While established principles and conventions are important with text typography, display type is more subjective. This has the benefit of allowing more latitude for creativity, but the subjectivity makes it more difficult to choose. It is usually easier to defend text type decisions for objective reasons than it is to defend display choices.

There is, of course, a much wider choice of display typefaces, and that wider choice covers a much wider range, from the sublime to the ridiculous, either of which (or anything between) may be appropriate, depending on the project.

LAYOUT

While text and display type are both parts of a layout, text exists as blocks; the look of the block is important. With display type, the location and appearance of a single letter can make or break an effective design.

OPENTYPE FEATURES

The OpenType standard was a joint effort by Adobe and Microsoft. Its format can contain either TrueType or PostScript font outlines. TrueType OpenType fonts have the .ttf file ending, and PostScript OpenType fonts end with .otf. OpenType features, such as contextual and other alternates, are valuable tools for the typographer. Apart from allowing refinements to text, they are valuable in display type, most particularly for script faces (see page 198). Informal scripts especially benefit from contextual alternates, because having repeated identical characters gives a certain incongruous sterility. The OpenType standard was a significant advance in typography. It not only made it more practical to set type in Arabic and other calligraphic scripts in page layout programs, it also enabled far more characters in both Roman and other scripts. OpenType features are supported in CSS.

Before OpenType, fonts had a limited number of places for glyphs, so if small caps, old style numbers, or any complex ligatures were needed, it was necessary to install a second font.

MULTIPLE MASTERS AND VARIABLE FONTS

In the late 1970s, Donald Knuth, a mathematician and computer scientist, designed the Metafont program, which controlled the form of fonts generated for his TeX typesetting system. It allowed designers to specify typographic form mathematically. This development was the first step in the path that has led to the introduction of today's variable fonts.

Multiple Master fonts were introduced by Adobe in the early 1990s. They contained two or more master character sets, such as light and bold, wide and narrow, and the intention was that a user could choose midpoints between them. These capabilities were never well supported by the software that might have used them, though the concept was used widely in font design software, in which fonts can be interpolated between different weights or widths. The Adobe Multiple Master fonts Serif MM and Adobe Sans MM are still commonly seen in PDF files as a substitute for fonts that can't be embedded in the file.

....

Colour SVG Opentype fonts

A recent development is that of colour SVG fonts, which can be designed with gradients and multiple colours. They are not yet fully supported by most software.

Above is Adobe's Trajan Colour Concept SVG font. Although this duotone version doesn't show the actual colours of the font characters, it shows how the colour and gradients work.

METAFLOP

Metaflop is a web application that uses Metafont to allow designers to visually modulate base fonts using sliders, with the Metafont calculations done in the background. The results can be generated as usable font files.

'Variable fonts' are the most recent iteration of this approach, developed by several software companies and based on Apple's TrueType GX format of the mid-1990s. A variable font is a single font outline file that can be varied along one or more axes. They are an evolution of the OpenType font specification that let the user generate fonts between axes, as the Multiple Master font was intended to do. They have better software support, and work on the Web, so are likely to be more successful than the Multiple Master format.

Variable fonts on the Web

A single variable font is faster to load than a number of separate fonts of varying weights and widths. Variable optical sizes and weights can also be used to better function at different sizes.

USE VARIABILITY WITH CAUTION

Using too many, or too subtly different instances of variable fonts can cause visual conflict, similar to using fonts that are too similar together. Only a few distinctive instances should be used, especially if they are used at a similar size.

PRINT MEDIA

Printing surface, or substrate, makes a difference to the appearance of text type. Rougher and more absorbent paper tends to swell type, while smooth paper retains the original form of the type. As some types are better with some ink spread, and the letterpress types on which some digital typefaces are based on would have spread a bit because of the printing method (e.g. Bembo, most Bodonis), it is important to investigate how a setting will work in its final form. For graphic design students, the final printing method is usually the same as the design proofs, that is, using a laser printer, but even laser type will appear differently on different types of paper.

Colours, too, will appear differently on different materials, depending on the absorbency and colour of the paper. Testing on the final before final printing, and thorough press checks, help ensure a final project appears as intended. Sometimes type that looks fine on screen may need tracking, resizing or a change to the colour when seen in printed form on a particular kind of paper.

VARIABLE FONT AXES

Bold

Light

Extended ⟷ *Condensed*

The principle of Multiple Master fonts and variable fonts is the same: fonts can be rendered in a range of versions. This models the 'weight' and 'width' axes of a lower-case 'a' from a two-axis font. The Univers system (see page 162) is an early model of the concept.

Optically large

Optically small

Old Style ⟷ *Modern*

This principle can also be applied to other visual axes, as in between historical styles and suitability for use at different sizes.

SCALING TYPEFACES: SOMETIMES IT MAKES SENSE

Although one of the common 'rules' of typography instructors is that type should never be scaled, subtle use of scaling is very useful for justification of type, and, occasionally, to make a typeface work better at unusual scales. Like most things in typography, scaling is a problem when it is overdone or done inconsistently. Inconsistency is often seen in signage, when the designer condenses a long line to make it fit into a limited horizontal space. Also like most things in typography, it is a rule that is breakable for good reason and with consideration.

Policy
Univers 55

Policy
Univers 55 scaled to 48%

Policy
Univers 55 scaled to 124%

Policy
Univers 55

Policy
Univers 49

Policy
Univers 53

Scaling typefaces changes their visual nature and distorts their forms. If condensed or extended forms are needed, you should find a type family that has such cuts. Note that condensing usually looks more oddly distorted than expanding.

Scaling typefaces can be useful if applied carefully in contexts where it makes sense.

Trade Gothic is a bit tight and narrow at caption sizes.

Scaling typefaces can be useful if applied carefully in contexts where it makes sense.

Trade Gothic scaled to 104% and tracked out by 15 units makes it visually and legibly better at this size.

Gill Sans   Gill Sans   Gill Sans

Gill Sans is very sensitive to scaling, as are most faces with 'normal' proportions. On the left is Gill Sans undistorted. The centre version is scaled to 90 per cent horizontally. The version on the right is scaled to 115 per cent horizontally. The scaled versions are visibly distorted.

Blackoak
As designed, 100%

Blackoak
Horizontally scaled to 50%

More unusual typographic forms and structures can sometimes be significantly scaled without the negative effects that we see in the Gill Sans.

Latin
As designed, 100%

Latin
Horizontally scaled to 125%

Antique Olive
As designed, 100%

Antique Olive
Horizontally scaled to 120%

CONCLUSION

Typefaces are the basic tools of typography. No matter how good a typeface might be in terms of form and appearance, it can be set badly, whether due to choices made by the designer in terms of design decisions or lack of attention to detail in setting.

A display face is a good choice if it works for the purpose intended. If a display face is going to be used in a series, it should be tested with different words and possible contexts. If it is going to be used a single time for a couple of words, it is only important that those words look visually appropriate and resonate with the content. Display faces work graphically as much as they communicate words. A less-than-ideal choice of a display face will undermine a design, no matter how well it is set.

Except for use in a very small amount of copy, a text face should be examined more rigorously. It should be relatively unobtrusive and have the necessary features and glyphs for any anticipated purpose. In the case of a serif face, a full set of ligatures, small caps and old style numbers are good to have around if you need them. A sans serif used in text should be of normal proportion and have a reasonable weight. Often various weights of sans serif are possible choices for text, while only a few serif faces have different weights suitable for text. Any typeface used for text should have punctuation that is easy to see without drawing attention to itself. Character widths and kern pairs should also be looked at; some typefaces have good forms but less satisfactory interletter relationships. This can be corrected by the designer in a display setting but not, at least practically, in a text setting.

Finally, typefaces should be tested in the final environment. Typefaces that print well on one kind of paper may not print well on another. Typefaces that work on paper may not show well on screens, and a face that works well on one operating system or browser may not work as well on another. Those that work well in two dimensions may not work in three-dimensional applications.

Once you have evaluated and used a typeface and found its strengths and weaknesses, it makes sense to take that knowledge and that typeface to other projects.

TORONTO

Helvetica Medium, horizontally scaled to about 55 per cent was used for this building feature of the University of Toronto's Graduate Residence. A true condensed face would work better typographically.

TORONTO

Univers 59 is a bold condensed typeface that needs only a slightly decreased horizontal scaling to fit the same horizontal and vertical space. The flat sides and vertical character better suit the structure of the architecture.

Setting type has, to some degree, become a lost art, left more and more to software defaults, and taught less and less in graphic design programs. This chapter discusses the aesthetic decisions that must be made, as well as how to best use software to execute those decisions. The importance of systems in setting up and executing long and complex documents is addressed, as well as how to make the subtle changes that make the difference between acceptable and good type.

Setting type

This chapter looks at how to make text and display type look good and work well, once the basic design decisions have been made. Again, just as the distinction between display type as a principally visual component of a design (with a semantic function), and text type whose function is essentially semantic (but with visual aspects) is crucial when *choosing* typefaces, the two functions are important to consider when *setting* type. Some of this chapter discusses mainly printed text, because web typography currently offers the designer less control over type. However, the principles apply to web typography in most cases. At the time of writing, the greatest amount of control over typography is available in print environments. As the current most commonly used page layout program is InDesign, there are several references to how to use it to apply the principles discussed.

Display type and text type have a lot in common: they have the same basic letter forms, they communicate language and have a visual quality. Communication of language is invariably required of text, and usually, of display type. (Graphic typography sometimes may not communicate language and become pure form).

However, the differences between display type and text type are in many ways more significant than their similarities when it comes to typographic design.

The details are not the details.
They make the design.

Charles Eames

Serifs are better for justified settings

Serif typefaces suit justified settings better than sans serif, as the serifs help disguise differences in spacing between letters. Sans serif faces with round forms, such as Avenir, are particularly hard to justify well, especially on measures with few characters per line.

CONSIDER CHANGING UNIT DEFAULTS IN SOFTWARE

Changing kerning and tracking settings from their defaults can help make your text improvements more subtle. For example, the default setting in InDesign is twenty thousandths of an em. Changing it in Preferences to five units makes for more refined adjustments.

Between the two extremes of unrelieved monotony and typographical pyrotechnics there is an area where the typographic designer can contribute to the pleasure of reading, and the understanding of what is being said.

Carl Dair, *Design with Type*

DISPLAY TYPE IS FIRST VISUAL, TEXT TYPE IS FIRST LINGUISTIC

Display type is first visual, while still carrying meaning. It is usually bigger than associated text type. It catches the eye, it telegraphs one important word or group of words, and its appearance often connotes either something about the words it is representing or the content associated with it. It creates the reader's first impression, and influences whether readers will pursue engagement with the content or not. Consequently, the relationships between words and individual letters of those display text will benefit from attention that would go unnoticed in text.

A text block and the typeface it is composed in undeniably have visual aspects, but a reader is not conscious of them when reading. Still, the patchy unevenness of badly justified type, or a wild rag on flush left type, will likely be a factor in whether a reader actually engages (or continues to engage) with the content.

SETTING TEXT TYPE

At a glance, there isn't always much obvious difference between well set and badly set type, but it often makes the difference between good and bad typography. However, the best setting in the world will not get readers to read content that they perceive as uninteresting, and text that is interesting to a reader is likely to be read in spite of some typographic obstacles, as long as the typography doesn't actually drive them away.

In most cases, the relationship of reader and text lies somewhere in between these extremes of the reader being very eager to read given content and actively not wanting to read it. If the reader must read a given text, for some reason, the typography will influence how thoroughly it is read.

Somewhat ironically, studies show that people who read text set in difficult-to-read typefaces remember and understand it better than when they are presented easy-to-read text. The problem is, of course, that in most cases, readers do have the choice of whether to read or not, and if type is difficult to read, they probably won't read it (see Chapter Five).

PRINT

The biggest potential pitfall in setting type for print is the relationship between screen and print. Word spacing and overall letterspacing may appear different on the designer's screen than they do in print. Type on screen is not the same context as print, and because we look at type magnified while setting it, it is impossible to judge final scale.

Another potential problem is that the printer we proof on may render type differently than the final printer. Printing test proofs and carefully looking at them will catch most problems. It is also a good idea to try to find examples at the same size of the typeface printed as it will be in its final form and on the final paper being used. If the final form is offset printing, there is a certain amount a printer can do to darken or lighten print by adjusting the ink, so being at the press to check the type when the job is being printed is something that should be done, if possible.

SCREEN

Good type on screen is a matter of good typographic design decisions in terms of typeface, size, leading and spacing for type in different screen sizes and formats. We can (with some effort) adjust kerning for display type, as well as track text type, and making adjustments to white spaces and the vertical space between columns. We can choose en or em dashes, apostrophes and how things such as drop caps or rules appear, but much of the traditional attention to details of typesetting is not yet possible. We have little control over rag, as type will reflow with the screen. And while justification can be specified, because of poor support for hyphenation, it is not yet a practical option.

FLUSH LEFT

To craft a really good rag requires more effort and intervention from the designer than does constructing a good H&J setting for justified text, at least if the line length is above fifty characters or so. The software algorithms of page layout software do not on their own (at least at the time of writing) reliably create a good rag, so to produce one, it is necessary to adjust some lines by breaking them, and with tracking, adding or changing hyphenation points, or adjusting word space.

The need to proof work

Working with print, architectural or other projects is removed from the final context. Although working with type on screen gives an idea of how it will appear in its final form, it can be misleading. We zoom in and out on screen and get an idea, but never a truly accurate one, of how the type will appear physically.

TYPEFACES AND JUSTIFICATION

Serif faces are not demonstrably more readable than sans serif typefaces, but they are usually better for justified settings, because the serifs help make variations in spacing between letters and words less noticeable.

Justified type on the Web

Though it is possible to set justified type on the Web, you don't often see it. Hyphenation is hard to control and doesn't always work the same on all browsers, and control over justification parameters is non-existent, unless the designer codes line by line, something that is impractical with responsive sites.

SMALL CAPS

True small capitals are relatively heavier and wider than regular caps. They are useful for making initialisms (such as HTML) or acronyms (such as NATO), as regular caps disrupt the colour of the page, and tend to draw the reader's eyes to them. They are also sometimes used for the first word or few words of a chapter title or new section. Page layout software or the CSS 'small caps' property will insert the small caps if they are available in the font, and will shrink the regular capitals if they are not, so the designer must pay attention when invoking small caps. Generally, it is better to choose a font that has true small caps than to imitate them, though this is not always possible.

ART'S POWER is in inspiration and the artistic conception. Craft's power is in execution and attention to detail. Today's practice of graphic

First two words set in font with true small caps.

ART'S POWER is in inspiration and the artistic conception. Craft's power is in execution and attention to detail. Today's practice of graphic

First two words set in font without true small caps.

ART'S POWER is in inspiration

Bad. *System Times Roman with automatically reduced capitals to 75 per cent.*

ART'S POWER is in inspiration

Best. *Times Roman with true small caps, in this case, Linotype's version.*

ART'S POWER is in inspiration

Okay. *System Times Roman with Caslon true small caps slightly resized.*

ART'S POWER is in inspiration

Okay. *System Times Roman with Caslon Pro Semibold capitals reduced to 75 per cent.*

The examples above show the difference between designed true small capitals and regular capitals that have been reduced in size. On the bottom is one possible solution if small caps are not part of the font: using the small capitals of another font or a semibold weight (as shown here) of a similar font is likely to work better. Generally it's better to find a font that includes true small caps. Check the glyphs palette if you aren't sure if the font has small caps.

WIDOWS AND ORPHANS

Debate exists between those who call widows a single word at the end of a paragraph, and orphans a partial line at the top of a page, and those who use the words conversely. However, most people believe that, whatever they are called, they should both be avoided.

We will use the first definition, though experience suggests that most people will say something like, 'Fix the widows and orphans', without consciously differentiating between the two. Like so much else in typography, there are varying degrees of severity. What some might consider a widow on a long measure would not be a problem on a short one. It is better to think about proportion: a last line shorter than 20 per cent of the measure should be avoided.

The tradition of craft production of type, with advances made by skilled crafts people who built closely on what had come before, continued until the beginning of the 19th century. It was then that the demands of advertising provoked the competitive development of more unusual faces in order to make ads stand out from their surroundings. They were often not designed with an eye to aesthetic subtlety but rather to be loud and attract attention. On the whole, they succeeded at this, but tended to be more novel than well executed.

A reaction set in against the garish typography of much of the 19th century by the Arts and Craft, Art Nouveau, Vienna Secession, Dada, Futurism, Bauhaus and so on.

The last line has two short words, but they are only about 10 per cent of the paragraph line length. This should be avoided.

Generally, however, some type that resulted from these movements was almost as problematic (though in a more interesting way) than they were reacting against. With an interest in artistic and philosophical principles, they were less interested in the function of typography as a means of semantic communication.

In these cases, the visual quality of the work was its message.

This short measure has only part of a word on the last line of the first paragraph, but it is about a third of the line length, so doesn't pose a serious problem, especially as the short line has an appropriately small paragraph indent.

Some orphans are worse than others. An orphan shorter than two-thirds of the line should be fixed, whether by saving a line earlier in the text or by pushing one over. Generally, an orphan is worse than a widow, so if spacing a line in earlier text causes a widow of at least five characters but solves a bad orphan, it is the lesser of evils. These can be controlled with software settings that keep at least two lines of each paragraph together, though it will make text block lengths uneven.

This orphan should be solved.

attention to detail.

This is not true simply of display type, where designers are generally successful in choosing typefaces and adjusting kerning, letterspacing, leading and word spaces. The designer must also set aside time for dealing with body typography on its own terms, taking a more exigent, craft-based attitude that is different from the general process of graphic design.

so will be understandably hard pressed to pay attention to every detail.

This is not true simply of display type, where designers are generally successful in choosing typefaces and adjusting kerning, letterspacing, leading and word spaces. The designer must also set aside time for dealing with body typography on its own terms, taking a more exigent, craft-based attitude that is different from the general process of graphic design.

This orphan is less serious, because there is enough space filled visually to hold the top of the page. By subtle adjustment of the paragraph starting on the previous page, it might be possible to gain another word for this line. Again, the lesser of evils principle applies. If gaining the word causes rivers in the rest of the paragraph, it is better to live with the orphan. Orphans are easier to solve in a ragged-right setting.

You can rename and replace style sheets that come in word processing documents, as well as fix local formatting that might be in the file. For example, if a paragraph style is set to Times, and the file provider has highlighted the text and changed it to Comic Sans, you can change the style sheet to Comic Sans, and then change it back to Times, thus getting rid of the Comic Sans, and keeping any other local formatting such as italics and bolds. Using 'search and replace' functions to replace formats with paragraph styles can also be useful for removing unwanted local formatting.

Word spaces after periods

In the late 1400s, the time of Nicolas Jenson, word spaces after a period were more or less optional. In the 1800s, an em space was often used after periods. In the era of typewriters, the monospaced letters made two spaces after a period the reasonable and accepted choice. Currently, among typographers the accepted correct amount of space after a period is a single word space.

When Eric Gill suggested that flush left type was a better design choice than justified type, he also preferred a tight rag, with approximately equal line lengths, which he proposed to solve in typesetting. In effect he suggested that we split the difference by setting type flush left but varying the word space slightly in order to make a more even line length, which is quite easy to do (though not automatically) with page layout software, if not with current css. (As you can see on the image on page 193 taken from *Essay on Typography*, Gill also sometimes used an ampersand instead of an 'and' in order to make the right edge more even.)

Not everyone agrees with Gill about the correctness of a tight rag. Some designers prefer a more 'toothy' rag, with more variation between short and long lines. Any rag will need some attention to be regular and not visually distracting. The narrower the measure, the more intervention is needed. Tools for adjusting the rag include increasing or decreasing tracking of the text, forcing line breaks with the shift return key, or doing what Gill suggested, adjusting the word space in a sentence.

With current page layout software, the best ways to improve a rag are first by rebreaking lines, second by subtle adjustment to the word space or tracking, applied line by line. (Not by plus or minus tracking entire paragraphs, which is a common approach among rushed magazine designers.) The 'adjusting word space' command is not usually accessible by menu, but the common page layout programs have keyboard commands available that allow the user to do this.

These refinements only work if the adjustments are subtle enough not to be noticeable. If they are obvious to the reader, they are often worse than the problems they are intended to address.

JUSTIFIED TEXT

Justified text is the most common setting for long reading in print. If the column width is wide enough, as in the sixty-five characters per line range, justifying type is both neat, with its two straight vertical edges, and, with modern page layout software, easier to do well than it was in the days of Eric Gill.

Given a long enough line length and a reasonable tolerance of hyphenation, using the parameters of page layout software (such as minimum and maximum preferred word space, tracking and glyph scaling) will let you do a decent job of setting justified text. No doubt the type will need some intervention (though usually less than a flush left setting). Programs that have a feature that highlights hyphenation and justification violations, such as InDesign, will be a great help. Currently, the designer has less control over the parameters of ragged text, and no highlighting feature exists for rag problems.

As previously mentioned, justifying type is still a problem in HTML/CSS (at the time of writing), not only because hyphenation doesn't work well, but because, depending on the design, if text is reflowing in a responsive layout, it may end up on too narrow a measure for even hyphenated justified text. This can be partly avoided with good responsive design breakpoints but still will make the designer's typographic life more difficult. This situation is likely to improve as web standards develop, though since flush left web type has become an accepted convention, there isn't much pressure to address this particular problem.

Flush right and centred type

Flush right type is hard to read, because the eye may have trouble finding the beginning of the next line. It is still useful as short text in cases where it is set against a visual object to the right, for example in a caption to the left of an image or as marginal material to the left of a block of text. Flush right can be used freely in display type.

Centred type is almost always used for display or other graphic typography such as pull quotes. It is seldom suitable for text, except in rare cases such as an epigraph after a centred head. The rag for centred type needs more attention than flush left. It should generally be more toothy and rhythmic.

Typewriter quotes

Every designer knows that typewriter-style or 'dumb' quotes and apostrophes are incorrect. But they are not inch marks either. Inches, feet, minutes and seconds should be indicated by 'primes', which can be found in the Symbol font. Depending on the typeface they are used with, they may need some size adjustment.

5′6″ not 5'6"

The same applies to latitude and longitude:

48° 25′ 43″ N
123°21′ 56″ W

**DON'T USE WORD SPACES
TO CREATE WHITE SPACES**

Here's why: you should be able to search and replace double word spaces, which appear commonly in text files, with single spaces.

If you use two word spaces instead of an en space for example, you will lose those if you globally replace multiple spaces with a single space.

White spaces:

thin space	≈ half a word space
quarter space	≈ one word space
en space	≈ two word spaces
em space	≈ four word spaces

This shows the hyphenation from a sample paragraph style sheet for a book with a line length of about sixty characters per line, justified. All page layout programs give similar control over when and how automatic hyphens are inserted.

REDUCED CAPS

If setting numbers or acronyms in text in a serif face, which don't usually have true small caps, the jarring effect of the larger characters can be subtly lessened by creating a style that reduces the size of the caps slightly, with some spacing and slight scaling to compensate.
So instead of:

UNICEF was created in 1946

you would have

UNICEF was created in 1946

The caps and numbers have been sized at 95 per cent of the text, tracked 20 em units, and the horizontal scale increased by 4 per cent.

Don't be in a hurry to bring original files into the final software. Unless the content has been edited to final form, it might make sense to go through it first in terms of grammar and spelling using the word processing program it likely originated in.

Besides the fact that the grammar and editing tools are more comprehensive than those in page layout software, an advantage of working in a word processing program is that it is easier to focus on the text and not be distracted by the design.

A similar benefit can be found later in the process by making unpaginated text-only 'galley' files in page layout software. Working on the typography in this way means you will be able to pay more attention to typographic details rather than being distracted by other design elements.

Be careful not to lose any formatting information that might be in the file. If you force all text into a style sheet, you will lose things like bold and italics. The more text you have to deal with, the more important this becomes. It may take a bit longer to keep such local formatting and any useful style sheets that might be in the word processing file, but, except for short texts, it is worth it.

If you are editing significant amounts of text in InDesign, the Story Editor is a useful tool. It shows the story text without formatting and lets you edit overset text, as well as text that is small or otherwise difficult to read in the default Layout View.

Justifying type

When type was set line by line, by hand or by machine, 'justifying' meant and making a block of text aesthetically pleasing and more readable by adjusting the word space, whether or not each line of type was the same length.

Now, however, 'justified' is generally used in typography to mean 'fully justified', a setting where all but indented or terminal lines are set at the same length.

Opinions on hyphenation vary. Some designers are uncompromising, saying, for example, 'never hyphenate ragged right text or proper nouns'. It is better to take a Tschicholdian 'lesser of evils' approach: you may prefer to avoid hyphenation, but often, it's better than the alternatives of a bad rag or uneven justification. Some hyphens are worse than others. Hyphens in long compound words makes sense between the compounds. For example, hyphenating 'multidisciplinary' as 'multi-disciplinary' is a natural break, as it splits the word by meaning. Breaking long words toward the end is preferred over breaking them near the beginning, as the reader probably already knows what word he or she is dealing with after the first part of the word. 'Multidisciplin-ary' is not quite as good as 'Multi-disciplinary,' but better than 'Mul-tidisciplinary.'

Hyphenation parameters

Generally, it is better to set hyphenation specifications to a minimum of three characters at the beginning and end of a hyphenated word. Having word breaks such as activi-ty or mi-gration is distracting. Sometimes, breaking a word after two letters can work, if it is after a prefix, as in 'un-likelihood' or 'de-contaminate, but these should be done case-by-case, with a 'discretionary hyphen' inserted in a word where necessary.

The hyphenation of proper nouns, such as the names 'Conway' or 'London', is undesirable, in spite of their two clear syllables. If you are dealing with a long name such as Wittgenstein or Baskerville, hyphenating is better than having bad justification or rag. Breaking Wittgen-stein and Basker-ville is better than breaking such names elsewhere, as the division relates to the original meanings. If dealing with a narrow justified column even Bas-kerville or Witt-genstein may be the lesser of evils. If it was you who made the decision to work with such a narrow column in a project where long names or words are common, you have only yourself to blame.

A page from Eric Gill's 1931 book Essay on Typography, *showing his idea of a good setting, including the use of an ampersand instead of 'and' to improve the rag.*

PARAGRAPH COMPOSITION VERSUS LINE-BY-LINE COMPOSITION

InDesign's Paragraph Composer setting generally produces better results than Single Line Composer if there is no intervention from the designer. However, if you want to refine a setting, the Paragraph Composer is difficult to work with, as it will change lines in the paragraph above where you are working. The Single Line Composer is better for typographers who normally refine their work.

Penguin composition rules

TEXT COMPOSITION

All text composition should be as closely word-spaced as possible. As a rule, the spacing should be about a middle space or the thickness of an 'i' in the type size used.

Wide spaces should be strictly avoided. Words may be freely broken whenever necessary to avoid wide spacing, as breaking words is less harmful to the appearance of the page than too much space between words.

All major punctuation marks – full point, colon, and semicolon – should be followed by the same spacing as is used throughout the rest of the line.

INDENTING OF PARAGRAPHS

The indent of the paragraph should be the em of the fount body.

Omit indents in the first line of the first paragraph of any text and at the beginning of a new section that comes under a subheading. It is not necessary to set the first word in small capitals, but if this is done for any reason, the word should be letter-spaced in the same way as the running title.

If a chapter is divided into several parts without headings, these parts should be divided not only by an additional space, but always by one or more asterisks of the fount body. As a rule, one asterisk is sufficient. Without them it is impossible to see whether a part ends at the bottom of a page or not. Even when the last line of such a part ends the page, there will always be space for an asterisk in the bottom margin.

PUNCTUATION MARKS AND SPELLING

If this can be done on the keyboard, put thin spaces before question marks, exclamation marks, colons, and semicolons.

Between initials and names, as in G. B. Shaw and after all abbreviations where a full point is used, use a smaller (fixed) space than between the other words in the line.

Instead of em rules without spaces, use en rules preceded and followed by the word space of the line, as in the third paragraph above.

Marks of omission should consist of three full points. These should be set without any spaces, but be preceded and followed by word spaces.

Use full points sparingly and omit after these abbreviations: Mr, Mrs, Messrs, Dr, St, WC2, 8vo, and others containing the last letter of the abbreviated word.

Use single quotes for a first quotation and double quotes for quotations within quotations. If there is still another quotation within the second, return to single quotes. Punctuation belonging to a quotation comes within the quotes, otherwise outside.

Opening quotes should be followed by a hairspace except before A and J. Closing quotes should be preceded by a hairspace except after a comma or a full point. If this cannot be done on the keyboard, omit these hairspaces, but try to get the necessary attachment.

When long extracts are set in small type do not use quotes.

Use parentheses ( ) for explanation and interpolations; brackets [ ] for notes.

For all other queries on spelling, consult the *Rules for Compositors and Readers at the University Press, Oxford,* or Collins's *Authors' and Printers' Dictionary.*

CAPITALS, SMALL CAPITALS, AND ITALICS

Words in capitals must always be letter-spaced. The spacing of the capitals in lines of importance should be very carefully optically equalized. The word spaces in lines either of capitals or small capitals should not exceed an en quad.

All display lines set in the same fount should be given the same spacing throughout the book.

Use small capitals for running headlines and in contents pages. They must always be slightly letter-spaced to make words legible.

Running headlines, unless otherwise stated, should consist of the title of the book on the left-hand page, and the contents of the chapter on the right.

Italics are to be used for emphasis, for foreign words and phrases, and for the titles of books, newspapers, and plays which appear in the text. In such cases the definite article 'The' should be printed in roman, unless it is part of the title itself.

In bibliographical and related matter, as a rule, authors' names should be given in small capitals with capitals, and the titles in italics.

FIGURES

Do not mix old style text composition with modern face figures. Either hanging or ranging fraction figures may be used if they are cut in the fount used for the text.

Jan Tschichold's composition rules brought consistency and quality to Penguin books. They were extremely influential in English language publishing. Although they were intended for the guidance of book compositors of the time, they are still useful to today's designer who is dealing with text typography.

In text matter, numbers under 100 should be composed in letters. Use figures when the matter consists of a sequence of stated quantities, particulars of age, etc. In dates use the fewest possible figures, 1946–7, not 1946–1947. Divide by an en rule without spaces.

REFERENCES AND FOOTNOTES

The reference to a footnote may be given by an asterisk of the fount body, if there are only a few footnotes in the book, and not more than one per page. But if there are two or more footnotes per page, use superior fraction figures preceded by a thin space.

Do not use modern face fraction figures in any old style fount. Either hanging or ranging fraction figures may be used provided that they are in harmony with the face used for the text. For books composed in any old face letter, we recommend Monotype Superior Figures F627, to be cast on the size two points below the size of the face used.

Footnotes should be set two points smaller than the text. Indent the first line of these with the same number of points as the paragraphs in the text matter. Use equal leading between all lines of footnotes, use the same leading as in the text matter, and put 1–2 point lead underneath the last line in order to get register with the normal lines.

For the numbering of footnotes use normal figures followed by a full point and an en quad. These figures may run either throughout the chapter, or even through the whole book, according to the special instructions given by the typographer.

FOLIOS

These should, as a rule, be set in the same size and face as the text, and in Arabic numerals.

Pagination should begin with the first leaf in the book, but the first folio actually appearing is that on the verso of the first page of the text.

When there is preliminary matter whose extent is unknown at the time of making up the text into pages, it is necessary to use lower-case roman numerals, numbered from the first page of the first sheet. The first actually appearing cannot be definitely stated, but may be on the acknowledgments page, or at latest on the second page of the preface. In this case, the first Arabic folio to appear will be '2' on the verso of the first text page.

Folios for any text matter at the end of the book, such as index etc., should continue the Arabic numbering of the text pages.

THE PRINTING OF PLAYS

The same rules should apply to the printing of plays as to the printing of prose. Names of characters should be set in capitals and small capitals. The text following is indented. Stage directions should be in italics, enclosed in square brackets. The headline should include the number of the act and the scene.

THE PRINTING OF POETRY

For printing poetry use type of a smaller size than would be used for prose. All composition should be leaded and the words evenly spaced with middle spaces. The titles should be centred on the measure, not on the first line. The beginning of each poem may be treated as a chapter opening, with small capitals, etc.

Extra leading, especially between verses of irregular length, may often be misleading, as it is impossible to see whether the verse ends at the bottom of the page or not. The safest way of recognizing the poet's intention is to indent the first line of every new verse, after which leading is not really necessary. Therefore, the first line of the second and following verses should be indented, unless the poet has indicated a shape not allowing for indentations.

MAKE-UP

Books should, with certain exceptions, be made up in the following order:
I. Preliminary pages: 1, half title; 2, frontispiece; 3, title; 4, Imprint or date of publication; 5, dedication; 6, acknowledgments; 7, contents; 8, list of illustrations; 9, list of abbreviations; 10, preface; 11, introduction; 12, errata.
II. The text of the book.
III. Additional matter: 1. appendix; 2. author's notes; 3. glossary; 4. bibliography; 5. index.

The above should each begin on a right-hand page, imprint and frontispiece excepted. As a rule, chapter headings should be dropped a few lines.

The preliminary pages should be set in the same face and style as the book itself. Avoid bold faces.

The index should be set in two or more columns and in type two points smaller than the text. The first word of each letter of the alphabet should be set in small capitals with capitals.

– *Jan Tschichold (1947)*

Narrow columns will need a greater tolerance for hyphenation and varied spacing in justified settings, or looser rags in the case of flush left text. Languages such as German, which has many long words, will need a greater tolerance of hyphenation than languages with fewer long words.

Bad spacing is bad spacing in any era.

Aaron Burns, *U&lc 17.2*, 1992

CAPITALS NEED SPACE

Capitals, particularly including small capitals, need more spacing between letters and words than lower-case type at the same size. Large type, on the other hand, needs less (and different) spacing than small type (see page 206).

Metrics vs optical kerning

Metrics kerning is determined by the typeface designer. Optical kerning is determined by an algorithm in a program. Presumably, the metrics kerning should work best, but because type designers may kern more with an eye to display settings, optical kerning is sometimes better. Kerning in CSS uses the metrics kerning.

If you are designing in a pre-existing system with narrow columns, this kind of problem may be unavoidable. Adjusting justification parameters can reduce, if not eliminate, the number of breaks.

Allowing one or two hyphens in a row is usually a good starting point for a justified setting of 60 characters or more. If you have a long measure, especially if it is flush left, you may be able to avoid hyphenation, though if there are long, compound words (such as 'multidisciplinary'), occasional hyphens might be needed.

If you are setting up parameters for a very narrow justified column, such as are found in newspapers, you might allow three hyphens in a row and allow two letters before and after a break. A measure this narrow, though, invites reconsidering the design.

If a project has several different settings, as many do, different hyphenation, as well as other justification parameters, are likely needed for each style, which is another good reason to have style sheets for all settings. For example, headings might have hyphenation turned off, as well as tighter word space and tracking. Text type will need different hyphenation and justification parameters for different typefaces, sizes, alignments and measures.

TSCHICHOLD COMPOSITION RULES

In 1947, Jan Tschichold worked with Penguin books in a redesign and development of production standards for their titles (see pages 194–195). As well as redesigning the covers, he specified every aspect and detail of typesetting text, and his composition rules remain influential today, particularly in the UK. The Penguin books were generally set justified, so Tschichold suggested — showing the pragmatic 'lesser-of-evils' principle that is valuable in making typographic decisions — that 'Wide spaces should be strictly avoided. Words may be freely broken whenever necessary to avoid wide spacing, as breaking words is *less harmful* (my italics) to the appearance of the page than too much space between words.' He recognized that while hyphenation may be undesirable, rivers of wide spaces are worse.

Whether or not you agree with Tschichold's specifications (and most typographers would agree that they are generally good, at least for the book setting they were intended for), it is useful to have defaults that work for you.

KERNING DISPLAY TYPE

Most typefaces have reasonably good kerning, so what is needed is a critical eye more than changing the spacing of every pair. A critical look is needed, though, because different words may need different kerning, and occasionally you might run into a typeface that has no kern pairs. Looking at a word upside down, or blurring it, can also be helpful. *Always look at three letters at a time, because the relationship between a single pair of letters in a word is more or less meaningless.*

Caraway

Metrics kerning from the font file, but this font happens to have no kern pairs for the problem pairs.

Caraway

Overkerning of some pairs.

Caraway

Hand kerned, looking at three letters at a time, that is, first looking at 'Car', then 'ara', then 'raw', etc.

OTTAWA

OTTAWA

The space caused by the two Ts forces the other letters to be more widely spaced to have even visual spacing. The top version shows default metrics, the bottom version is adjusted to mitigate the problem.

YARROW   ΜΟЯЯAY   YARROW

By looking at the type upside down we look at the formal qualities rather than reading. Blurring the type does something similar but gives us a better idea of the overall density of the type.

BIDWELL HENNIG, ART DIRECTOR FOR KENLY/GUNCH/ELDER, IS IN A PANIC.
THE TYPE HE'S JUST SPECIFIED HAS TO BE ON THE BOARDS BY 10 A.M. TOMORROW.

This typositor type from a type shop ad in the 1970s is, ironically, a perfect example of over-kerning, and the danger of not looking at three-letter groups. (Look at the 'PAN' for a particularly notable example of uneven visual spacing.)

BIDWELL HENNIG, ART DIRECTOR FOR KENLY/GUNCH/ELDER, IS IN A PANIC.
THE TYPE HE'S JUST SPECIFIED HAS TO BE ON THE BOARDS BY 10 A.M. TOMORROW.

This is a digital version of the same typeface, ITC Tiffany Heavy. The metrics kerning is not perfect, but it is much better than the hand-kerned version on the left.

LIGATURES AND ALTERNATE CHARACTERS

Use of ligatures is a design decision, but some typefaces need ligatures more than others, so this often ends up being a typesetting more than a design decision. Their use depends on context: for example, they should be avoided in large or tracked-out display type. Using ligatures makes sense for most (but not all) serif typefaces. Here we look at places where they cause problems and where they do nothing at all. They can also be useful for script faces, which may have alternate versions of letters that help to maintain the natural look of handwriting.

If a serif font you are using doesn't have ff or ffi ligatures, consider whether it is better to leave ligatures turned off. Also, some typefaces have upgraded versions, sometimes called 'Pro', which have the 'ffi' and 'ffl' ligatures among other features.

The ligatures and contextual alternates can be turned on (if available) in the Character options OpenType menu in InDesign, or with font-variant-alternates in CSS.

fine   office   office

The fi ligature in this face is both a bit forced and unneeded; there is no visual conflict between the f and i when they are together. Ligatures should be turned off.

fine   office   office

The fi ligature looks good here but not when it is beside an ordinary f. The f and i look okay, because the terminal of the narrow f is far enough away from the i. Ligatures aren't needed.

fine   office   office

In this case, the fi is a bit tight, and the font has a very nice ffi ligature. The ligatures should be on.

fine   office   office

Here, the fi ligature is the usual f and i set on a single glyph, so whether or not the ligature is on makes no difference.

The suffice factor
The suffice factor
The suffice factor

Garamond Premier Pro has a full set of ligatures and alternate characters. The fi combination is awkward, and ligatures should be turned on. The historically based Discretionary Ligatures (e.g. the ct ligature), on the other hand, are too mannered for a modern setting.

The suffice factor
The suffice factor
The suffice factor
The suffice factor

The italic has Contextual Alternates, which only make sense in decorative work. They should be used sparingly, if at all. Here, having one at the end of every word breaks up the line too much.

analysis

This word set in Mayence Premium shows how contextual alternates can give a more natural look to a script font by substituting varied letterforms for repeated letters.

SYSTEMS HAVE LIMITS

Still, relying too much on set rules is a bad idea. Tschichold's rules worked well enough for typesetters executing a systematic design program. The compositors were not employed as designers but as craftspersons. Design, by definition, requires rethinking the job in each case. If we are not rethinking, we are executing a system rather than designing (though a good typographer will execute that system better than a non-designer). Good execution may often be achieved by following rules; good design takes creative thought and constant questioning.

What is right for one typographic system might be wrong for another. Typeface, type size, layout, setting decisions and parameters all depend on content, audience and medium. Changing any of these suggests rethinking the others.

Page layout programs and fonts are themselves systems which have limitations which may influence design. As long as we are aware of this, we can accept or reject those influences. For example, since page layout software is more helpful in producing good justified type than it is in producing good ragged text, it will usually take less time to produce well justified text, given a reasonably wide measure. These might influence our design decisions on our choice of justification or measure. Fonts have built-in widths, spacing and kerns, which might affect our perception of their suitability, even though these characteristics can be adjusted. As long as we are aware of these influences, recognitions of the strengths and weakness of a system can make for good decisions. If we don't recognize these factors, then we either don't benefit from systems, or unconsciously design to accommodate them, which may take away from the design being as strong as it might otherwise be.

PAGE LAYOUT PROGRAM
COMPOSITION RULES OF THUMB

General

- Avoid setting justified type when average line length is less than fifty characters per line.

- Hyphenation: three characters before, three after a word break.

- No more than two hyphens in a row in a line with fifty or more characters per line. In a shorter line, three hyphens may be the lesser of evils.

Ragged type

- Hyphenation zone set to zero (in InDesign).

Justified type

Use Single Line composer (in InDesign) in order to make adjustments.

- Allow no more than 5 per cent variation in letterspacing (e.g. –1 to +4%).

- Allow no more than 2 per cent difference in glyph scaling (e.g. 99% – 101%), except in very narrow justified settings, where you might go as high as 98% – 102%

- Check justified type with 'Highlight H&J violations' (in InDesign).

These three-metre tall letters made of steel, aluminium and polycarbonate, standing in front of Toronto's City Hall, make the loose spacing between the R and O particularly obvious.

JUSTIFICATION SETTINGS

The settings below are really too narrow to be justified. But in cases where they might have to be, even more time than usual should be spent to determine the best hyphenation and justification settings. For a narrow measure, allowing more hyphenation and variation in letterspace, and even a bit of horizontal scaling makes sense. It all should be checked for typographic colour before final printing. The narrower the setting, the more it is likely to need intervention by the designer.

When phototype and digital type were introduced, the problem of the same typeface being used for all ranges began to creep in, whether because of the manufacturer of the typesetting system, or by decisions made by the designer, whether inadvertent or not, to use inappropriate cuts for given sizes. This was exacerbated by the means that the letterforms were carried, that is, no longer in metal but on film or digitally, by the more or less simultaneous replacement of letterpress by offset print (where the letterforms are not pressed into the paper.

Bad setting (word space varies less, letter spacing varies widely).

When phototype and digital type were introduced, the problem of the same typeface being used for all ranges began to creep in, whether because of the manufacturer of the typesetting system, or by decisions made by the designer, whether inadvertent or not, to use inappropriate cuts for given sizes. This was exacerbated by the means that the letterforms were carried, that is, no longer in metal but on film or digitally, by the more or less simultaneous replacement of letterpress by offset print (where the letterforms are not pressed into the paper.

Bad setting (word space varies less, glyph scaling varies widely).

When phototype and digital type were introduced, the problem of the same typeface being used for all ranges began to creep in, whether because of the manufacturer of the typesetting system, or by decisions made by the designer, whether inadvertent or not, to use inappropriate cuts for given sizes. This was exacerbated by the means that the letterforms were carried, that is, no longer in metal but on film or digitally, by the more or less simultaneous replacement of letterpress by offset print (where the letterforms are not pressed into the paper.

Better setting (a balance of word space, letter spacing and scaling).

HYPHENATION SETTINGS

Some page layout software (in this case, InDesign) allows options for hyphenation that affect ragged and justified settings. The larger the number in the hyphenation zone the looser the rag is allowed to be, and with justified settings. There is also a slider that influences whether there is more hyphenation or better spacing. All set with Paragraph Composer and default H&Js. Any of these could improved with intervention by the designer.

Hyphenation is not currently reliable with text on the Web, but in print, especially justified settings, it needs some consideration. Opinions on hyphenation vary. Some print designers take a uncompromising approach, for example, 'never hyphenate ragged right text,' or 'never hyphenate proper nouns'. It is better to take a 'lesser of evils' approach: you may prefer to avoid hyphenation, but often, hyphenation is better than the alternatives of a bad rag or uneven justification. Some hyphens are worse than others. Hyphens in long compound words make sense between the compounds. Breaking long words toward the end is preferred over breaking them near the beginning, as the reader probably already knows what word he or she is dealing with after the first part of the word. There is still much debate about hyphenation, and every designer has their own opinion. A current tendency to prefer avoiding hyphens is allied to a current preference among designers for flush left settings. However, justified settings are still the norm for many kinds of settings, particularly for extended reading

Slider set to fewer hyphens, hyphenation zone in set to 3 picas.

Hyphenation is not currently reliable with text on the Web, but in print, especially justified settings, it needs some consideration. Opinions on hyphenation vary. Some print designers take a uncompromising approach, for example, 'never hyphenate ragged right text,' or 'never hyphenate proper nouns'. It is better to take a 'lesser of evils' approach: you may prefer to avoid hyphenation, but often, hyphenation is better than the alternatives of an awkward rag or uneven justification. Some hyphens are worse than others. Hyphens in long compound words make sense between the compounds. Breaking long words toward the end is preferred over breaking them near the beginning, as the reader probably already knows what word he or she is dealing with after the first part of the word. There is still much debate about hyphenation, and every designer has their own opinion. A current tendency to prefer avoiding hyphens is allied to a current preference among designers for flush left settings. However, justified settings are still the norm for many kinds of settings, particularly for extended reading.

Slider set to better spacing, hyphenation zone in set to 1 pica.

Hyphenation is not currently reliable with text on the Web, but in print, especially justified settings, it needs some consideration. Opinions on hyphenation vary. Some print designers take a uncompromising approach, for example, 'never hyphenate ragged right text,' or 'never hyphenate proper nouns'. It is better to take a 'lesser of evils' approach: you may prefer to avoid hyphenation, but often, hyphenation is better than the alternatives of a bad rag or uneven justification. Some hyphens are worse than others. Hyphens in long compound words make sense between the compounds. Breaking long words toward the end is preferred over breaking them near the beginning, as the reader probably already knows what word he or she is dealing with after the first part of the word. There is still much debate about hyphenation, and every designer has their own opinion. A current tendency to prefer avoiding hyphens is allied to a current preference among designers for flush left settings. However, justified settings are still the norm for many kinds of settings, particularly for extended reading

Slider set to fewer hyphens. Hyphenation zone doesn't apply to justified settings.

Hyphenation is not currently reliable with text on the Web, but in print, especially justified settings, it needs some consideration. Opinions on hyphenation vary. Some print designers take a uncompromising approach, for example, 'never hyphenate ragged right text,' or 'never hyphenate proper nouns'. It is better to take a 'lesser of evils' approach: you may prefer to avoid hyphenation, but often, hyphenation is better than the alternatives of an awkward rag or uneven justification. Some hyphens are worse than others. Hyphens in long compound words make sense between the compounds. Breaking long words toward the end is preferred over breaking them near the beginning, as the reader probably already knows what word he or she is dealing with after the first part of the word. There is still much debate about hyphenation, and every designer has their own opinion. A current tendency to prefer avoiding hyphens is allied to a current preference among designers for flush left settings. However, justified settings are still the norm for many kinds of settings, particularly for extended reading.

Slider set to better spacing. Hyphenation zone doesn't apply.

WORD SPACE

Word space is suitable for text in most typefaces, but it's worth looking at, especially in display type where the word space should often be less and the individual space between words can often benefit from adjustment. One rule of thumb is that the word space should be around that of a lower-case 'i' or the width of a counter of an 'n'.

Wordᵢspaceᵢshouldᵢbeᵢaboutᵢthatᵢofᵢaᵢlowerᵢcaseᵢ'i'

word space

This Bembo Semibold Italic font has a word space that is too wide. Setting it at about 70 per cent will give a better setting, slightly less than the width of the 'i'.

word i space

word space

Capitals need more space

CAPITALS NEED MORE SPACE

Because word space is the same for capitals and lower-case characters, but capitals are taller, they need more space. Here the lower-case setting has 100 per cent of the font word space, while the capitals are set to 130 per cent word space, keeping the proportion between letter height and width of space about the same.

HYPHENS AND ENDASHES IN RANGES

25–28 May

29 May – 1 June

June 1-3

In a text setting, for a range of numbers or other alike things (such as May–June), an endash without space is correct. If the range is between unlike things (such as May – 1), then it is clearer to add space around the endash.

With display type, appearance trumps 'correct' punctuation. In this case, the endash is too long, so a hyphen is used (and raised a bit, as hyphens and other dashes are designed to be used with lower-case characters).

Visual
Visual
Visual
Visual
Visual
Visual
Visual
Visual
Visual
Visual

Larger type needs tighter spacing to appear to have the same spacing as smaller type. The 5-point type at the top is tracked +25 units, while the 38-point type at the bottom is tracked −30 units. If they were all tracked the same, the small type would appear to be set tighter than the large type.

. . . .

Editorial punctuation styles

There is no 'correct' editorial style. Whether single or double apostrophes are used in a given case, when commas are appropriate, whether emdashes or endashes are used for parenthetical divisions, are all to some extent up to editorial discretion. Some of these tend to be associated with UK or US style – the dominant English writing traditions – others are more idiosyncratic, depending on house style or a particular editor's taste. The most important thing is consistency within a project.

Organization of work

Without an organized approach to a big or complex project, you will spend too long making adjustments and then redoing them, because a change to copy has made earlier adjustments useless.

This may happen due to decisions, made by others, that mean you have to redo or readjust work already done. It maybe caused if some text is entirely replaced, rendering all your careful typographic adjustments and reconciliations wasted, but it can also be caused by someone making a change that adds or subtracts as little as a single line, which may cause a new series of orphans (or widows).

Time spent adjusting individual lines of type before the copy has been more or less finalized is likely to be a waste of time. If the type size and line length have been determined, though, hyphenation and H&J parameters, if available, as they are in page layout programs, are well worth developing early in the process.

A clearly organized work flow and efficient use of style sheets and master pages will make production faster and less error prone, giving more time for design and attention to typographic detail.

OTHER ADJUSTMENTS IN TEXT

If you have control of them, the hyphenation and justification parameters deserve attention for every type of setting, and even within the same setting, as different paragraphs can come with different problems.

Before computerized type, increasing the space between letters in text (tracking) was impossible or impractical; adjustments to text settings were done with word spacing and hyphenation. Kerning in text was not possible. With computers, it became possible to adjust not only the relationships between letters, but also their horizontal scale. Some typographers prefer to avoid adjusting tracking, and even more prefer to avoid scaling type.

However, others, following the 'lesser of evils' principle, will allow a minimal amount of tracking (and even scaling) if it makes for a better setting. Don't overuse these, because if they are noticeable, it has a terrible effect on both reading pace and appearance. The adjustments have to be subtle, and more or less imperceptible.

SETTING DISPLAY TYPE

Setting display type has more to do with the visual relationships between individual letters and lines. Display type is also, like text blocks, a part of an overall page composition.

Unless you are deliberately causing tension with active space manipulations (as in the work of David Carson, for example), spacing should be visually even. Display type should normally be set tighter than text type, both in terms of interletter space, word space and in leading, unless there is a good reason for doing something else. And there may well be a reason to do something else. Setting text type doesn't have much room for the unconventional, while display type does.

Display type can be set vertically, at an angle, even upside down, though upside down is rare if the type has is meant to be read. Display type can be used as a mask, distorted, printed, scanned and manipulated, or otherwise treated visually in a way that would be unwise with text type.

For website design, it may make sense to set large display type as an image if visual effects are added. Whenever possible, though, keeping type 'live' is better. It will scale without problems, and will appear in search engines.

Type as display succeed or fail on its graphic qualities, both in terms of its compositional function and in how its appearance resonates with its meaning. It still has to be legible to be read. The degree of legibility necessary depends on the context. In a billboard on a highway, the type has to be read quickly to be effective. In a situation where a reader will have more time with it, legibility can be marginal, if the type is visually effective.

IT'S BETTER TO UNDER-KERN THAN OVER-KERN

Adjusting kerning has caused more harm to letter relationships than it has improved them. See page 197 for a glaring example.

Hyphenation on the Web

Although web hyphenation is not well supported at the time of writing, it is on its way in theory. It will allow extensive control over hyphenation similar to that available in page layout programs. When these changes are fully implemented by browsers, justified type will be a practical alternative to ragged right text.

KERNING WORD SPACE

Page layout programs such as InDesign and Quark Xpress have keyboard commands that will slightly increase or decrease the kerning only in word spaces of selected text. Used on individual lines, this is useful for adjusting line length in ragged text and display type without affecting the tracking of the words themselves.

OPTICAL ALIGNMENT IN DISPLAY TYPE

As with many things in typography, what looks right to the eye is not always what makes strict geometric sense. In most cases, the larger the type, the more important graphic refinement becomes.

"Time flies whether you are having fun or not."

"Time flies" whether you are having fun "or not."

Centred type needs adjustment to be visually centred. Punctuation in particular can make a setting appear to be not centred. The top block above is centred but doesn't look like it. The bottom block has been adjusted by hanging the punctuation outside the lines and looks centred. Using optical alignment in InDesign would mitigate the problem but not solve it.

**ALPHA
BRAVO
CHARLIE
YANKEE
TANGO**

Not bad
Type set without optical margin alignment. The C, T and particularly the Y appear slightly too far to the right.

**ALPHA
BRAVO
CHARLIE
YANKEE
TANGO**

Good
Type adjusted visually to create an optical alignment.

**ALPHA
BRAVO
CHARLIE
YANKEE
TANGO**

Bad
Type excessively adjusted visually to create an optical alignment. Lining up the stems of the Y and T makes the letters appear too far to the left.

Headline

To successfully manage the production of finished work, designers needed a deep understanding of both the affordances and potential problems of the heavily code-based text type systems and the photographic display type systems. The systems were not 'user-friendly': the complex systems that work in the background of modern page layout systems needed attention from and control by the extensively trained operators.

Because each character in a font has proportional space on each side, a large character in the same text box will have more space to the left than a small one. In this case, it causes the head to not visually align with the text below. This can be addressed by indenting the text slightly.

ADJUSTING RAG WITH WORD SPACE

Often, a good way to adjust rag is with word space and rebreaking lines if necessary, rather than using tracking. Slight line-by-line tracking can help, but with some typefaces even slight tracking is visible, and so affects the rhythm and colour of the type.

Working in different typographic environments means that there are different rights and wrongs. Things that make sense for a wide measure and long reading for book-type texts on screen or on paper may not make sense for type in narrow columns, and may be almost completely irrelevant for display or architectural applications (for example).

Round-bowled typefaces, such as the Avenir shown here, are quite sensitive to tracking. Here, the difference between tight and loose lines is noticeable.

Working in different typographic environments means that there are different rights and wrongs. Things that make sense for a wide measure and long reading for book-type texts on screen or on paper may not make sense for type in narrow columns, and may be almost completely irrelevant for display or architectural applications (for example).

Without changing any tracking of words, the rag has been improved on this block of text by subtly adjusting only the word space, a command available in most layout programs.

OPTICAL ALIGNMENT IN TEXT

Optical alignment in text is a mixed blessing. It solves some visual problems but causes others. It cures the visual indent caused by quotation marks but can conversely give them too much prominence, which is more distracting than the indent.

Optical alignment of text often causes more visual problems than it is worth. It generally works well with hyphenation, as the hyphens are (relatively) visually insignificant, which means they leave a slight visual indentation in the edge of the text. However, in other cases —such as with emdashes, they are visually distracting. This is true of double quotation marks. To give an example, "The double quotes hang unnaturally into the margin."

Optical margin alignment creates odd margins when treating anything but hyphens, commas and periods. Here the emdash protrudes too much.

Optical alignment of text often causes more visual problems than it is worth. It generally works well with hyphenation, as the hyphens are (relatively) visually insignificant, which means they leave a slight visual indentation in the edge of the text. However, in other cases —such as with emdashes, they are visually distracting. This is true of double quotation marks. To give an example, "The double quotes hang unnaturally into the margin."

While the hyphens do affect the straightness of the right margin, since we are used to it, it is not usually noticed.

Tehran

Kerned for display use

Tehran is the capital of Iran.
Although many cities have
served as the capital, Tehran
is the most recent.

Tehran

Kerned for text use

*Appropriate kerning is different for display text,
both in terms of overall tightness and in relative
tightness of pairs that need kerns. We see the
space between the 'T' and the 'e' in display as
being too large. At small sizes, the density at
the beginning of the word seems too high.*

Tehran is located in
Tehran province.

*The first example of 'Tehran' in the sentence
above has been treated as in the top version. It is
too tight overall, and the 'Te' is much too tight.*

In most cases, fonts are kerned for text use.

sabon
sabon

*If you are working with a page layout program
such as Quark XPress, you can edit kern pairs
within the program to readjust the pairs. In the
example above, the kerns between the 's' and
'a', and the 'a' and 'b' have been adjusted.*

Hyphenation in display type

Display type (such as titles) generally should avoid hyphenation,
unless there is a good reason for it. Sometimes it may make
sense as a design element but not as normal practice. If a
hyphen is necessary with a long word, it should break in the
most logical place, e.g. typo-graphic.

KERNING

Kerning is most relevant in display type. In the days before computer fonts, text type was unkerned, unless two characters were cast on a single sort, or part of a letter extended beyond its sort. Today, more problems are caused than solved by designers adjusting the kerning. This often seems to be due to a designer focusing on a single pair of letters. *It is impossible to correctly kern by looking at only two letters in a word.* A group of three letters need to be looked at when kerning any pair, and then the word looked at as a whole.

The most common problem of kerning in text type is when the foundry has over-kerned, sometimes caused by kerning for a display context, sometime by the tunnel vision of focusing on individual pairs rather than the overall relationships between characters. If the kern pairs have problems, this can be dealt with by using optical kerning if it is available, or even by turning off the kerning, which, while not ideal (because we have become accustomed to some kerning in text), is better than overkerning.

Kerning is more necessary with all capital settings, because the relationship between capital letters is more likely to be awkward. In mixed case settings, the most common problems pairs are between the T, V, W, Y and, depending on the typeface, F and P, and the vowels that often follow them. Other pairs may need slight adjustment, but are unlikely to cause noticeable problems.

Most browsers support the kerning embedded in the font. If you want to refine that, type can be custom kerned in HTML, though it is more difficult than it is in page layout programs. Or kerning can be turned off if that works better, which it might well in text settings.

METRICS KERNING, OPTICAL KERNING, HAND KERNING

Metrics kerning is part of the font software, and is created by the type foundry; in most cases it should be used. Optical kerning is done according to algorithms in software. If the foundry font metrics are not good, as sometimes happens, applying optical kerning will override the kerning decisions of the foundry. Generally, it is only practical to adjust kerning in display type, though if you are using software that allows editing of the kern table, corrections to the metric values can be made. The Stempel Garamond shown here has over 1600 kern pairs, which is more than necessary. Around 500 should be enough; any kerns of less than 5 units can be omitted. Display type is likely to benefit from a designer's fine-tuning, as good kerning will depend on the word and setting.

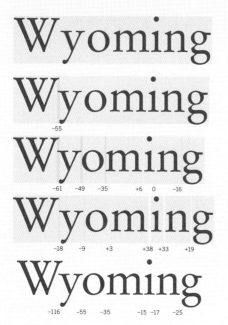

This is Bauer Bodoni with kerning set to 'none'; all the other relationships are defined by the widths assigned to each letter by the founder. These will work for text settings, but clearly, a Wy pair would help

In this word, the only kern pair assigned by the foundry for this typeface is the Wy. The kerning is the same at all sizes. These foundry pairs are what would apply on the Web.

This is Adobe's optical kerning* algorithm applied to 100-point type. It is quite good for display settings, though could benefit from some adjustment.

This is Adobe's optical kerning applied to 8-point type. This looser setting makes sense for smaller settings, but the pair adjustments are more suitable for display settings. It can be useful if the metrics pairs have problems.

This shows type hand kerned for a display setting.

*Adobe optical kerning
Adobe optical kerning sets large type tighter than small type. This generally makes sense, but it can cause problems if the designer is not working at actual size, as in some environmental typography projects, where the design file may be sized at a small percentage of the full-sized project.

An example of when optical kerning is the best choice for text or other non-display type.

TO WAVERLY PLYWOOD PANIC
To Waverly Plywood Panic

This setting is set to 0 kerning. The all caps setting is very awkward, while the mixed case setting has relatively minor problems, the only serious one (in this typeface) is between the T and o. The Wa and Pa could be a problem in some typefaces.

TO WAVERLY PLYWOOD PANIC
To Waverly Plywood Panic

This caps setting with metrics kerning is mostly better than the caps setting above. The mixed case has improved only slightly, and both have become worse than the 0 kerning. The benefits are outweighed by the problem that the 'word space-W' pair is overkerned in the font, making the first two words appear much too close together.

TO WAVERLY PLYWOOD PANIC
To Waverly Plywood Panic

In the optical setting, while the kerning is not perfect The 'ER', 'RL', 'PL' and 'NI' are a bit tight, as are some of the lower-case letters, it is better, because it does some kerning, and most important solves the problem of the 'word space-W' problem in the font metrics.

LEADING AND OTHER ADJUSTMENTS IN DISPLAY TYPE

Display type usually needs less leading than text type, and negative leading often makes sense, especially with caps settings, because they have no descenders (except from punctuation such as commas or from letters such as J or Q that may drop below the baseline).

Pathos Logos Ethos

30 points

30 points

The leading is equal, but the relationship between the ascenders and descenders on the second and third lines makes them seem much tighter. This is an extreme case, but adjustment of leading will often improve stacked display type.

Pathos Logos Ethos

30 points

35 points

The leading looks more even here, even though there are five more points of leading between the second two words. If you just look at the caps, it's clear, but we tend to look at the whole world as a unit.

LOOK, LISTEN, REACT

Very tight leading works for all caps settings, though commas and semicolons, as well as Qs and Js, might need accommodation.

"Can this program fail?"

This setting of display text has one obvious problem: the quotation mark on the left would be better hung in the margin. There are other adjustments that can improve it, which are often neglected. The leading appears to be greater on between the first and second lines the font kerning, while appropriate for text, is uneven in terms of visual relationships between letters, and the word space is also designed for text.

"Can this program fail?"

Hanging the punctuation, adjusting the leading to even the visual effect of ascender/descender relationships, reducing word space, adjusting the tracking and kerning, and setting the quotes separately to adjust the spacing are all things that can make for better display type, and which would never be applied to text type. There is no formula for these adjustments, they need the designer's attention and judgement in each case.

CONCLUSION

Text type and display type need different kinds of attention from the designer and get different kinds of attention from the viewer/reader. Text type requires more attention to the design of the setting such as point size, leading, measure, number of lines and placement on the page; and the adjustment of typographic parameters such as tracking and hyphenation and justification settings, and the shape of a rag in non-justified settings.

Display type should be visually striking, appropriate to the content, and convey the right connotational and expressive effect, as well as being well crafted. Readers should not feel misled: no matter how attractive the type is, if it creates unfulfilled expectations in readers, they are more likely to abandon the text, even if they might read it if properly prepared by their initial perception. Type designer Steve Matteson once wrote 'Type is the clothes that words wear.' We might add, 'Display type and layout are the clothes that text type wears.'

Both text and display type need craft, though the craft is of different kinds. With text type, the craft is setting up systems that work in terms of appropriateness to content and readability, looking carefully at the type, and ensuring that details are correct.

With display type, the craft is in thinking about what you want to accomplish, making decisions that will work with the content and reader, and paying attention to its visual aspects. It should work well compositionally (which might include adjusting leading line by line), have good optical spacing, and, of course, be a typeface that works conceptually and aesthetically with the content and the rest of the design.

······································

Emdashes or endashes

Endashes are used for ranges of numbers in text, and as what we might call functional emdashes, with spaces around them, particularly in the UK. Emdashes in some typefaces are an em long, that is to say, they are 12 points long in 12-point type; others, particularly in more contemporary or informal typefaces, are shorter.

I think so—I'm not sure.

I think so—I'm not sure.

I think so — I'm not sure.

The Caslon at top has a traditional emdash, the same length as the point size. The Warnock emdash in the middle example is shorter. The Futura Condensed emdash at the bottom is even shorter. A dash as long as a traditional font em would look very long when set with a condensed typeface.

CATCHING ERRORS

Your job probably doesn't include catching editorial errors, but if you do, it will enhance your reputation for quality design work, even though it doesn't really have much to do with design.

Typographic principles are essentially the same in all media. However, the way users interact with or experience type on screen is different than on paper, and the organizational structures are potentially more complex on screen, as organization is not usually linear but divergent. There are also possibilities on screen for changing colours, positions, shapes and interactions. Screen designers must consider the different contexts in which type appears, as typographic design adapts to different screen sizes and formats.

Type on screen

Just as printed typography is a technological extension of hand-writing, screen typography is a technological extension of printing. Although the screen has added possibilities and differences in the way type is organized and presented, the principles and experience of actually reading text and the aesthetics of typography are largely the same in both media. This is why the conventions of print are often referred to in discussions of screen typography.

Even before the internet and other screen media were added to communication design options, there were many decisions involved in deciding what form a typographic project should take. Should a print design use letterpress, offset lithography or rotogravure? Should flexography or silk-screen be used for printing on object surfaces? Which materials should be used for type for architectural and signage applications? These were the kinds of questions that needed, and continue to need, consideration in the context of the intended purpose of the typographic communication. Technology and the Internet have added more options to the possibilities for communication. Each technology has its own typographic limitations and possibilities.

A web designer has to be willing to accept, challenge and manipulate the constraints of the Web.

Mark Boulton, *Designing for the Web*

antialiasing
antialiasing

Antialiasing gives the impression of higher resolution than the actual resolution by using grey or coloured subpixels (there are three coloured RGB subpixels per screen pixel) to smooth the representation of angled lines on a vertical/horizontal grid. As you can see, this is needed more on angled or italic type. It becomes less important the higher the resolution of the screen.

. . . .

Hinting

Hinting is part of font software that regularizes pixels to improve type rasterization at low resolutions. High-resolution screens and anti-aliasing have reduced the importance of this. It still applies to small type on laser printers.

hinting

No hinting: every pixel touched by the red outline representing the shape of the font is turned on.

hinting

Hinted: stems and serifs are adjusted to improve the regularity and the weight.

hinting

Hinted: italic doesn't align as well with the vertical and horizontal grid, even when hinted.

TYPE ON SCREEN

This chapter does not address how to code HTML, JavaScript, Java or other coding that is relevant to screen typography. It does discuss what can be done with CSS and what makes for good typographic practice when designing for screen.

The limitations of typography on screen were significant in the past. Until twenty years ago, television screens had an image of around 600 horizontal scan lines. Early Macintoshes had black-and-white monitors (with no greyscale and thus no antialiasing) with a resolution of 512 x 342 pixels, and 72 pixels per inch.

Resolution and colour limitations have largely disappeared because of improvements in screens; limitations on typographic form also have disappeared or are disappearing.

There are websites that refer to traditional print typography, or to Robert Bringhurst's print-oriented *Elements of Typographic Style*, and hold them up as models for type on the Web. Still, while reading on screen has a lot in common with other forms of reading, there are differences. These are in the visual character of the screen, in navigation and access to other sites and type, and in the culture of how readers use the internet.

Although the amount of non-screen type is increasing in the public environment (more architecture, vehicles and public furniture have surfaces that carry typographic content), screens, both public and private, are the main means by which we are exposed to the typography of information, commercial, opinion and other communication content.

Most people get increasing amounts of their exposure to type on screens, and decreasing exposure to type in print. This trend will continue. So unless a designer makes the economically challenging choice to focus on print in their practice, that designer will increasingly be asked to design more for screens, and less for print and other physical applications.

ontology recapitulates phylogeny
ontology recapitulates phylogeny

On the top is a hinted typeface, on the bottom an unhinted typeface, both displayed at text size on a PDF on screen. In the unhinted type, the base line and x-height vary, and the 'a' has almost lost its aperture.

Some aspects of typography, particularly those that relate to the human eye and, to a lesser but significant extent, those of reading culture, are essentially the same in print as on screen. Other aspects, such as possibilities of organization and motion and user control of the typographical experience are different, with many more options than physical type. Scrolling and clicking are very different from the individual presentation of the page spread in book form; and the possibilities for instant navigation of typographic content are much greater for the screen. Nevertheless, screen navigation elements are conceptually similar to print structures.

MUTABILITY

Perhaps the biggest difference between print and screen typography is mutability. Even the most ephemeral print is more permanent than a web page. To look at it one way, a web page is replaced 70 times a seconds or whatever your screens refresh rate is. This means that video and animation is possible. Content can be, and often is, changed several times in a day. It also means that the importance of typographic error is less. Putting up pages with typos is still not a good idea, but can at least be rectified with no significant cost. Websites are updated, sometimes by their authors, sometimes by other websites, sometimes by data which may come from users or things such as RSS feeds.

Typographic content becomes unpredictable. In these cases, as with responsive design, typographic design becomes anticipatory, the rough equivalent of using 'lorem ipsum' text for print design in cases in which the text for a print design is not yet available, or akin to designing for a book series for which some of the content may not yet have been written.

SCREEN TECHNOLOGY

The light emitting nature of screens also affects the typography. Type on LED pixel boards and seven-segment displays, whether LED or liquid crystal, continue to provide a significant amount of our typographical experience. These offer little opportunity for typographic craft, except perhaps as inspiration. However, the increasing resolution of screens, at lower costs, suggests that these displays will be increasingly rare.

Typography on early screens

The Mac Classic had 72 dpi and could show only black-and-white pixels so antialiasing was not possible.

Twenty-four and 12-point type at actual size as they would appear on an early desktop computer display.

Das Kabinett des Dr. Caligari, *Robert Wiene, 1919. An early example of motion typography.*

At the time of writing, resolutions of over 200 device pixels per inch are not uncommon, and antialiasing and subpixel rendering make these resolutions perceptually better than a 600 dpi printer. Ironically perhaps, hinting, which used to be most important in the rasterizing of linearly described forms on coarse screen resolutions, is now more important in laser printing, as 600 dpi laser prints are usually (large public displays aside) the lowest resolution that we regularly encounter now. As screen displays usually antialias type, the laser printer, which only prints solid colour, is usually the lowest effective resolution of type that we encounter.

> Users don't read web pages, they scan. Scanning means they only stop to read when something catches their eye.
>
> Nick Babich

AUTO KERNING ON THE WEB: NORMAL, AUTO OR NONE

Currently, most web browsers default kerning to 'auto', which enables whatever kerning is embedded in the font file, so is the same as 'normal'. In the past, 'auto' used kerns for larger type and disabled it for smaller (usually 20 pixels or less) to reduce processing time. Although 'none' was used for greater speed, it sometimes works better for text type.

```
font-kerning: auto; // default
font-kerning: normal; // enables
kerning
font-kerning: none; // disables
kerning
```

Subpixel rendering

Pixels on current screens are composed of three coloured pixels (RGB). By using them, programmers can render type at an apparently higher resolution than the pixels per inch of the screen. ClearType screen rendering technology uses this strategy.

Type size, device pixels and CSS pixels

A device pixel is not the same thing as a CSS pixel, a relative unit that can be thought of as roughly $\frac{1}{96}$ of an inch (.26 mm) as seen from 28 inches (71 cm), which is a 'standard' viewing distance. Points in print are approximately $\frac{1}{72}$ of an inch, so the equivalent of 12-point type is about 16-pixel type. As a result, type will appear the same size on different resolution screens. In practice, people read print and desktop screens at an average distance of about 40 cm. However, people tend to hold handheld devices closer to their faces (an average of 32 cm, according to a study published in the journal *Optometry and Vision Science*) when they are looking at websites. So type on devices can be considerably smaller than on larger screens.

INTERACTION

Interaction in print involves things like turning pages, using tables of content and indexes, and we may, by following a reference by looking at a different document, in effect follow a link. The Web allows users to move effortlessly from one document to another. This gives the user more freedom, but makes it easier to abandon a page.

Interaction makes the designer's job more challenging. In addition to the basic typographic decisions, there are additional layers that have to be dealt with. More complex structures, rollovers, hover states, and responsive features mean that more decision have to be made, both on the large scale of page appearance and navigation structure, and on the detail level, such as the size and treatment of buttons, links, the size of rollovers, etc.

FORM

In terms of typographic form, a way to think about type in print and type on screen is that print type is static, while screen type is liquid. The parameters you set for characters and words will be affected by the style sheet containers that hold them, which in turn are affected by the medium on which they are seen. Good screen typography often consists of anticipating how type will work in the containers that hold it.

Users also have explicit control over typographic form. They can resize windows, magnify the screen or decide which screen to view it on.

Interactive screens have also changed the way that people deal with type on screen, as they can easily zoom in and out while looking at a page. This suggests that in the context of devices, the relative size of type forms becomes less important, as the user is not constrained to a 'distance' from the type but instead can virtually move towards and away from it.

The internet both invites user-led digression, and makes that digression easy, leading users to create their own relationships between different texts.

Users may choose other pages within the site, links to other sites, or different sites found by using a search engine, from which they may or may not return. Long and continuous reading is much less common on the screen than it has been, and continues to be, in books.

DIFFERENCES BETWEEN SCREEN AND PRINT

A typeface that would work for a project in print might not work well for the same project on screen. If the project will exist in both media, this bears thinking about. How text type renders on screen may be a reason for choosing or avoiding a typeface in print.

Testing a setting of type on different browsers and systems is the best way to find out, though there are web-based services that will let you emulate this. (Type can appear differently on os x and Windows machines even using the same browser.) Typefaces with thin strokes may suffer when the light coming from the screen overpowers the letterforms. Display type, while its form is more

The F and Z patterns

F PATTERN

Research done by the Neilsen Norman group and others using English language websites shows that with dense content, users tend to look at the site in an F pattern, first scanning horizontally, usually across the upper part of the content area. This initial scan forms the F's top bar.

Next, users move down the page and then read across in a second horizontal movement that tends to extend less to the right, forming the F's lower bar.

Next, users vertically scan the content's left side from top to bottom. This last motion forms the F's stem.

Z PATTERN

Pages that have less dense information are looked at in a faster Z pattern. First the eye scans horizontally, then diagonally to bottom left of the screen, and then across the bottom.

Any content that catches the user's interest will alter these movements.

CSS VIEW WIDTH

Setting type sizes as a percentage of view width will (mostly) retain line breaks and rags, but will result in type that is very small on narrow screens, and too large on wide screens. However, combining this approach with media query break-points can help give more control over typography.

Arial

Tahoma

Trebuchet

Verdana

Courier

Georgia

Times

Comic Sans

Impact

The faces above are installed on almost every desktop computer. For this reason, a few of them are still often used in CSS font stacks. Before web fonts, they were the only safe choices for designers, so almost all text for websites was chosen from this list.

FLASH OF UNSTYLED TEXT (FOUT)

Type on a web page may appear for a moment as a system font, such as one of the typefaces above, while a web font is loading, causing a 'Flash of Unstyled Text'. This can be changed by hiding the type until the typeface loads, giving a 'Flash of Invisible Text' (FOIT), Both are minor but annoying problems that can be mitigated using tools such as the Google Fonts Web Font Loader. The viewer won't get a FOUT if you choose from one of the fonts above, but most designers would agree that such a drastic action isn't worth it.

---

or less the same on screen as it is in print, will have a different aesthetic effect at different sizes, and in different relationships with other page elements in responsive type applications, suggesting that in responsive designs, different typefaces (or versions of typefaces) should be considered for different contexts (see page 225).

The basic ways that people read on screen are, in terms of culture and biology, the same as they are for reading type on printed surfaces, but the differences between the media mean that some behavioural and visual aspects are different (i.e. scrolling and light-emitting rather than page-turning and reflective).

Although the possibilities of the appearance and movement of type are well recognized, text type on screen gets less attention and tends to be conservative. Conventions such as using line spaces to indicate paragraphs and using 16-pixel type for text are usually adhered to. These conventions should be recognized, but shouldn't be accepted as rules. Text type needs the same attention as other aspects of website design.

Typographers might prefer to avoid layouts that allow the number of characters per line to change, because they take typographic control away. However, effective use of CSS media queries can address at least some of the potential problems with a liquid layout, by changing the type face and other specifications to work better in different situations.

Type and design
Type and design

Individual pair kerning is possible, though awkward, using CSS. The top version uses only the CSS font-kerning property, which accesses the kerning information in the font. The version on the bottom is kerned individually using the CSS letter-space property as shown here:

```
<span style="letter-spacing: -.15em">T</span>ype
<span style="letter-spacing: -.03em">a</span>
<span style="letter-spacing: -.04em">nd</span>
<span style="letter-spacing: -.04em">d</span>es
<span style="letter-spacing: -.04em">i</span>gn
```

As you can see, this is more difficult than visual kerning, as you must make adjustments, then refresh a browser to see the effect. There are JavaScript tools available which can help with this

WEB FONTS

One of the most significant developments in web typography is the availability of web fonts. In the early days of the internet, any fonts used on websites had to be installed on the computer of the user, so unless type appeared as a graphic, for designers to be sure that it would display properly on a user's computer, they had to use one of the typefaces listed on the previous page.

With web-based fonts being supported by all major browsers and offered by large and small type foundries, and with the establishment of paid services, such as Adobe Fonts and Fontstand, and free ones, such as Google fonts, there is a now a wide choice of typefaces for use on the Web.

Not all web (or print) typefaces are good. They may have problems of letterform design, or technical problems such as rendering badly at small sizes or on small screens due to lack of hinting or other technical shortcoming, or bad spacing or kerning. These kinds of problems are difficult to predict without testing, especially if you are designing for screen. As with print, this suggests choosing typefaces that you already know work well, particularly for text.

Type size choices are affected by the context. (Perhaps obviously, small screens and pages suggest smaller type. Less obviously, larger screens and pages suggest larger type.) Size of page is not the only factor; the distance of the viewer's eye from the text varies with the medium, as people look at screens from varying distances. Some screens have higher resolutions than others, which also influences the practical minimum size of type. As screen resolutions improve, this becomes less of a concern, with users' vision often being the limiting factor.

PROS AND CONS OF SCREEN TYPOGRAPHY

There are attributes of screen typography that are inherent in the medium. Some of them are, from a design point of view, negative. There are restrictions and compromises compared to the print environment, and there is an absence of opportunity for the material choices that can enrich printed or other physical typography. Designers, especially those from a print background, can find the relative lack of control of type frustrating.

TESTING TYPE ON BROWSERS

Type that looks good on an Apple device may look significantly different on a Windows or Android device. So testing is important. Even if there are no obvious problems with the layout, how the type details work on different systems, browsers and devices should be looked at carefully. Web-based browser testers, both paid and free, are a good (and fast) basic way to test how your type will work in different environments, though seeing type on a desktop screen is not the same as seeing it on a device in your hand.

Characteristics of web type

1 Preserves semantic structure (text is not only graphic, but can be used by search engines, e-readers, etc.)

2 Hypertextual: text can be an active link to other text.

3 Text is not static, but is treated more as a liquid poured into containers of variable form.

4 Text can move and be interactive.

The original responsive design

The early Web was responsive in a sense: the text would reflow to fit the window. This lets type fill any width of window, but it doesn't make for good typography or design, as leading and type size remain the same. This would be rarely seen these days, except for the fact that the very popular Wikipedia still uses this model.

Typography goes deeper than how something looks, it is how information is structured, it is how information in understood, it is how words and language is conveyed.

Mark Boulton

Typography reacts to the users

Survey graphics, such as pie charts, typically reflect the choices of the users who respond to the survey. Followed links typically have a typographic difference from unfollowed links. Using this affordance of the Web can suggest interesting typographic design possibilities.

On the other hand, there are also possibilities and potentials in screen typography that let you do things that are impossible in print. More complex hierarchies, motion typography, the ability to scale type to user preferences, the potential for making documents more accessible, and the ability to make type reactive and interactive make screen typography interesting and challenging. The traditional linear structures of printed material have, on screen, become, for better or worse, complex networks.

There are other things to consider when comparing print and screen. A page with a lot of white space that would work in print may be overpowering on a light-emitting screen or have too much contrast between the type and the background. Some conventions that are accepted in print are not accepted on screen, and vice versa.

In many cases, a typographic design must be adapted to many media. The content of a website will be seen in various formats for mobile devices, laptops, desktops and, perhaps, print.

Responsive design approaches

The variation in screen sizes used has led to different philosophies of design for screen: responsive design (designing in such a way that a website works well on all media platforms), progressive enhancement (designing the website so it works at a basic level on small screens, with enhanced features that work on large screens), and finally, mobile-first (which suggests that the site be designed first for small screens, and that this be used as a basis for larger screens). In practice, these different philosophies produce similar results.

Type on screen is more in the control of the user than print type is. The user can change the size, adjust contrast or brightness, window size, or on devices, change the format. Type on the internet also has unique interaction possibilities. For example, clicked-on links can create an index of the pages that have been visited.

Going beyond this, type can react to a user or users, as mouse clicks can change the size, opacity or location of type, making the user even more a collaborator in the typographic design.

COLOUR AND MOTION

In print, colour costs money, and motion is impossible. Beyond the labour of designing and production, it is easy and costless to put complex graphics and motion on screen. There is a temptation to use these even when they don't contribute to the communication or add to the user's experience.

Because colour and images are so common on screen, using fewer colours and avoiding unnecessary graphics is worth considering to make your work more original and effective. In a context where colour, particularly, so widely used, a minimalist one- or two-colour (for example) website can stand out in contrast to pages competing for the reader's interest.

The same applies to motion; using too much motion is distracting, and devalues its worth.

CHANGES IN SCREEN TECHNOLOGY

As screen technology and resolutions improve, the task of choosing typefaces for screen display and choosing for traditional paper printing have become more similar. Type on screen now looks comparable on type in print. This means that print and screen designs can more easily have a common aesthetic. Type foundries spend increasing attention on developing fonts for screens.

With differences between screen sizes, CSS can be used to adjust typography to the screen, so we can not only do such expected things as change a layout from one to more columns, depending on the width of the screen. We can also change the leading depending on the number of characters likely to be on a screen, or change a typeface that works well at a large size on large screens, to another that works better at a smaller size on smaller screens.

ELECTRONIC PUBLICATION FONTS

Historically, fonts were designed differently for small sizes than they were for large sizes. The advent of versions of fonts designed for screen use has reproduced this approach. These have been around for a while. Minion Web, for example, was issued as part of the Minion family in the 1990s. However, fonts designed specifically for screen use are becoming more common.

....

'Mobile first' vs 'graceful degradation'

Because websites may be seen on everything between a large desktop screen and the smallest phone screen, responsive web typography has to work on a range of screen sizes. The 'mobile first' approach involves designing for the smallest format first, on a simple grid, then adjusting and adding structural complexity when the site is seen on a larger screen.

'Graceful degradation' starts with the largest and more complex format, and then simplifies the grid and other features at smaller sizes.

Because of the proliferation of handheld devices, the mobile first approach has become more popular.

Typefaces
Typefaces

The top is an image of Font Bureau's Benton Modern, the bottom is Benton Modern RE, which is designed for screen use at text sizes. Somewhat ironically, this 'new' development is similar to the historical approach that was common before the computer: making different drawings for typefaces used at different sizes.

SCREENS

Personal computers have light emitting screens. Electronic paper displays, such as are used by e-readers, are like black ink on paper: they are reflective rather than light-emitting. With sufficient resolution, the visual experience (if not the auditory, tactile and olfactory experience) of reading electronic paper could be more or less identical with reading printed paper.

If you watch people reading print, or text on a handheld device, you will see that many will adjust the distance from which they read according to the size of the type. On the desktop computer or laptop, users tend to look at the screen from a certain distance, and are more likely to change the size of the type, if necessary, than move nearer to or farther from it.

COLOURED WORDS FOR EMPHASIS

Setting some words in type of a different colour might work in a print job, but doing the same thing with a web design isn't a good idea, because readers will assume that the coloured text is a link and click on it.

Halation makes light type on a dark background harder to read.

This reproduces the halation effect (meaning that the type acquires a halo of light) that occurs with bright white letters on a dark background. More leading and letterspacing can help reduce the problem, as can choosing a sturdy typeface, such as the Plantin shown here.

Light emitting screens

Most computers, tablets and phones depend on emitted light. A white reflective page (such as paper or high-contrast electronic paper) with a light text (such as Baskerville) may work well. The same setting on a large computer monitor is likely to result in an overpowering white field, with the type disappearing in the glare.

Bolder typefaces without very thin strokes work better on light-emitting screens, especially at small sizes. This is true whether the design uses dark type on a light background or light type on a dark background.

Dark text on a light background is better in most circumstances. The screen is light, so the user's pupils are somewhat smaller. With a black screen, little light is being emitted, so the white text is bright and dazzling, and the user experiences a halo around it.

The exceptions are things like instrumentation in a dark environment, where, for the same reason, a bright screen will temporarily impair night vision. If light type is on a dark background, the type can be letterspaced and made grey to reduce the dazzle.

All other things being equal, sans serif faces will be more likely to work well on screen (their vertical strokes also line up better with the screen pixel grid), and their strokes are all substantial. Even bold serif typefaces often have very thin strokes as part of their structure (see page 169).

However, type foundries are starting to make versions of fonts designed specifically for screen, which are very similar in relative appearance to the small cuts of typefaces of the pre-computer era. Such typefaces are likely to work better at small sizes, including in print environments.

TYPE ON HANDHELD DEVICES AND TABLETS

Device screens are a case of an environment in which type is by necessity small, and this is where the traditional characteristics of small type become valuable. Larger x-heights and relative re-duction of the contrast of thick and thin strokes (in serif faces) and the increased spacing all work to make smaller type more legible and readable. The increasingly high resolution of small screens means that the limit to minimum typographic size is often the user's vision rather than screen resolution.

TYPOGRAPHIC NAVIGATION

The design of navigation of a complex website is a complex prob-lem. You might not think of this as being typography as much as information design. However, just as in print design, the navi-gation of complex information is both the responsibility of the designer, and depends on the organization and typographic treat-ment of navigational information. Because screen design permits hierarchical design and layered information, accessed by links, navigational typography is more complex and difficult to achieve effectively. Many websites, particularly complex ones, don't manage this well from a user point of view: it can be difficult or frustrating to find the specific page or information you want. Typographic navigation on screen needs more attention than is generally given, and testing typographic design structures with users is likely to significantly improve the experience of navigating a site.

....

Symbols, icons, indices

These categories are generally associated with the work of the semiotician Charles Peirce.

A symbol is something that we agree means something. It has no actual relationship with what it represents. An example is the 'eject' symbol: ⏏

An icon is an image of what it represents. An example is the 'speaker' icon: 🔊

An index is an image of something that is associated with what it represents, like the rhetorical device of metonymy. An example is the gear graphic, meaning 'settings': ⚙

....

States

Hover and mouse-click states are a useful tool for guiding the increased structural complexity of the internet and in appli-cation design, as well as being a common interactive experience on websites. Although colour is the most common way of using states to indicate clicked links, hover states can also be used to give more typographic information. Anything possible on the computer is an option for mouseover states, including sound as well as text.

WEBSITE STRUCTURES

Websites allow for more complex organizational structures than books, which is both an asset and a liability. The structure can allow for much more complex navigation, but can also make it difficult to find specific information on a given page. The fact that there can be links between pages at the same level, or between levels above or below, increases the options as well as the potential difficulties.

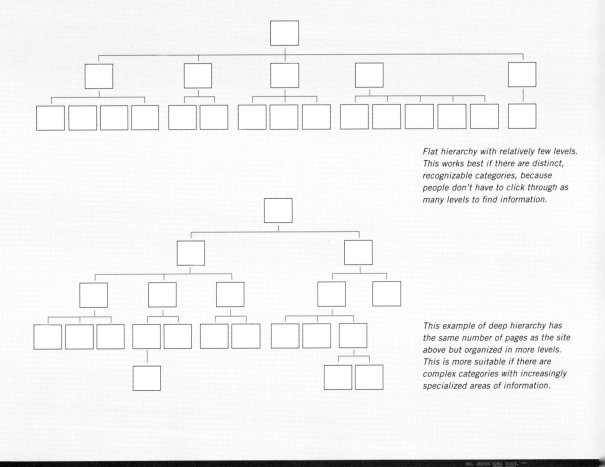

Flat hierarchy with relatively few levels. This works best if there are distinct, recognizable categories, because people don't have to click through as many levels to find information.

This example of deep hierarchy has the same number of pages as the site above but organized in more levels. This is more suitable if there are complex categories with increasingly specialized areas of information.

The archaic structure of the horizontal scroll (though with navigation links to different parts of the single page) is just one of the structural possibilities of a website.

Menus are the initial orienting structure for most interactive sites. They are usually typographic and, on some websites, may be offered in various languages from which users can choose their preference. This is most commonly seen in non-English sites, where there is a greater awareness of linguistic diversity. (This is relatively simple if the scripts are of the left-to-right traditions, more complex if including Arabic, Hebrew or one of the other right-to-left scripts.) The development of widely understood logographic icons for navigation suits the international nature of the Web, as well as saving screen space, something that is particularly valuable on small screens.

SITE STRUCTURES

While websites have largely supplanted books and printed matter as sources of typographic information, there are many structural similarities as well as differences, and traditional forms are reflected on the Web both literally and metaphorically.

Typographically, the physical book form we have used traditionally (the 'codex') is essentially linear (if not as linear as a scroll or 'rotulus' as the Romans called the scroll form of the book), though books are not necessarily used in a linear way. With the exception of reference books, or collections of essays, the implied structure of a book in the Western tradition is that one starts with the fore-edge on the right, then turns pages until one reaches the end, with the fore-edge on the left.

Screen affordances

The screen enables juxtaposition of structures that in the past were separate. For example, the scrolling page usually has fixed navigation and search elements, analogous to having a copy of the table of contents and index on every page of a book.

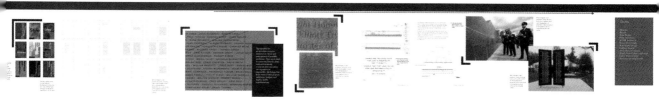

Electronic writing is a
radically unstable and
impermanent form, a form
in which the text exists
only only from moment to
moment. The reader joins
with the author in building
the text.

David Jury, *About Face*

Like websites, books and their pages are often organized by subject (in parts and chapters) and can be navigated (if they are not intended to be read continuously from beginning to end) by general topic or other division (in the table of contents) or by specific topic organized alphabetically (if the book has an index).

Websites can have links that connect both horizontally and vertically within the site, or with other sites or specific pages of other sites. Although linear in their physical organization, books may have a largely hierarchic content structure. Technical and reference books are good examples; we do not normally read them from beginning to end. Instead, we navigate to the part that we are interested in. A website (or interactive PDF) is able to organize this kind of information more easily than a printed book, because it is easier to click on a link than turn to a page, and search fields can be used to find a topic more easily than an index can.

PIXELS, EMS AND REMS

Control of size of type and other typographic measurements in HTML/CSS can be done in three ways.

PIXELS are relative to the screen. Using them gives the designer more typographic control but makes the website less accessible, as type specified in pixels overrides user-set browser preferences.

EMS are calculated from the parent size of type in a div. This can be confusing, because if a div specifies 2-em type as the basic size, that size becomes the em, so then if a child (e.g. the leading) of that is specified at 2 ems, it will be actually be 4 ems.

REMS (or 'root ems') are based on the root element type size, so are always the same size in a way that ems are not. A few old browser versions may not support them.

Icons

Icons offer an opportunity to create typographic ideograms. Though we generally use the word 'icon', they are often more specifically indices or symbols (see page 221). Simplifying and abstracting works best, mostly because icons are small, so complex images don't work well. Icons are more efficient in terms of space used than descriptive words (so very useful for devices), and, if well designed, also result in navigation that is less 'English-centric', something that is important for websites that may be viewed from anywhere in the world.

Websites *can* be linear, the way a book is. However, they seldom are. There are more possible ways to organize a website than there are a printed document, which is why we have to spend a considerable amount of time on the design of the logical structure of any complex website, as well as its look and feel.

This might seem to be getting away from typography, but it is not: however the site is organized, both the navigation itself, as well as the text, is communicated typographically.

RESPONSIVE TYPOGRAPHY

Although type will appear differently on different screens, the use of media queries and breakpoints means we can use typographic principles to adjust the type elements for different screens and aspect ratios. Because a limiting factor for legibility is size, text is necessarily relatively bigger on small screens, leaving less space available for image and white space.

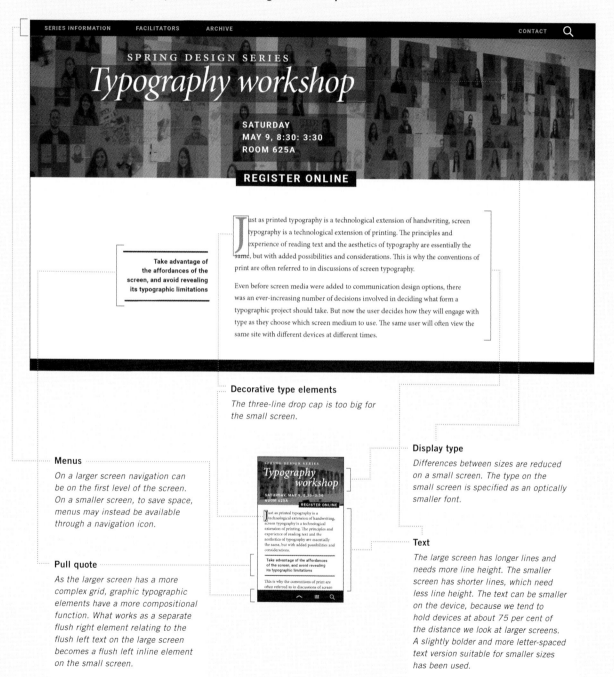

Decorative type elements

The three-line drop cap is too big for the small screen.

Menus

On a larger screen navigation can be on the first level of the screen. On a smaller screen, to save space, menus may instead be available through a navigation icon.

Pull quote

As the larger screen has a more complex grid, graphic typographic elements have a more compositional function. What works as a separate flush right element relating to the flush left text on the large screen becomes a flush left inline element on the small screen.

Display type

Differences between sizes are reduced on a small screen. The type on the small screen is specified as an optically smaller font.

Text

The large screen has longer lines and needs more line height. The smaller screen has shorter lines, which need less line height. The text can be smaller on the device, because we tend to hold devices at about 75 per cent of the distance we look at larger screens. A slightly bolder and more letter-spaced text version suitable for smaller sizes has been used.

Just as scribes, printers and designers incorporated new printing technologies and methods into their work over the centuries, the designer, now directly responsible for typography, must be familiar with the different and evolving ways of creating, executing and presenting typographic form. The codex that we use today was a technological advance over the scroll that had been used up until that point.

Just as the codex allowed random access to the reader, as it could be opened at any page, instead of having to roll all the way through a scroll to get to a particular point, leading to the development of the table of contents and the index, the navigation of websites also invites (or demands) different ways of navigating. It also enables them, allowing links to pages within or outside the site and being able to present live data from elsewhere.

RESPONSIVE TYPOGRAPHY

One of the most interesting, and frustrating, parts of responsive design is the quality of typography. If the same content is set differently as far as characters per line go, as type reflows to the viewport width, the kind of adjustments we might make to the rag in print typography will be useless. Trying to set up good justification parameters or a better rag on screen will be wasted. Lack of fine control over type makes consistent good rags and good justified type on Web pages almost impossible anyway.

Tools that address some of these will no doubt arrive in the near future. For now, css media queries and breakpoints can address many other aspects of responsive typography and make overall typography good, if not always great. Typographic specifications that we can adjust to better suit different screen sizes are:

- Font
- Size
- Leading (or line height)
- Tracking
- Alignment
- In some cases, kerning, as larger display type may suggest different kerning relationships than smaller display settings.

LINE BREAKS IN DISPLAY TYPE

Responsive type can lead to bad breaks at some screen widths. This can be addressed with spans (breaking the head into two blocks) or media queries (to manage the width so the line never breaks with the 'it' on a separate line). One simple approach is to use a non-breaking word space.

How to design it

This head works fine unless it breaks.

How to design it

Responsive websites can lead to settings like the one above.

How to design it

In this case, putting a non-breaking word space between 'design' and 'it' makes both words come down if the container gets too narrow for the whole head.

Reading responsive typography is more or less the same as reading anything else. What is different is that we have to anticipate, rather than specify, the way type will look and work in different contexts. Defining good typographic parameters is possible: perfect line-by-line typography is not.

MOTION TYPOGRAPHY

Motion typography (or kinetic typography) is found on everything from animated web banners to film titles. Although type on screen is usually static, the typographic designer's practice may include, or possibly be largely made up of, motion graphics. The use of JavaScript and HTML5 has led to at least some typographic motion on many websites. Although the basic principles are the same as static type, the designer can use motion typography to move from illegibility to legibility and back, to control pacing and information hierarchies, and to add an expressive dimension to typography with the basic tools of opacity, directional movement, change in size and colour, and relationships between letterforms, as well as using software filters that allow particular effects.

Much of graphic design has a narrative aspect, whether literal or implied, and motion typography, whether alone or in relation to image, lends itself to the development of compelling narrative.

There are really only five basic parameters, though they can be further broken down, or combined. You can move type, change the size, change the orientation of letters and words, change the form of letters or words, assemble or disassemble, and change opacity, colour or other visual property.

Things like easing (the rate at which movements accelerate or decelerate) and the particular motion or visual effect that you assign to letters or words can make the difference between great and not-so-great work. Pace is one of the most important aspects of motion typography. There is a tendency to pace typography too quickly, as in the process of design, the designer becomes very familiar with the material, so tends to hurry it along. Reading text typography aloud as it appears on screen is helpful to put oneself into the position of the viewer. Getting feedback from others helps with this.

Effective motion typography is often dependent on its relationship to the physics of actual motion. Smooth acceleration is a factor in creating 'realistic' movement.

POSSIBILITIES OF MOTION TYPOGRAPHY

These are the basic possibilities for motion typography. Any one of them can be done in an infinite number of ways. Generally, though, a simpler approach will be more effective for communication; too much movement and too many visual effects, like static typography, will distract from communication.

CHANGE IN SIZE three dimensions, approaching, vanishing, threatening

MOVING two dimensions, passing, narrative, anticipation

CHANGE IN ORGANIZATION movement, creates/resolves tension, involves viewer

 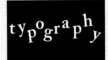 

OPACITY / COLOUR revealing, drawing attention

BROKEN / SEPARATED LETTERFORMS

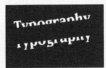  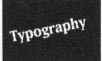

ADDITIVE movement, narrative, active

 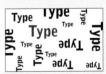

THREE-DIMENSIONAL ROTATION OF TWO DIMENSIONS movement, depth, revealing

DEGRADING / UPGRADING TYPE implies time, physical processes

It can be tempting to use too many of the features that software offers, something that people new to motion typography tend to do. This doesn't mean that we should avoid anything available to us, but too much visual activity will likely hinder communication and impair the overall experience of the viewer.

Basic typographic principles of contrast apply to motion as well. For example: one typographic element moving on a static background, or vice versa, or one element moving in a different direction from the other elements, will be what the viewer focuses on.

CONCLUSION

The computer screen as a typographic medium is relatively new. For much of the history of the internet, there were few typefaces that could be used (except as graphic images), the low resolution of earlier screens limited how well type could be rendered and there was little control over typographical parameters. The improvements in screen resolution, antialiasing approaches, greater control of typographic detail, and availability of typefaces means that those limitations to typography have disappeared or are disappearing, though control of type's behaviour on screen is still lacking.

The environment of the computer, where it is easier to be distracted, suggest that web typography has more need for points of entry, and that readers are likely to have less patience and be more likely to abandon reading if there are any obstacles or if their interest is not maintained, as something else is only a click away.

On the other hand, the new dimensions of interactive and motion typography have the potential to engage the reader in a way that print can't. Since the purpose of typography, whether in print or onscreen, is usually to communicate content, that engagement must include reading. Engagement with websites is often measured by views and clicks, but without the viewer actually engaging with the typographic content, the website will probably be ineffective.

Today's designer is faced with many more options and possibilities in terms of media and how to use them. Choosing the best options for organizing and presenting typographic content has become a bigger part of the designer's job.

I try to make the type do what it says.

Kyle Cooper, film title sequence designers

MOTION CONTRAST

The principles of contrast work with motion typography; motionless type will stand out if all other typographic elements are moving, and moving type will stand out if the other type is still.

While tradition is a powerful cultural force in typography, new technologies influence and provide new opportunities for typographic exploration. A systematic investigation of what can be done with type can give the designer more ways of creating original typographic treatments. Computers give us more options, and the traditional methods of physical experimentation are still available and can be integrated with new technologies. There are also completely new areas in animated, generative and interactive typography. The computer also offers the opportunity for creative interaction with users and data.

Creative typography

Typography has had a creative and experimental aspect from the beginning. If Gutenberg's experimentation was mainly technical, in order to reproduce a current writing style, by 1500 experimentation with layout had begun. Experimenting with the form of letters themselves didn't really take off until the innovative typefaces of the Industrial Revolution. The integration of type form and layout began in the 20th century, and the computer and graphic software expanded it once again.

Typographic creativity and experimentation can be turned to practical purposes but often begins, at least, as independent practice by designers. These investigations may or may not be developed into usable typography for design applications.

The computer and screen have increased the possibilities and avenues of exploration. Interactivity, both between user and typography, but also between typography and data, has almost unlimited room for exploration.

In terms of form, creative typography is most often useful in display type, where the visual aspect dominates. Experimentation with the visual qualities of text type is worth doing but is unlikely to directly result in improved communication. However, it can move the typographic design discipline forward, in a way that experimenting with the aesthetics of display type is less likely to.

> Proclaiming novelty today can seem like historical ignorance on a designer's part.
>
> Peter Bil'ak, *Experimental typography. Whatever that means.*

. . . .

Experimentation vs research

All the visual resources of the Internet mean that the balance between the primary research of design and secondary visual research skews too far to the latter. We have a huge number of inspiring examples. This can lead to not doing original experimentation and exploration. Using media other than design programs, whether physical or software, is a way to lead ourselves to innovate.

e e e

They clearly have very different aesthetics and potential uses, but the essential topology and orientation of these three 'e's is the same. To work as a typeface, even the most unorthodox of letters has to be recognizable.

𝖀

This A from Fette Fraktur is not recognizable as an A to a modern audience accustomed to Roman type. It shows the dangers of letterforms diverging too much from current practice if they are expected to be read.

APPROACHES ASPECT COMMON COMMUNICATION COMPUTER CREATE **CREATIVE** **DESIGN** DEVELOP **DIFFERENT** DISPLAY DO NOT ENVIRONMENT EXAMPLE **EXPERIMENT** **EXPERIMENTATION** EXPLORATION **FORM** GRAPHIC INTERACTIONS LAYOUT LEAD LETTERS LIKELY **MATERIAL** METHOD ORIGINAL PHYSICAL **POSSIBILITIES PRACTICE** PROCESS PROJECT PURELY RELATIONSHIPS REPRODUCE **RESULT** SKEUOMORPH **SOFTWARE** SOMETHING STYLE **TECHNIQUES TEXT** TREATMENT **TYPE** TYPEFACES **TYPOGRAPHIC** **TYPOGRAPHY** USED VISUAL **WORK**

A word cloud is simple example of the interaction between data and typography. The typeface and relationships are decided by the designer, while the data and algorithms give an unpredictable result. This example shows the most frequent words in this chapter, but could be a constantly changing representation if interpreting data from a website.

The intersections of the dual nature of typography (that is, between aesthetics and communication) show where experimentation can exist. Experimental type for communication makes as much or as little sense as experimental linguistics. In terms of the aesthetics of typography, though, experimental approaches are necessary create work that responds to changing cultures and environments.

Display type usually has to communicate linguistic information, though occasionally may be a purely visual use of letterforms. It often falls somewhere in between, and uses words to both communicate language, and to evoke emotion or other reaction that relates to that language.

So display type is where much of the practical opportunity for typographic creativity lies. This is why posters are such a popular project in design schools, while text design projects are less so. Display type reflects, reproduces and creates culture in the sense of reproducing language but also in the sense of visual culture.

In most cases, the more creative text type is, the less readable it is, even if it might be arguably legible. For example, very large type might be very legible, but will make long text hard to read.

Creative organization of type, type relationships and textual relationships is possible in print, but the natural environment for this is web-based media. Text can be located, parsed, and represented, and users can be invited to participate in its organization and expression.

PRINCIPLES OF CREATIVE TYPOGRAPHY

Where does creative typography reside? Traditionally, in originality of concept, form, medium, composition, treatment and organization. With the web and software systems we can add conceptual and interactive dimension of creativity to those.

Typography creativity is time-consuming, because it involves experimentation, and most experiments don't directly lead to something usable, which is why in design practice it most often is developed outside the time constraints of a project with deadlines. For many, a graphic design education is the only time when typographic experimentation is encouraged for its own sake, outside the necessity of meeting a practical design brief.

A lot can be learned from a 'failed' experiment. It may simply eliminate a direction, or it may lead to another, more successful, approach or method. If you don't experiment, your typography may be well executed but is unlikely to be very original.

Text type in graphic design practice may benefit from a creative approach, if that type is either representing language that is not important, or is provided elsewhere, as graphic designer David Carson showed when he famously set part of an interview for *Ray Gun* magazine in Zapf Dingbats as well as (apparently grudgingly) also setting it more conventionally.

CREATIVE APPROACHES TO TYPOGRAPHY IN PRACTICE

Given that the choices available to a designer are essentially infinite, it is surprising how easy it is to find oneself returning again and again to one particular approach. (This may have the useful result of giving a designer a distinctive typographic style, but may also end up in the designer doing less design, and spending more time adapting a few established design methods and styles to every project, which is not why most of us practice.) Some of this may be due to pressures of time, since systematic experimentation and exploration of various typographical possibilities may not provide a solution to a particular project. Creative exploration does keep you aware of possibilities that might not otherwise occur to you. Finding time for it is what results in design breakthroughs and truly original work.

Keeping records of experiments and the analysis of creative and experimental work helps give designers the kind of creative depth that will enrich both personal and professional practice.

Some common approaches to experimenting with type form are scaling, cropping, projecting, spacing, deconstructing it, layering it or processing it with software. The possibilities are unlimited. Most non-software techniques have been tried before, and software itself tends to reproduce techniques that were developed before computer typography. However, the nice thing about typographic exploration is that any technique you use will probably be different than previous explorations in at least some way, depending

Blending between two typefaces can result in interesting and unexpected results that can be taken further by editing and refining.

FRAGMENT

Experimenting with deconstruction of the forms of letters challenges the norms of typeface design.

Type treatment/hand work. By painting these Helvetica letters very approximately on brick, the typeface becomes more friendly and human.

Detail of Ed Fella event poster, handlettering and pasted-up type, photocopied, 2006, designed by Ed Fella.

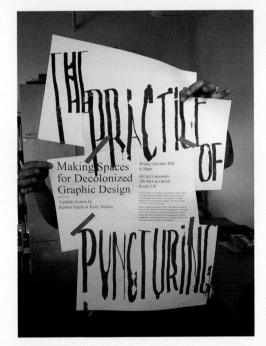

Handlettering and media experimentation can produce pieces that working on the computer alone would never lead to. Eduardo Villar-Martinez.

This poster uses laser printed type distressed with water and physical processes, and composed and scanned back into the computer. Courtesy of Donald Zhu.

on the content and context. Any systematic exploration of different techniques is likely to help make your work original and, with some luck and judgement, excellent.

Avoiding the crowd

Like typefaces themselves, creative techniques come into fashion, then get overused, then become unpopular, then after a time of not being used, are rediscovered and revived. It is more creatively productive to work with typefaces and techniques that are not widely used by contemporaries at any given time.

Creative approaches can be taken to the grid itself. The context of the grid led to many creative approaches by Josef Müller-Brock-mann and other designers of the Swiss style. Giving yourself constraints, such as working within a particular grid, in only one or two colours, or using a single typeface, can lead to creative work that leaving the possibilities completely open would never lead to. Devising unorthodox grids also can lead to interesting work.

Treatment of the type itself can make the difference between a compelling piece and a less compelling piece. Type can be moved from the computer into the environment and back again. This might involve technologies (e.g. photocopying, photography) or human intervention (e.g. tracing, copying, cutting into pieces and recomposing) or using computer coding to create or process typographic form.

EXPERIMENTAL / GENERATIVE / ACCIDENTAL TYPOGRAPHY

There are different kinds of experimentation. Experimentation can be purposeful, if you want to achieve some effect and, not knowing how, you try different methods or media as a way of achieving it. Or it can be purely experimental, when you are just working for your own pleasure, to see what happens.

Almost all typographic design has aspects of experimentation. We try something, then see if it works or not. So design is an editing process: what we choose to develop is a large part of the difference between one designer and another. Giving the same text, grid and typeface to two designers is likely to produce very different results.

technology
technology
technology
technology

Varying treatments of the same typeface, in this case, Adobe Caslon, make a difference to its visual and connotative effect. First, the standard typeface, second, the face run through a roughening filter, third, an autotrace of an image of the type, and fourth, three-point printed on a 600 dpi laser printer.

Working with experimental ways of setting text gives good opportunity for working with composition and exploring ways of questioning or challenging content.

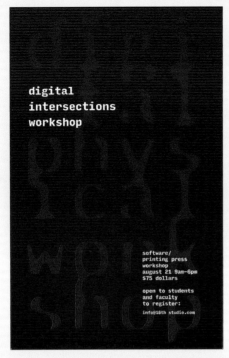

Typography treated with software effects usually
applied to images.

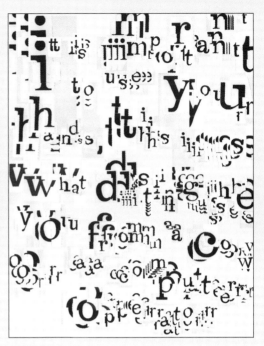

Printing out type on a laser printer, cutting it up and pasting it
down is the basis of this experimental work. The copy says
'It is important to use your hands, this is what distinguishes
you from a computer operator,' paraphrasing Paul Rand.
Courtesy of David Hong.

Augmented reality software lets
designers put typography into the
environment by integrating it with
the camera of a device. Looking at a
scene on a device screen can overlay
a typographic layer.

Exploration of form. Magazine cover, 2018, editing
Persian characters. Courtesy of Kaveh Ashourinia.

In another sense there is something contrary between the word 'design' and 'experimentation'; design by definition has a purpose, and experimental typography is purely exploration. But by no means does this mean we shouldn't experiment as part of our design practice, even if it isn't directly a part of our professional practice (which are not quite the same thing), because if we don't experiment, then we don't come up with something new.

Using computer software filters experimentally can produce interesting work. It might be sneered at by some, but like all design processes, the development of new techniques and work can come from experimentation. The thing to avoid is just being impressed by a mistake, and leaving it at that; it is learning to control and develop what is found out by accident that is worthwhile.

Typography that interacts with RSS feeds or data sets is another avenue for generation of unforeseen typographic results.

CREATIVITY VERSUS NOVELTY

Novelty implies something new. Creativity is something different: as the word suggests, it's created rather than just new. That is not to say that novelty and chance operation may not provide part of, or lead to, a creative typographic approach. The difference is that creativity is intentional, while novelty in itself has no intention.

Much of current typographic practice is carried out on the computer. As a result, getting off the computer can result in original and creative ways of approaching typography both directly, and as a way of inspiring and informing work on the computer. An iteration of a design that incorporates physical iterations of type can have much more presence and visual interest than one entirely executed on computer.

Filippo Marinetti was a pioneer of this kind of practice in the early 20th century, when he used letterpress and photolithography for typographic design. Much of typographic innovation comes from work that investigates form or work that straddles communication and exploration. Kurt Schwitters and other Dada typographers, David Carson, April Greiman, Ed Fella, Marian Bantjes, Si Scott, Elliott Earls and Martin Venezky are examples of practitioners of this kind of hybrid typographic work.

I don't think that type should be expressive at all.

Massimo Vignelli, in *Helvetica*

Experimental type treatment exploring alternatives to stencil letters for use in architectural applications, most often steel.

Software filters offer visual effects, and can also suggest techniques in other media.

Materiality may be actual, as in the case of paper choice, printing and binding techniques, or represented, as when the image of materiality is captured, usually digitally, by means of a camera or scanner. Actual materiality is only possible in physical iterations of design, most commonly with things like books, designed objects or architectural typography.

TECHNIQUES / APPROACHES / OPTIONS

The following pages have suggestions for creative approaches. The examples are by no means exhaustive but show some areas that typographers focus on when experimenting with type. Many of them may intersect or move from one area to another in the process of experimentation. Results that don't work for an intended purpose may well work in another context. Part of good typographic design is recognizing when creative approaches fit with the project, and when they are better saved for a future project.

Neville Brody's Blur is the result of a face being blurred in software, then image traced to create the font outlines

This piece is the result of projecting typography onto dancers and recording the result.
Courtesy of Magdalena Vasko.

EXPERIMENTAL LAYOUT

Although typographic practice depends on conventions that make communication of language possible, typography can critique texts rather than simply presenting them as effectively as possible, the usual (and expected) function of graphic design. The relationships between typographic elements can comment on, subvert or question content. In even the most functional design, structural and navigational elements such as table of contents or running feet can be treated with more latitude, and relationships between text and supporting elements, such as footnotes or commentary, can be designed in unorthodox ways without negatively affecting the main text.

TYPE FORM

We tend to accept type form as given, but there is opportunity to challenge those forms, whether through creation of new forms or by altering or manipulating them either physically or on the computer. They can be altered into forms that challenge the viewer, or take a principle and explore it or push it farther. Typefaces such as Thomas Huot-Marchand's Minuscule (see page 243 or Peter Bil'ak and Pieter van Rosmalen's Karloff are examples of this.

SOFTWARE TYPE TREATMENT

Type treatment may be related to form. Neville Brody's 1991 typeface Blur is a case of treatment (blurring) leading, via autotracing, to a different visual form, in this case, moving from a vector font, to a bitmap form, then reinterpreted back to a vector font. Such approaches may be purely experimental or may be deliberately used to create a particular effect or style. Typographic texts can also be translated into static or dynamic typographic form using Web-based or other software.

The free open source program Processing allows generative and interactive typography. This shows a captured screen from a random particle generation 'sketch' animation.

This variable typeface, Plastic, by Jitka Janečková and Ivana Palečková, takes a creative approach by having the serif length as one of the two axes.

Laser-cut type into wood as a test for
letters that were eventually cut into steel
with a water jet as part of a park installation
naming species of local and migratory birds.
Plant Architect.

MATERIAL EXPLORATION

This might include cutting up and reassembling type, 3-D printing,
laser cutting letters into wood or other material and photograph-
ing or making letters with different materials. Marian Bantjes, for
example, creates new physical and digital typographic forms using
traditional as well as less traditional materials.

GENERATIVE TYPE

Type on the computer is the manifestation of a confluence of
decisions made by software designers and computer coding. The
designer is the final link in a chain of interactions. Underlying the
appearance is computer code which can be manipulated or which
uses existing type forms and performs further operations on it. The
open-source program Processing is a widely-used tool of people
working with the coding of generative and interactive typography.

PERCEPTUAL EXPERIMENTS

Typographic form can be used as a basis of experiments with visual
perception. Optical illusions, experiments with low spatial resolution, or working with the figure ground relationships or other
aspect of perceptual psychology can be applied to typographic
investigations.

CREATIVE INTERACTIONS WITH THE ENVIRONMENT

Type can be projected onto architecture, or be placed in a context
in which it is not normally found. Technology can be employed
to interact with the environment or the public. Augmented reality
software makes it possible to integrate software with the 'real'
environment through devices and VR headsets.

While playing with figure/ground relationships is not novel, it involves the reader's
eye and mind in an uncommon way.

The computer allows the creation of visual effects that
would be difficult to do with traditional methods.

MORPHOLOGY

In his book *Designing Programmes*, Karl Gerstner proposed a morphology for creative approaches to wordmark design. Adapted to a wider field, a morphological approach can be useful in a systematic approach to typographic creativity, as below. The designer can create these for themselves to encourage original approaches. Below is an example of a typographic morphology. Elements can be ignored or new elements added.

Type form

Type form					
Case	majuscules	minuscules	normal mixed	abnormal mixed	other
Typeface	serif	sans serif	other	combination	other
Typeface structure	low contrast	high contrast	combination		
Weight	light	medium	bold	combination	
Size	small	medium	large	combination	
Set width	narrow	normal	wide	combination	
Characters	normal	cropped	mixed chars	blended chars	
Direction	horizontal	vertical	diagonal	circular	

Type treatment

Type treatment					
Effects	fragmenting	blurring	subtracting	adding	combination
Dimensionality	none	orthogonal	perspective	combination	
Materiality	none	physical	physical > digital*	digital > physical*	
Distortion	none	linear	radial	random	other

Composition

Composition					
Balance	symmetrical	asymmetrical	combination		
Grouping	none	separated	touching	overlapping	combination
Proximity	none	close	far	combination	
Rhythm	regular	irregular	alternating	syncopated	
Texture	fine	medium	coarse	combination	
Repetition	few	many	random	combination	
Rotation	none	slight	moderate	extreme	combination

Other elements

Other elements				
Bullets, etc.	none	normal	symbols	combination
Rules	none	type oriented	independent	combination
Rule weight	none	light	heavy	combination

*Refers to moving between the physical and digital environments.

This large physical type both attracts attention and suggests the sculpture that makes up an important part of this museum's collection

Dimensionality

Dimensionality may be actual, as when letters are made from materials, or it may also be implied, as when, for example, two-dimensional type is treated in a way that appears to be three dimensional. Common ways of attaining this may be simple (as in the use of drop shadows or extruding type into three-dimensional space), or more complex.

SKEUOMORPHING

Skeuomorphing, the practice of imitating or alluding to material aspects of something other than the medium being used, is a common (and unmodernist), technique, which has been widely used in websites but also throughout the history of typography: Gutenberg's type can be considered a skeuomorph of the contemporary style of writing. Type of the Victorian era often had skeuomorphic aspects, suggesting three-dimensional characters. Some modern typefaces consciously imitate the look of worn metal type of the past. The computer has made skeuomorphic typography easier, with designers able to imitate things like distressed wood type or neon lettering. On-screen publications with pages that 'turn' are another common skeuomorph.

In the computer interface design, it means something different: using a visual representation of a real-world object as a metaphor for a computer function. The garbage can icon is a classic example.

A typical skeuomorph typographic approach: imitating the appearance of neon letters.

Glitching provides interesting if unpredictable results.

Glitching

Glitching is one of the most the out-of-control method of experimentation, and can result in interesting form, though it usually takes many tries to get something good. It can act as inspiration, because sometimes results can be reproduced in other programs with better control. A common method is using a text editor to edit an image file. It works best with colour files. Glitching typography is basically a try-and-edit process, as the result is always a surprise.

CONCLUSION

Creative and experimental typography is where a lot of the fun in design is found. It is often an area of personal practice for designers, but it is likely to inform and enhance their professional practices. A typographer who doesn't experiment with unconventional work and approaches may well produce conventionally competent work, but is unlikely to produce highly creative or innovative design.

Creative typography is useful in practice for display typography and layout. In text type it can be an adjunct to more conventional communication design. Experimenting with text type is less common, and so in many ways, is more interesting to other designers and theorists. Typefaces and setting that embody a theoretical approach to text, such as Minuscule, are more likely to work as display type than they are as text.

Creative experimentation in typography has many different avenues. It can be material experimentation, whether using physical type forms, handlettering or working with collaged printed typography. It can be generative, working with programs such as Processing, or the features and effects of software. It can incorporate photography or other media. It can mean creating new letterforms and fonts.

The combination of software and data also offers potential for typographic experimentation. Creative typographic interpretations of data can communicate information in radically different and unexpected ways.

Creative typography is also an important part of design culture; designers build visual culture with the interchange of experimental work. It is also the kind of work that attracts and engages other designers, and one's professional reputation is not only dependent on happy clients. The reputation that we have with other designers is just as important. Other designers don't have to like your work to respect what you bring to the discipline.

Technology has greatly changed the practice and experience of typography over the last forty years. No doubt there are challenging and fascinating creative possibilities to come.

Experimental letter forms. Minuscule Deux, designed by Thomas Huot-Marchand to function at settings as small as two-point, develops the work of 19th century ophthalmologist Louis Émile Javal.

Type set at an angle on screen is rare, even though it is not particularly difficult to do. This particular treatment used to be more difficult, and the edges of angled type would 'stairstep' on a low-resolution display, something that has been largely solved with high resolution screens and better antialiasing techniques. There are historical reasons for this, stemming from the pre-CSS days, but there is no current reason to adhere to them.

One of the most purely typographic of practices, in that much of it deals with the form of letters, with the only context being the other forms in the font, is typeface design. Working with type forms gives a better understanding of typography in general. The ability to use font software at a basic level is also useful to a designer in other ways; for logo development, to add custom characters to a font or to adjust weights or other aspects of typefaces. Handlettering also offers an opportunity for designers to expand their practice beyond using type.

Customizing / creating type forms

Vector illustration programs let designers modify, redraw or create letterforms, whether directly or by converting images into vector format. The availability of font editing software makes it possible to incorporate those forms into usable fonts. As a result, designers' practices may include the production of typefaces for clients as part of larger projects for individual clients or as a focus of practice. Even if typeface design is not part of what you do, font editing software can also be very useful for creating fonts of special characters for a particular purpose, such as custom icons, or simply as a drawing tool, as the way that font editors deal with Bezier curves are well suited to the development and adjustment of vector forms such as logos.

It is a big job to develop a complete typeface, and many typefaces should be made and perfected before you offer typeface design as a service. Although font editing software is quite easy to learn and use, at least on a basic level, creating a reliable and complete font is more complicated and takes up a lot of time.

You are always building on what came before. If you're ignorant of it, you're probably going to repeat it by mistake.

Christian Schwartz, Commercial Type

ABCDEFGH

In the early 1800s, Vincent Figgins was one of the first designers of type that created the illusion of type being three-dimensional, one of the many typographic innovations of the Industrial Revolution.

imum possibili
new Sprinter C

THE VOLVO SE

\nd you thou

Custom typefaces commissioned by Mercedes-Benz and Volvo are a part of their visual branding.

abcd
efghij
klmn
opqr
stuv
wxyz

These six primitives on the left were used to build all the red lower-case characters of the admittedly simple typeface above. The other lower-case characters (in black) could be built out of them as well, with minor adjustments and alterations.

Type design is a finicky
craft in which the
smallest details require
inordinate care.

Rick Poynor

CUSTOMIZING TYPE FORMS

Altering type forms for wordmarks and logos is a way of giving an organization a distinctive typographic presence. The changes can be subtle, such as shortening the length of ascenders and descenders of a wordmark, or adjusting forms to make the letters in a name fit together better, to more radical changes such as redrawing every character of a name.

CREATING TYPEFACES

A custom typeface can strengthen a visual identity. It also can make financial sense for a large company, as the licensing cost for a corporation to use an off-the-shelf typeface or family can far outweigh the fee for a typeface designer to design a typeface or type family for which the rights are assigned by the designer to the commissioning organization. A display face is less of an undertaking than a text face, as fewer characters are usually necessary, and are usually used in fewer environments.

It's beyond the scope of this book to deal with all the matters of designing a typeface. This kind of project should not be taken lightly; learning how to make a professional quality typeface, with consistent characters, good spacing and kerning, and reliable behaviour in various browsers, is a big job. Sketching letterforms, getting type editing software and taking a typeface design course are good places to begin. If you propose to create a complete typeface for a client, collaborating with or consulting an experienced typeface designer is advisable.

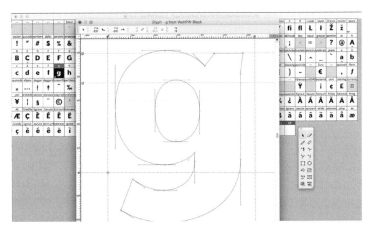

Character in FontLab 5, a font editing program. The character is drawn with Bezier curves. These can be created in the program itself or imported from a vector editing program, such as Adobe Illustrator.

End user license agreements

If you want to experiment with modifying an existing typeface, start with an open source font, so you are not in danger of breaching a type foundry's End User License Agreement (EULA), and thus liable to civil prosecution, in the case of your ending up distributing such a font or using it for a client's public materials. To be on the safe side, read the EULA of any font you want to modify. Open source typefaces often have conditions about modifying the typeface, which often have to do with giving credit to the original designer in the font file itself.

There are several commercial font editors of varying prices and varying capabilities. Some have free trials, so you can get a feeling of how they work, and some have cheaper 'light' versions that are adequate for simple font projects. FontForge is a capable free open-source program, though it takes a certain amount of willingness to deal with computer operating systems to install and use, particularly on Apple machines.

The most important things are to maintain logical consistency among the letters, which can be helped by creating 'primitives', that is, elements that can be reused in many letters, and to make sure that the interletter relationships work, which means you must test all likely relationships.

Type design takes time

The last five percent of executing a typeface design will often take something like 95 percent of the total time. You make great progress at the beginning, but perfecting the typeface takes much longer, with smaller and smaller improvements.

Sketching, and then making progressively more refined drawings, is one approach. You don't necessarily have to draw all characters, unless you are making an informal script typeface. For a normal standard font, drawing a 'b' will give you a good idea of

The relationship between the bowls of these letters is clear, but they are also clearly not identical.

Letters derived from forms made with a
software spiral drawing tool.

ᴀᴙᴄᴇᴀᴎᴇ
ᴇᴉᴀᴆᴅ ᴙᴇ
ᴉᴅᴇᴙᴄᴅᴆ

Calligraphy by German architect Karl
Adalbert Fischl in the early 20th century.

BALLOON
BALLOON

In the top version above, the two 'l's
and 'o's are identical, while they vary
on the bottom version. Typefaces that
are intended to represent informal
hand lettering need alternative versions
of characters to avoid undermining
the effect caused by repeated letters.

what a 'p' should look like, while an 'h' will give you an 'n', and 'o' is related to 'c' and 'e'. An 'H' will show the weight of vertical stems and horizontal strokes of caps. All letterforms in a font will be related to each other, so some parts can often be used for many letters, though they may need slight adjustment for each letter. The vertical stroke will be essentially the same across the lower-case letters. The vertical strokes of the capitals will likely be slightly heavier than the lowercase, but will be the same for most of the capitals. Informal script faces have the least internal consistency.

TYPEFACE REVIVALS

The past has been a frequent source of typographic design for the last two hundred years. In the 1800s, William Morris looked back 300 years to Nicolas Jenson's work for the inspiration for his Golden font. Stanley Morison in the 1920s looked to the past for the model for Times New Roman, as well as supervising revivals of other historical typefaces, including Bembo, Francesco Griffo's work of around 1500 for Aldus Manutius. Most of the text type-faces used today are either revivals of or have been inspired by historical typefaces. Typefaces from the past that have been by-passed by other type designers are worth investigating. There are many unusual and interesting typefaces and lettering styles that haven't yet been the inspiration for typographic revivals.

Victorian advertising and early 20th-century Germany are good sources of inspiration for 'innovative' typefaces.

OTHER SCRIPTS

Most typeface development by far has been of Roman typefaces. Other traditions have more need for new typographic develop-ment. While designing a script such as Chinese is a daunting task, any alphabetic or syllabic script is worth tackling if you have a background in reading and writing it. William Caslon got his start designing an Arabic face, though he had no knowledge of Arabic himself, though it is not recorded how good native Arabic readers may have found it. Scripts such as Cyrillic and Greek have more in common with Roman but still have their own cultural contexts, which mean that familiarity of the originating culture is necessary to successfully work with (or design) typefaces.

Paradigm

Paradigm

Dyadic

Dyadic

gestalt

gestalt

Using a vector editing program, such as
Adobe Illustrator, to refine existing type forms,
from subtle to more dramatic.

graphics

Mixing forms from different typefaces.

plasticity

Blended fonts using font editing software.

sidewalk

Hand-drawn (or scrawled) forms converted to
a font.

auslegen

Typeface revival. Typeface found in G magazine,
a German art and architecture journal of the
early 1920s.

SPECIAL PURPOSE FONTS

A font with only four characters created to make
setting a catalogue hundreds of pages long much
faster, as it saved the designer from positioning
.eps files for each entry.

An icon font made for an outdoors magazine that
visually communicates information about different
locations and activities.

BBBB

The Modern typeface was the starting point for the first variations of the Victorian era. By changing the weight relationships in a current Bodoni 'B', we can recapitulate some early Victorian typefaces. By exaggerating the thick strokes, we see the model of the Fat Face. By thickening the thin strokes (and bracketing serifs), the Clarendon style was created. Finally, by reversing the thin and thick strokes, we see a reverse stress French Clarendon.

Beowolf
Beowolf
Beowolf

Beowolf was a font that was run through a program that randomized each point as it was printed, making the forms degrade progressively. Though this programming was not part of the font itself, it shows how programming and typography can relate.

This letter was originally drawn on paper with a half-dried-out felt-tip marker. The process of vectorizing doesn't capture the original appearance perfectly but does represent it convincingly at smaller sizes.

DIFFERENT APPROACHES TO CREATING ORIGINAL TYPE FORMS

There are many approaches to creating new letterforms. These are a few of them. They can be used alone or in combination.

EXAGGERATION OF EXISTING FORMS/EXTRAPOLATION

This was a common strategy of Victorian typeface designers: 'fat faces' were exaggerations of the modern form with thick strokes greatly thickened, with the thin strokes remaining more or less unchanged. Clarendons took the current serif model and thickened everything, including the serifs. Radically condensing or expanding overall letter forms was another common approach.

TRANSLATING MEDIA

Scanning forms drawn on paper or otherwise produced can be transformed into vectors or be turned into typefaces. Scanning, rather than using a vector program, helps to avoid the excessively geometric forms that can result from starting character design on the computer.

TYPE 'MIXING'

Interpolating between different typefaces by using a blend tool is one way of mixing typefaces. Another is using parts of different typefaces together, for example, taking the serifs from one typeface and joining them to another. (See page 233 for examples of both.) These techniques were popular in the 1990s but are used much less now. This kind of thing may violate End User License Agreements, so read them before going to far with this.

PROGRAMMING

If you are interested in programming, the Python programming language, developed by Guido van Rossum, is a language widely used in type editing programs, and it is suitable for writing macros that can both automate repetitive tasks in typeface design programs and make generative changes to type forms.

The 1989 Beowolf typeface created by Erik van Blokland and Just van Rossum (Guido's brother) is an early example of the intersection of programming and the appearance of type forms.

No matter how you start, whether on or off the computer, most typefaces will end up as Bezier curves. They are easy to edit in

Illustrator or font-editing programs, and are the 'standard' format of fonts. However, if you are working with textures and complex colours, having a set of letterforms in bitmap form can work. It is also possible to make OpenType svg fonts that have colour bitmaps, which are increasingly supported by software (see page 179).

CONCLUSION

Customizing and creating type forms gives you control over typography beyond the traditional designer role of choosing a typeface. This can range from experimental creation of forms to the practical solving of problems for a client. Being able to make a refined and distinctive wordmark is a valuable professional skill. Designing a typeface also gives you the opportunity to put your own theories and preferences into action. The careers of such people as Matthew Carter, Zuzana Licko and Rudy VanderLans (the founders of Emigre), Erik Spiekermann, Carol Twombly, John Hudson, Fiona Ross, Jonathan Barnbrook and Christian Schwartz (among many others), show that typeface design can be a focus of both commercial and academic practices. Working with letterform creation also increases your understanding of typography and type forms. Taking a typeface design course is useful even for those who have no ambitions to be a typeface designer.

Hand lettering

Hand lettering has acquired new value since the advent of the computer and the availability of thousands of typefaces. Because typography is so easy to produce, it has become commonplace and taken for granted, and so there has been a resurgence of appreciation for calligraphy and less formal styles of lettering.

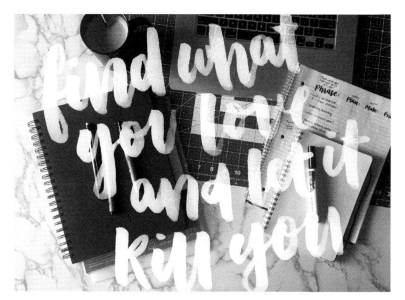

Hand lettering has gained value because 'perfect' typefaces are so easy to produce.
Courtesy of Talia Abramson.

Acknowledgements

My thanks to Commissioning Editor Louise Baird-Smith and Senior Production Editor Leafy Cummins at Bloomsbury for their initiation and facilitation of this book, and to OCAD University for granting a sabbatical to complete this project. The attention given to the draft manuscript by the reviewers was also very helpful, as were Bloomsbury's editors and proofreaders. Thanks to many colleagues for their encouragement, wisdom and advice on technical matters. This project also owes a lot to the interest and enthusiasm of the students at various schools at which I've had the pleasure of teaching over the years, who gave me insight into what makes up the important elements of a typographic education. Much of what I have learned about typography over the years is thanks to the many excellent employers, collaborators and diverse clients with whom I have worked since I started my typographic career over 30 years ago.

Much of the work on this book was done in the company of my siblings, Andrew and Judy. Finally, my thanks to Berry Choi and Jeremy Hunt for their support and tolerance as this project progressed.

Index

The text of this book is set in 10 on 13½ point Adobe Caslon, designed by Carol Twombly, based on William Caslon's specimens of the mid 1700s. Headings and captions are set in different sizes and weights of Trade Gothic, originally designed by Jackson Burke for Linotype in 1948. Chapter numbers are set in Franklin Gothic Extra Condensed, originally designed under Morris Fuller Benton of American Type Founders in 1906.